MRS GRIFFIN
SENDS HER LOVE
and other writings

MRS GRIFFIN
SENDS HER LOVE

and other writings

Miss Read

Edited by Jenny Dereham
with a foreword by Jill Saint

First published in Great Britain in 2013
by Orion Books
an imprint of the Orion Publishing Group Ltd
Orion House, 5 Upper St Martin's Lane,
London, WC2H 9EA

An Hachette UK Company

1 3 5 7 9 10 8 6 4 2

Copyright © Jill Saint 2013

For further copyright information see page 315

The moral right of Miss Read to be identified as the
author of this work has been asserted in accordance with
the Copyright, Designs and Patents Act of 1988.

A CIP catalogue record for this book is
available from the British Library.

ISBN 978 1 4091 4790 9 (hardback)
ISBN 978 1 4091 4791 6 (ebook)

Typeset at The Spartan Press Ltd,
Lymington, Hants

Printed in Great Britain by Clays Ltd, St Ives plc

The Orion Publishing Group's policy is to use papers that are
natural, renewable and recyclable products and made from wood
grown in sustainable forests. The logging and manufacturing
processes are expected to conform to the environmental
regulations of the country of origin.

www.orionbooks.co.uk

To
CAROLINE
with love

and gratitude for a lifetime's friendship
between two families

and
my love and heartfelt thanks to
JENNY
without whose unstinting hard work and eye for detail
this book would never have been published.

Thank you for your unswerving dedication to Miss Read
over so many years – both the editing and the loyal friendship.
She was always aware of your part in her success, and immensely
grateful for your support. I know she would have approved
of this collection. She would probably have called it

Whatever Jenny Thinks Best.

Contents

*

THE JOYS & PERILS OF TEACHING

THE HEART OF THE VILLAGE

THE VILLAGE YEAR

COUNTRY MATTERS

THE JOY OF WORDS

A MEDLEY OF OTHER WRITING

THE BIRTH OF MISS READ

TALES FROM A VILLAGE SCHOOL

Occasional notes in italic at the beginning of an article are by Jill Saint.

Foreword by Jill Saint

*

Long before Miss Read was born, Dora Saint was an active writer. Although from the mid-1950s she became best known for her Fairacre and Thrush Green novels, from the end of the Second World War she regularly wrote many light essays, short poems, entertaining monologues based on her teaching experience, and more serious pieces about country life. She was a practical person, with very little self-importance, but she was proud to be able to say, 'I started with *Punch*.' At that period she also wrote regularly for *The Lady* and *The Countryman* and had the occasional success with *Country Life* and national newspapers. She continued to write some of these shorter pieces after the Miss Read books began, but not as many.

She contributed regularly to *Woman's Hour*, wrote scripts for BBC Schools Broadcasting, and reviewed school and children's books for the *Times Educational Supplement*, as well as writing articles for them. All this continued well into the 1970s, and she would often be consulted by the *TES* or a publisher for her opinion on a new book or series, usually for primary schools, though she reviewed a number of books for older children.

Dora could turn her hand to many types of writing. In fact, she originally wanted to be a journalist, but her father felt this was far too rackety a career for a girl at that time, so she trained as a teacher. This was at Homerton College at Cambridge, a city which meant much to her all her life. There she was also introduced to the work of Rupert Brooke, another life-long passion.

She was a Londoner by birth, but a countrywoman at heart. She attended a village school in Kent from the age of seven, and this made a great impression on her. After the war, she and Doug lived for a couple of years in Newbury, but in 1947 moved to the small village of Chieveley on the edge of the Berkshire Downs. So, from their mid-thirties onwards they were able to follow a rural life. These experiences, and of course her teaching, had a great influence on her writing, both fiction and non-fiction.

In her Foreword to *Tales from a Village School*, published by Michael Joseph Ltd in 1994, she wrote: 'I still value the light essay and feel happiest when employing it. It is, I believe, the perfect training for most types of writing, for it needs tailoring to a desired length, a strong beginning and ending, and the power of holding the attention of the reader. It forces the writer to be brief, discriminating and alert to the response of his public.'

I read all the Miss Read books in manuscript and occasionally made a suggestion or correction. Dora wrote in exercise books, each full-length novel taking about ten exercise books, and these were eventually bound in handsome red buckram. I still have them but, at Dora's suggestion, they are ultimately to go to Reading University. Their archive department is now housed with the Museum of Rural Life, which seems most appropriate.

I remember reading the manuscript of *Christmas Mouse*, and enquired, 'What are you calling this child, Simon or Stephen?'

'What have I called him?' my mother asked.

'Both.'

'Oh! Stephen, I think, then. Go through and cross out Simon, would you?'

A pragmatic writer.

Dora wrote each day if possible, at fairly regular hours, which was typical of her practical approach to writing – no waiting for inspiration to strike. She would begin when the house was quiet, after my father – who was a history teacher in Newbury – and I had left for our respective schools, and finish around tea-time. Occasionally she would have a deadline for a book review or a commissioned piece, and would need to work outside these times, but this was rare.

I tried not to disturb her during the day. One day I needed to speak to her mid-morning, and apologised for ringing then.

'That's all right,' she said. 'I'd stopped, actually. I'm trying to decide whether to kill off Bertie.'

'Oh!' I said, 'what a shame! I like Bertie.'

'I like Bertie, too,' she said, thoughtfully.

'Mightn't you need him for another book?' I suggested.

'Yes, I might. Oh, well, never mind, perhaps I'll just have his foot off. What did you ring about?'

I have long thought that a collection of my mother's shorter pieces would make an attractive book, and am delighted that this is to appear in her centenary year.

From the Foreword to
Tales from a Village School

*

I spent three happy years at a Kentish village school in the 1920s. Later in life, I had short spells of supply teaching at various Berkshire schools, which confirmed my own belief that a well-run village school is the ideal place for a young child to begin its education.

I always wanted to write and I am often asked how I started. My approach was practical rather than poetic, but as I would prefer to be Anthony Trollope rather than Percy Bysshe Shelley, it is possibly just as well.

I had always been attracted to the light essay, admiring its brevity, grace and wit achieved by many writers from Hazlitt and Charles Lamb to the eminent essayists of my own youth such as Hilaire Belloc, A. A. Milne and E. V. Knox. The last two I came across mainly in *Punch*, which was one of the few magazines accepting such work when I began to write after the Second World War. I determined to get into *Punch*. Perhaps I was setting my sights too high for a beginner, but in time I achieved my purpose.

There was a more practical side to deciding to write light essays. Our young daughter was at school, and I had the house to myself. With any luck, I could draft an essay of 850 to 1000 words in that time.

I also wrote short verses, not only for *Punch* but for *The Lady*, *Country Life* and any other journal which seemed to welcome 'corner-fillers'. This was in the early 1950s when Kenneth Bird, better known as the brilliant cartoonist Fougasse, was editor of *Punch*. It was during his reign that I began to contribute more regularly with a series based on an infants' teacher's monologue, called 'The Forty Series'.

It had often occurred to me when I was teaching that a recording of the idiotic outpourings heard in the infants' room might be diverting. (Joyce Grenfell perfected this art.) I would hear myself saying: 'I'm looking for a well-behaved frog for our play, and three really trustworthy rabbits.' I wrote a number of such frivolous essays which *Punch* took; the *Times Educational Supplement* also took many country school articles.

But perhaps I was most fortunate to appear in the *Observer*. 'The Lucky Hole' came out in 1953 and led to an invitation from the publishing house of Michael Joseph to write my first book *Village School*, and to form a happy relationship with that publisher which has lasted forty years.

I later had a long spell of most interesting work for the BBC Schools Programmes.

Memories of my own Kentish village school and spells of supply teaching influenced my work greatly, as examples here show. Later, my novels about Fairacre and Thrush Green echoed the country school theme as well as my feeling for the changing seasons in the English countryside. These two interests, I believe, find a ready response in the majority of my readers and, after all, my aim is to entertain them.

I still value the light essay and feel happiest when employing it. It is, I believe, the perfect training for most types of writing, for it needs tailoring to a desired length, a strong beginning and ending, and the power of holding the attention of the reader. It forces the writer to be brief, discriminating and alert to the response of his public.

I enjoyed writing these stories very much.

Miss Read, 1994

MEMORIES OF CHILDHOOD
& SCHOOLDAYS

From Time Remembered

On the second day of March 1921 I went with my mother to Hither Green station in South London to go to our new home. We were bound for Chelsfield, only a few stations down the line, and I looked forward eagerly to the journey. It was a weekday, and I really should have been in school, which made the whole adventure more exciting.

I was seven years old.

We chugged along steadily through Grove Park, leafy Chislehurst and Orpington.

'Chelsfield next stop,' said my mother.

I was glad to hear it. It had been a long haul, I thought, between Chislehurst and Orpington through the fields and with not much to see.

The high embankment changed to a lower level, until we began to run between chalk cuttings. We were nearly there now and my mother prepared to descend from the train. It drew up with a squealing of brakes, and a hissing of steam. We climbed down, carrying our one piece of luggage, a basket with a picnic lunch in it, and I stood dumbfounded.

There was no one on the platform except for the guard of the train. I had never seen a station like this. There were no posters, no trolleys, no litter bins, no milk churns!

Furthermore, once the train had pulled away, everything was still and quiet. Before me, on a green bank, sheltered from the wind, primroses were growing, and somewhere, high above, birds were singing, which I learnt soon after were skylarks, indigenous to this chalky North Downs country.

We crossed by a footbridge, our footsteps echoing hollowly, to the up platform. Here things were much more station-like to my eyes. There was a shirt-sleeved porter, and metal posters advertising Waverley pens and Nestlé's milk. There was even a chocolate machine where a penny would buy a bar of the delicious stuff.

The porter took our tickets and pointed out the way to our destination. It led across the station yard, through a gate, and on to a footpath beside a wood.

The peace of a spring morning enveloped us as we climbed the gentle slope, the wood on our right, and the deep railway cutting on our left.

We were both glad to stop now and again to have a rest. The wood gave way to fields of springy turf which made a pleasant resting place. There was a sturdy black metal sign set just inside the wires separating the railway property from our path. It said: *Trespassers will be fined £2.* It seemed a pity, as already a few early blue violets could be seen there. However, there was enough to enchant us on this side of the fence.

Tiny plants, which I should recognise later as sheep's-bit scabious and thyme, were pressed under my legs. The larks were in joyous frenzy above. The sky was blue, the now distant wood misty with early buds, and the air was heady to a London child.

A great surge of happiness engulfed me. This is where I was going to live. I should learn all about birds and trees and flowers. This is where I belonged. Any qualms about a new school vanished in these surroundings.

This was the country, and I was at home there.

It was a knowledge that was to stay throughout my life.

My Country Childhood

I became a country child at the age of seven. Before that I lived with my parents and my elder sister Lil in south London. My maternal grandmother, two unmarried sisters and a bachelor uncle all lived nearby in a Victorian house. They introduced us to such pleasures as Beatrix Potter, decorous walks in suburban parks, Sunday School, trips to the theatre and the London shops.

My mother's ill-health uprooted us and we moved to the village of Chelsfield in Kent, a few stations down the railway line which runs from London to Folkestone. Suddenly, for me, life began. I felt like a minnow released from a jam jar into a stream. Here, I knew instinctively, was my true element.

In the first place, the country was quiet and blessedly free from crowds which I had always loathed. The sky was higher, the horizon farther away and the whole place teemed with new delights. I discovered dog violets and harebells in the North Downs countryside, as well as old friends like buttercups and daisies.

Instead of London plane trees, scabby-trunked and bobble-hanging, there were walnut, beech, yew and holly which flourished in the chalky soil. Instead of strutting pigeons and Cockney sparrows, there were finches of all kinds and larger birds like pheasants and bottle-shaped partridges. It was a brave new world indeed, and I was enchanted.

My first Christmas centred around the parish church of St Martin's where my father and mother sang in the choir. Both the church and village chapel had celebrations, tea parties, evenings of sacred music and the like. I remember a nativity play enacted in the chancel of St Martin's, the crib dimly glowing among the shadows, and the sharp, aromatic scent of yew, laurel and cypress with which the church was decked.

At the village school, we had our own Christmas fun. The glass and varnished wood partition creaked back to make one long room to accommodate parents and friends who had been invited to our concert. The desks were dragged to one end, and planks lodged across them to make a stage. Here another eight-year-old and I opened the proceedings with an Irish jig accompanied by ominous thumps from the makeshift stage and Miss Ellis at the piano. The climax of the evening came when the big boys and girls acted a scene from *Oliver Twist*. I can hear their voices now.

'Oliver Twist has asked for more.'

'Asked for more? Compose yourself, Bumble!'

That first country Christmas confirmed my initial impression. This was the place to live.

The summer of my eighth year was one of intense and prolonged heat and my city socks-with-garters and liberty bodice were replaced by loose cotton frocks (with matching knickers) and open sandals in which one's bare toes were soon powdered with chalky dust. Never had I felt so free, so happy, and only a straw hat, anchored by elastic under the chin, reminded me of my former confining raiment.

Our school was about a mile from the house, and here again the contrast was favourable. My early school years had been spent in a large three-storey building, where my Aunt Rose taught. There were about fifty children to a class, discipline was strict, and there was constant goading to work harder and faster. At break time, the playground seethed with noisy children, boisterous at being released from sitting up straight and in silence for so long.

But at Chelsfield School, the playground was shaded by lime trees, and there were wooden seats beneath them. The classes were small and there was no urgency about our working methods. Our headmaster was blessed with a fine bass voice and at the drop of a hat he would sing to us. We tried to accompany him in ballads from dog-eared copies of *The National Song Book*, our wavering trebles following his powerful voice like fledgling ducklings trailing after their parent.

School life went on at an ambling pace which suited me well. As a foreigner, I realise now, I might well have been ostracised, even bullied, for the children were often related, and had certainly known each other from babyhood. However, they were a kindly bunch, and I soon made friends.

But it was not all rapture. There were aspects of country living which repelled me. I hated to see poor dead rooks hanging upside down from sticks among the crops, their black satin wings opening and shutting macabrely in the wind. I feared the hostile geese which emerged from the farm to chase me with outstretched snake-like necks. Cows, bees, wasps and sad, ferocious dogs chained to their kennels all appalled me.

There were other horrors. As a town child, I had been used to unlimited water, to baths with taps and lavatories with a chain which released a flush of cleansing water. Our new home was equipped with these amenities, but some of the rural homes I visited still had an earth privy at the end of the garden. These 'little houses' were usually embowered in elder, flowering currant or even lilac bushes. Their wooden seats were scrubbed to ribby whiteness, but I still lived in dread of having to visit them.

But these were only minor blemishes in an otherwise perfect world. The happiness that had engulfed me, when I arrived in the country at the age of seven, told me that this was the place for me. Luckily, it still is.

Sweet and Sticky

Every morning, just before nine o'clock, a small gaggle of schoolchildren swarm into the little shop in our village. The shop sells everything. Bottles of camphorated oil, lashed by elastic to bright cardboard backgrounds, repel the winter ills and dangle beside tubes of suntan which offer summer comfort. Boxes of onions, bananas, tomatoes and oranges jostle each other on the floor. Indian tea, French dressing, South African apricots and Dutch cheeses stand cheek by jowl on the counter – the pick of the world is here.

But the children ignore it all. They make their way from the jangling door, with an air of dedicated concentration, towards a small side counter which bears a fine array of sweets. There they stand, one shoe rubbing up and down the other leg, in agonies of indecision over their choice of elevenses. 'Anything for a penny?' asks one young hopeful. The shop does not betray his trust. He is directed to a box which holds a number of tiny packets and bears the notice ASSORTED CHEWS. Blissfully, he scrabbles while his sister, three years older and a seasoned shopper, hands over threepence for a bar of chocolate without any preliminary shilly-shallying.

'Buck up!' she urges the scrabbler. 'Bell'll be going!' She retires to the door, jigging up and down impatiently as the brother wavers between STRAWBERRY and PEAR. Two little girls, their arms entwined affectionately across the backs of each other's home-knitted jumpers, plump for pink and white nougat. They lisp their thanks for the change in unison, for both have lost their front milk teeth.

It would seem from casual observation that the children in this particular group spend about threepence each a day at this absorbing counter. Dark rumour has it that children elsewhere are given the whole of their children's allowance as soon as it is collected at the Post Office, with an indulgent 'There, love! There's your sweet money.' But somehow the mind boggles at accepting this statement, and I cannot imagine it happening in our prudent village. The thought of rebellious young stomachs and dental cavities offsets the blissful vision of mounds of marsh-mallows, piles of peppermints and hundredweights of humbugs.

Nevertheless, it would seem that children nowadays eat more sweets than we did when I was young. Looking back to those halcyon days of the early twenties, I know we had no daily sum to spend on sweets, although naturally one accompanied any friend who might be in need of purely disinterested advice in the spending of a penny at Mrs Jenner's village shop. The little girls, I remember, were somewhat conservative in their choice of sweets. They were in their apparel, too, though this was not their fault. I was considered very avant-garde with my pink check gingham knickers matching my frock. More sedate maidens in my class still wore white cotton drawers with crochet-edgings which left a fascinating pattern on the back of the thigh after prolonged pressure against a school bench. Usually the girls came away with bars of chocolate or toffee, though the more venture-some might branch out and buy long black liquorice boot laces or black liquorice birds' nests embellished with sugar eggs of fearsome pink and green.

My own partiality was for sherbert dabs with a dear little toffee spoon which grew tragically smaller as the sherbert was sucked from it. Sometimes Mrs Jenner offered sherbert dabs which had a short liquorice pipe emerging from the yellow triangular bag, and although these sometimes had the added attraction of a Union Jack sticking from the top I always refused them. Painful experience had taught me that to suck sherbert 'down the wrong way' was one of the hazards of this mode of eating.

If the genuine sherbert dab was not available, I found coconut tobacco, realistically presented in brown shreds, a satisfying substitute, though pink and white coconut chips were equally acceptable. Chocolate animals were a temptation, but rather expensive, and the dreadful pang which one felt on biting off their heads could not be overcome.

But the best bargain of all was Mrs Jenner's home-made toffee, which cost twopence a quarter. There were two sorts, demerara and fig, and they lay in two flat silver tins, glistening with good-ness. A small metal hammer lay athwart the tins, ready to knock the smoooth expanse into glorious smithereens. A sizable splinter of Mrs Jenner's toffee in the mouth made speech impossible for ten minutes. It had a glutinous quality which I have never met since – a clinging-to-the-teeth which was amazing. My sister and I regularly bought the demerara variety when our milk teeth were laggardly in coming out and there had been parental hints about 'helping with a clean hanky'. That toffee never failed us, and I have never met a pleasanter method of tooth extraction.

But our sweet-buying was comparatively rare. We had sweets given to us at home, of course: a piece of good chocolate or a horribly wholesome boiled sweet from a hygienically sealed jar, but no child counts that. Kind aunts presented us with pretty boxes of confectionery, which were warmly appreciated, though only one uncle gave us anything approaching our own choice. A young bachelor, he had brought us pink and white sugar whistles which got messily and inextricably entangled with the long-haired hearth-rug, much to the disgust of my mother. 'Fancy George bringing such *silly* things for the children!' she said wrathfully, after the guest's departure. But we thought the choice was inspired – and I still do. Dear Uncle George!

When I see the daily shoppers clutching their coins in the village shop here, I can understand the phenomenon of present-day parties, where the honey-spread scones and the banana sandwiches lie untouched while the anchovy toast and the cheese straws vanish rapidly. Is it surprising that today's children prefer savouries to sweets when they can feast so bountifully at the local confectioner's? May they get as much joy there as I did at Mrs Jenner's.

The Real Thing

There seems to be a mistaken idea that learning by doing is a new thing. In reality, of course, it is as old as the hills. From the moment when a harassed cave-woman besought her husband, doodling on the living-room wall, to give the child another burnt stick to draw on the space lower down and allow her to get on with the cooking, children have been enjoying numberless activities, and learning, all the time, from their successes and failures. In the centuries that followed, the system of apprenticeship was soundly built on this sensible concept.

But the wholehearted adoption of learning through activity throughout primary schools as we see it flourishing today, is new. It has grown rapidly in a lifetime. One has only to look back to one's own early days at school to realise that the lessons which are remembered are usually those which involved objects and their manipulation rather than something taught orally or by reading. In my first year at a big London infants' school, I can remember with pleasure several sessions with a shoe-lacing apparatus which, I suspect, was one of Mme Montessori's ideas.

An early drawing lesson sticks in my mind. We were given two beautiful red cherries, gleaming and seductive, to copy with our red crayons. The fragrance of the fruit rising from twenty or more double tables was agonising and no doubt the final thrill of being allowed to eat our models has kept this particular lesson ever-fresh for me.

The infants' school had other joys. Plasticine rolled into a noisy flapping worm with the palm of one's hand before turning it into a neatly coiled basket with a weak, flaccid handle, bead frames bearing ten beads on each wire rung which clicked satisfyingly against the wooden frame as we flicked them along, chanting:

> *One and nine make ten,*
> *Two and eight make ten,*
> *Three and seven make ten,*
> *Four and six make ten,*

rising to a magnificent crescendo in the emphatic

> *Five and five make ten,*

as we slammed home the five red and five blue beads together before embarking on the second half of the incantation.

But once in the junior school, at the sober age of seven, things changed. Life was real and earnest, and every morning had its loathsome spell of table practice. The red-tipped pointer leapt from side to side like a gadfly, and we followed faint but pursuing. Books and papers took the place of bright toys. The warm, strong feel of wood, the cold prettiness of china beads, the handling of such diverse and elemental substances as clay, water, sand and stone, with all the deep inexpressible joy which it engendered, was largely replaced by the cold impersonality of paper and the cramped holding of a new pen. Hands which had given so much pleasure were now the servants of a refractory nib and an inkwell which seemed always to be filled with black honey. They did not make things any more – at least, not in the mornings – they simply guided a pen, painfully and haltingly, and through it tried to put down the urges which could have been so much more happily expressed in other media.

There were moments of reality, of course, which stand out from their gloomy background like lamps in a dark street. I can remember the excitement of poking broad beans, fat and deliciously mottled, between wet pink blotting paper and the side of a jam jar, and the tricky stage of edging them under the shoulder of the pot without letting them slide, with a plop, into the water at the bottom.

There was a magnificent lesson, too, about a fruit cake, given by a student (from Goldsmiths' probably). This enlightened young woman, with one eye fixed apprehensively upon her tutor's figure at the back of our classroom, mixed the cake in front of our entranced gaze. Flour, sugar, butter, currants, peel, spice were shaken in and their names put on the blackboard. Happy indeed were the lucky few who were allowed to pour in the milk and stir the mixture. Our greatest worry was time, I recall. Would the cake be cooked before we went home? We watched the student's return from her sorties to the school kitchen with increasing anxiety. The aim of the lesson was to learn the spelling of the words on the blackboard, but I am sure that many of us also learnt to tell the time that afternoon as we watched the hands of the clock creep inexorably towards home time while our lovely cake baked all too slowly.

If we were lucky enough to be drafted to Division B of Upper Four then we made steak and kidney pie or ironed shirts instead. But all that lay far ahead of the junior school where we struggled with copper-plate writing, a crossed J nib and a penholder that tasted of chewed wood and salt tears.

Today the middle-aged visitor to the classroom may well wonder what on earth the children are doing. Some pour water from milk bottles into jugs, others are being measured against the wall, a game of quoits is being played on the floor. Children flow from cupboards to desks and back again fetching and carrying apparatus. Can this really be an arithmetic lesson, the bewildered visitor wonders? And, if so, are they really learning anything that they will remember?

Her own early memories will supply the answer to that last question.

Delectable Distractions

It is easy to forget, when one is grown up, the awful boredom of the schoolroom. Our village school was livelier than most forty years ago, the surroundings were pleasant and the teachers enlightened. But I can still recall the ennui which overcame me and, no doubt, my fellows, imprisoned as we were in our double desks.

Various factors contributed to our state of mind. For one thing, the desks were confoundedly uncomfortable. Worse still, they squeaked abominably when wriggled upon, and so called down the wrath of the teacher. Then so often, it seemed, we had to share reading books. This nearly drove me wild as my co-reader always seemed to be abysmally slow and was only halfway down the page when I had finished and was waiting impatiently to turn over.

Satan obligingly found mischief for my idle hands to do during these maddening interludes. Dredging the inkwell with one's pen passed a few pleasurable moments as one lifted delicious jelly-like blobs of foreign matter and arranged them prettily round the rim. Dropping the pen to the floor and counting the number of times it stayed embedded upright by its quivering nib was another good game but apt to be frowned upon by pettifogging authority. Small pieces of pink blotting paper, torn from the precious three-by-four allowed, were surprisingly nice to eat, and occasionally an obliging fly would settle on the arid desk top and create a diversion.

But the most successful time-waster was given to me by a discerning uncle. It was a pen with a glass holder. This hollow tube was filled with a delectable rose-coloured liquid in which a large fat air bubble floated gently up and down, turning the whole magnificent thing into a rudimentary spirit level. This wonderful object kept me sane while my desk mate made his laborious way down the page, or the headmaster was tediously explaining fractions. When at last it was accidentally scrunched underfoot by a clumsy schoolfellow, and translated into a wet and glittering circle on the floorboards, my grief was bitter. I still hope to come across another one.

There were objects on the walls, of course, to interest us but they had been there for generations and soon palled. There was a glass-fronted case, I remember, showing the life history of a lump of cotton. It ended up on a reel – as we knew it would – and did little to whip us into a state of exhilaration. Now and again we had a new calendar or a poster about buying savings stamps, but our teachers had never heard of visual aids, and apart from the occasional picture or diagram drawn on the blackboard we had little to catch the eye. True, there was a sepia photograph of King George V, resplendent in uniform, hanging over the fireplace, and one of Queen Mary behind our heads, wasp-waisted in beautiful lace, but that was all.

It was small wonder that we welcomed visitors as a diversion. Even nurse, who came to inspect our heads, and whose ministrations we found a trifle humiliating, made a break. The managers were even more welcome, particularly a dapper little man with a pointed beard. He always read our names from the register and could be relied upon to pronounce more than half of them wrongly, thus  giving exquisite pleasure to all. But the one we liked best was a good-natured motherly person who unfailingly brought a box of sweets with her. Her visits were never too frequent for us.

Occasionally, someone from the great world outside the village came to see us. Once it was an earnest individual whom we remembered as 'The Temperance Man'. One hot afternoon, he warned us of the evils of strong drink, although the chance of *any* sort of drink on such a day interested his captive audience in their hard desks. He illustrated his talk with gruesome diagrams of the human inside. I don't think any of us had the remotest notion of anatomy, and the sight of all those tubes, coloured blue and red, inside a man who had no face but only a head like the rubber interior of a golf ball, quite appalled us. When he flipped over the final wall sheet and displayed a lurid heart the size of a bullock's, the handsomest boy in the school (nearly thirteen and practically grown up) slumped to the floor in a dead faint. He had all our sympathy.

But such exotic birds of passage were rare in our schoolroom. We were certainly lucky in the top class for we had two teachers to look at. Our headmaster, though neat and clean, seemed always to be dressed in the same suit. It was of navy blue serge with shiny elbows, knees and seat, and his ties were undramatic.

The other teacher, who taught Standards 3 and 4 in the same room, was a cheerful person who seemed to us to be tottering on the verge of the grave although, looking back, I realise that she could not have been much more than thirty at the time. Her clothes were as regrettably subfusc as the headmaster's, and consisted of sensible skirts and blouses in colours guaranteed not to show the dirt. But one day she came to school wearing a modest engagement ring, and this, in its sober surroundings, flashed upon our dazzled eyes like a shooting star.

Nowadays when I go into schools and see the host of teachers in their bright clothes, the galaxy of pictures on the walls and the acres of pastel paint, I feel a slight twinge of pity for my lost childhood. And when I observe the children actually getting out of their desks and walking unchecked about the classroom, then I am consumed with envy.

On the other hand, would they get as much illicit pleasure, I wonder, from a glass-filled penholder with an air bubble? I doubt it. One has to be securely trapped in an uncomfortable desk to savour a thing like that to the full.

Time for Dinner

Before the days of school dinners, the time from 12 noon until 1.30 or 1.45 was hallowed indeed. For the majority of young children, it was a complete break from the bondage of school.

At our village school, I suppose that less than a dozen children out of almost a hundred stayed within its walls munching their sandwiches at midday. The rest of us roared out from the cloakrooms, dragging on our coats and buttoning them anyhow as we snuffed up the glorious fresh air of the Kentish countryside.

Most of the children lived within a stone's throw of the school and their dinners were less than ten minutes' running or hopping or skipping away. One lucky family lived right next door to the school, and at playtime the eldest child could hang over the railings and yell piercingly, 'What's for dinner, Mum?'

A vague mumble would come from within, accompanied by tantalising whiffs of stewed rabbit with onions, or the fragrance of boiling bacon, and the rest of us, pausing in our play, would envy one who lived so close to home.

My own dinner waited for me over a mile away. With luck I was at the table by half-past twelve, replete and washed at one, and on my way back to reach afternoon school at one-thirty. There were a great many things to waylay a child on that homeward mile, although hunger usually drove me on fairly smartly.

I knew where to find the first blue and white violets. I knew where toothwort grew, as pink and fleshy as piglets. I picked the seed-pods of stitchwort to pop, and parted the fine grass to find wild strawberries on the bank. There was a hollow damson tree which sometimes sheltered a robin's nest – and there was a pond. Occasionally, half a dozen fierce geese would leave the pond and waddle menacingly across my path.

'You want to shout at them,' said the farmer when he found me in tears with a pecked leg. In the farm kitchen, he anointed the wound with iodine, applied with one of my tormentor's wing feathers. 'Bullies always run away if you fight back!'

At certain times of the year, great heaps of grey flints for road mending were tipped at the side of the road and these also took some time to negotiate.

Perhaps because they knew of these hazards to my dinner

hour, my parents sometimes let me ride a scooter, and on fine days I made record time charging rhythmically along those traffic-free roads with the sole of one shoe wearing out rapidly on the gritty surface.

But better by far than the scooter was the system of lifts which I soon worked out. On Wednesdays and Fridays the fish van travelled from the village past my house soon after noon. He was an obliging man who kept a look out for me as we tumbled down the school steps, and I rode in style on the scale-flecked seat beside him, while cod and skate, haddock and kippers slithered about in the boxes behind. Sometimes the builder (he who owned the duck pond) was in the village on business, and I would wait hopefully by his Ford van as the precious minutes went by. I dared not wait longer than a quarter past twelve or I should never be back in time.

He very rarely left me waiting. I was dropped at his builder's yard, still a quarter of a mile from home, but I was duly grateful, and watched him turn into his yard where the white planks were planed and the aromatic shavings warmed the feet of those who worked.

But best of all I liked the corn merchant's covered wagon for my lift. I did not save much time by this transport for the great carthorse plodded more slowly than I ran, but to be so high, to smell the grain in the sacks at the back, and to watch the horse's massive haunches moving beneath the worn leather harness made this a blissful occasion.

Occasionally, when my parents had to be away for the day, I joined the sandwich-eaters. In the winter time, we drew chairs round the fireguard and balanced our paper packets in our laps. While we examined the egg or cheese fillings, before demolition, we exchanged village gossip or played 'I Spy' or 'Bird, Beast or

Fish' in a haphazard way. It was pleasant enough, but I enjoyed summer dinner hours far more.

Near the school was an enchanting place called the 'Rec'. I doubt if any of us knew its full name, but we all knew its delights. There was a vast expanse of short grass for rolling on, and plenty of tall grass, dusty with pollen, in which to hide from friends. There was a lop-sided swing and a battered see-saw that operated with an ear-splitting squealing. There were daisies for making chains, buttercups for ascertaining whether one liked butter, plantains for playing 'Knock-off-his-knob', and sunshine over all. It was heaven.

And then came glory of a more sophisticated kind. It happened that on Thursdays there would be no one at home, and arrangements were made for me to have my midday meal in solitary state in the baker's shop. My mother would have ordered for me two eggs, bread and butter, and milk. I was allowed to choose one cake from the display in the window for my pudding.

The shop had two marble-topped tables with intricate

cast-iron legs which reminded me of our treadle-machine at home. I perched on a high round-backed chair and felt alternately shy and lordly as the baker's wife set out two brown eggs, with the bloom of recent laying upon them, a plate with bread and butter, and a large glass of milk standing on a saucer – a refinement which I had not met before. She was very kind and welcoming, begged me to ring the steel bell on the counter if I wanted anything, promised to 'look in again' and then retired behind a glass door to her own dinner. The glass was decently screened with a curtain of spotted muslin. I could not see the baker or his wife and family, but I could hear knives and forks at work, and envied them not one jot. Poor things, they might be having to face tripe, or liver, or a frightful tapioca pudding, I thought to myself, as I thwacked the top of my first egg!

Whilst eating, I gazed at the two pictures on the wall. One was of a little girl draped in her grandmother's black shawl and peering through gold-rimmed spectacles. She was drinking, I believe, Mazawattee tea, and was of only passing interest to me drinking my milk. But the second picture was much more

intriguing. It showed a haughty lady dressed in a tight Edwardian costume of peacock-blue velvet. There were a great many gathers flowing from a wasp-waist, braid, frogging, and an incredibly beautiful hat above the patrician features. She was reclining (it is the only word for such controlled disposal of the limbs) on what I took to be a park seat – an iron green-painted affair with slats and curlicues. She looked rather weary, I thought solicitously, as if she had collapsed elegantly there in the park on her way home from the shops, for she was burdened with a quarter of a pound of Horniman's tea dangling from a gloved forefinger, and may well have found the strain too much for her delicate constitution.

Under her disdainful gaze, the eggshells empty, I waited patiently for the baker's wife to reappear. I could not bring myself to ring the bell. My second course presented an agonising problem. There were three kinds of cakes in the window, and which should I choose?

The tray of sticky currant buns glistened temptingly. Next to it the doughnuts lay plump, fragrant, frosted with sugar and containing, I knew, a generous spoonful of raspberry jam. But then the third tray held queen cakes in adorably frilled paper cases, and each one was crowned with a glutinous glacé cherry. I loved them all with an eight-year-old's greed, and there must be only one.

The baker's wife generally settled matters for me. No doubt 'standin' around an' sufferin'' while I hovered from tray to tray helped her to make up my mind for me. Five minutes later, replete, I said farewell to her, and to the two ladies on the wall, and made my way out into the village street. There was still a glorious half-hour before afternoon school to rush about the 'Rec' and shake the food down.

I don't envy modern children their well-balanced, hygienically-cooked school dinners. No one doubts that school dinners are excellent in every way, but the biggest snag is that *one has to have them in school.*

And, let's face it, who honestly likes that?

Lament for the Secret Places

There is a lot to be said for the wide green lawns that surround so many schools. For one thing, they create a pleasing setting for the buildings and for the brightly clad young figures racing about. They also, of course, provide a place for organised – and unorganised – activities.

You can see, in one sweeping glance, that this is their main function. There is the cricket square; there are the tennis courts. If the pupils are not old enough for such sophistication then you may notice the sand pit, the climbing frame and the chute. Here and there will be trim beds of flowers, snapdragons or salvias neatly planted in rows, or some tidily pruned bush roses. Everything is delightfully gay and open. You feel at once that any spry teacher, alone on playground duty, could see a private fight the minute it began and could take immediate steps to suppress it before it blew up into gang warfare.

All this, I suppose, is to the good, but I feel a sneaking regret for the children who are thus blessed. For where is the *secrecy*, the *mystery*, the fun of hiding from those in authority to be found? Some of the pleasanter places of my schooldays, I remember, were frowned upon by those in charge, and thus rendered even more desirable.

At my village school, there was a brick structure with a large flat wooden lid. If one took a good run at it, and a colossal leap, it was just possible to scramble on top and take possession of this delectable plateau. It was a perfect place. For one thing, there was a wall behind it which made a useful prop for one's back and the aspect was southerly. Here one sheltered from the keen winds of the North Downs, warmed with the sun reflected from the flat lid, and enjoyed the feeling of superiority given by one's apartness from the hurly-burly of the playground a yard or so below. Any bold invaders could easily be repulsed by the out-thrust of a sandalled foot. It was true that there were rather a lot of flies, but their buzzing added to the somnolent atmosphere. I resented very much the peremptory demands to 'come down this minute!' which so often terminated a siesta in this choice spot. It was years later that I learnt that it was the school rubbish dump.

It was at the same time, incidentally, that another mystery was explained. The green metal boxes, with an intriguing clenched fist on the side, which I had vaguely supposed to be litter bins fixed far too high on the classroom wall, and into which I had tossed many an apple core, were really ventilators, I discovered. It is my guess that many a child today is as mystified as I was about the things.

There was certainly plenty of mown grass at my next school. There were hockey pitches, netball courts, cricket squares and tennis courts, in profusion. But, mercifully, there were also dozens of places for private, as well as corporate, activities. In a large shrubbery – planted, no doubt, when the school was built in 1905 – was a broken-down garden seat, thrust there hurriedly, I imagine, to be out of sight, and subsequently forgotten. It was black and sooty, as were the branches and trunks of the ageing shrubs which hid it. Here the air was damp and acrid among the shadows. Underfoot, dead laurel and holly leaves made a rustling carpet. Above, flaking bark and withered leaves rained down gently upon one's American bob, or light-starved skinny twigs successfully tweaked the hair slide from one's locks. It made a perfect place for the meeting of secret societies, and many a list of rules for members was made here on pages torn cunningly from the middle of our spelling books.

We were lucky enough, too, to have a brook running through our grounds, separating the old fields from the new. A wide stout bridge spanned its three feet of water, but naturally it was much better to jump it and have the excitement of missing the farther bank and ending up with black stockings and speckled plimsolls well soaked. Balsam bushes, willows and long grass shaded the water, and wild mint and forget-me-nots added colour and scent. Here one could find frogs and water beetles if one felt adventurous, or could simply hang over the bridge and watch the crisscross currents sway the underwater reeds if one were in the contemplative mood which followed school dinner. Nearby, three or four ancient elm trees offered shade and solitude for those who sought them.

I should not like to give the impression that peace and quiet were all we longed for in our out-of-door life. Team games in the wide open spaces necessarily claimed much of our attention, and a dozen or so little gardens, each about the size of a hearth-rug, were there to be tended by pairs of gardeners. For some reason, those in authority preferred two to be responsible, which is why I weakly gave in to a friend of mine, called Ethel, and agreed to become co-gardener.

Ethel was an ambitious gardener: I was not. We had London Pride and marigolds and pinks in our small plot. To my mind, these were quite enough. With the groundsel, chickweed, dandelions, docks, thistles and other native flora with which nature bountifully provided us, the garden was adequately covered, in my view. But Ethel thought otherwise, and insisted on putting in some vegetables which needed an enormous amount of care. The stand-pipe, from which we filled our watering-cans, was a considerable distance from the gardens, but I willingly lugged the cans back and forth rather than bend and weed, for I had – and still have – a horror of worms, and the thought of a chance encounter under the groundsel was more than I could face. I quite enjoyed watering the fruits of Ethel's labours, gossiping amicably with her, as she tugged at the weeds. We usually poured the last few drops from the can into a metal contraption which stood, for some reason unknown to us, in the middle of the gardens. We learnt later that this was the rain gauge.

But, looking back, I can see that it was the quiet secret places which held the greatest attraction, and still do, for children. I have stood in the stony wastes of country school playgrounds and watched the children making for their favourite spots – the lair beneath the clump of elder trees, the hide-away between the coke bunker and the nut hedge, the mildewy corner where the churchyard wall meets the wall of the infants' room and over-hanging lime branches screen a child from sight.

I should like to make a plea to those who design school grounds. No one in his senses expects a romantic grotto, a dripping cave, or even a miniature forest to be incorporated in the proposals, desirable though these would undoubtedly be in the children's opinion. But the clean, bare look is not all. Let us have an overgrown shrubbery or two, and some jungly grass with tall, tough weeds to provide cover.

Distant Afternoons

In those far-off days of the early twenties, when 'I Want to be Happy' and 'Tea for Two' wailed from every gramophone and my mother was busy running up a charming low-waisted frock from three yards of material (dead straight and reaching to the knees), I was attending school in a Kentish village. It was a glorious place. The headmaster was a rollicking fellow with a fine bass voice, and he had two assistants, one for the infants and the other for the juniors. Altogether, I suppose, we must have mustered eighty or ninety children and, looking back over the years, they seem to have been a very friendly collection.

The only unpleasant feature for me was the number of needlework lessons. I was appalled to find that the first fifty-five minutes of Monday, Wednesday and Friday afternoons were devoted to this detestable subject. The girls trooped into the junior room, and the boys trooped into the senior room where they had drawing lessons under the eye of the headmaster. (On Thursdays, we all had a drawing lesson, so the boys, with four sessions weekly, should have been excellent draughtsmen in later life.) While we were incarcerated on one side of the partition with small grubby pieces of calico which smelt of dog biscuits, the boys worked laboriously at something called Mechanical Drawing, for which they had a separate book full of the most dreary-looking pencil work, with dotted lines and shading. Rulers were much in evidence, and the little boys used to march in from the junior room next door, stiff-legged, with yellow rulers protruding from their sock tops. Meanwhile, we languished with our seams. The clock stood still. Outside the sun shone and the villagers gossiped. The lime trees rustled, swifts screamed past the windows and still the clock said five past two. Only when I found myself demoted from seam-unpicker to cleaner-of-rusty-knitting-needles, with a limp piece of threadbare emery paper, did the clock on the wall appear to move at all.

The Thursday afternoon drawing lesson was much more interesting. We were reminded, before going home at noon, to bring a 'specimen'. Good children brought daffodils, roses or sprays of autumn leaves, but forgetful ones – about three-quarters of us – were driven to criminal ends to obtain their needs.

Reminded by the smug rose-holders sniffing self-righteously at their blooms, we would rush down the school steps to old Mr Baker's front garden. His house was weather-boarded, in the pleasant Kentish fashion, and painted white. Unfortunately, it had a monstrous regiment of lace-shrouded windows, so that we could not see if we were observed. A large privet bush grew by the path, and from this we would snap small twigs and, breathless with excitement and guilt, tear back to school. Poor Mr Baker, frail and white-bearded, would hobble down his path, furious and gesticulating. Sometimes he caught a few tardy culprits, but not often, for we ran like the wind. His privet bush became remarkably one-sided, and the percentage of privet-sprig drawings compared with those of flowers was incredibly high.

After play on Thursday afternoons came poetry lesson. We were supposed to learn a poem a week from the anthology that lay in our desks, and it was the headmaster's custom to call a child to the front of the class to recite his new poem. The girls did occasionally learn a new one, but the boys never. Years before, probably in the infants' room, they had learnt a poem which began:

> *The cock is crowing,*
> *The stream is flowing,*
> *The small birds twitter,*
> *The lake doth glitter,*
> *The green fields sleep in the sun.*

This was their great stand-by. Boy after boy would come out, draw a deep agonised breath and gabble this interminable work with varying degrees of accuracy and fluency. The girls preferred 'I once had a sweet little doll, dears', or a rather lugubrious saga called 'Somebody's Mother'.

By far the most exhilarating afternoon lesson took place on Friday after play. The whole school crowded gleefully, three in a desk and some standing, into one classroom. We shared tattered copies of the *National Song Book*, one of the women teachers played the twanging piano and our headmaster's magnificent voice rumbled among the pitch-pine rafters. We roared out 'The Golden Vanity' and 'Marching Through Georgia', and cooed through 'Shenandoah' and 'Killarney' in obedience to the red-tipped cardboard pointer. When it came to 'Charlie is my Darling', there was no holding us; geographically, we could not have been much farther from the Highlands, but our hearts were most certainly there.

Looking back, I wonder sometimes just what we did learn on those distant golden afternoons. Nothing? Everything?

Sweet Memories

It is astonishing to find how many teachers are incapable of playing the piano these days. It is particularly astonishing when you consider how many of them had music lessons in their early years. I am among this disappointing band, and when, on supply, I am approached by anxious headmasters bearing hymn books open at 'Let All the World in Every Corner Sing' in five flats, I have to confess my uselessness.

'I can manage "Hushed was the Evening Hymn",' I offer gallantly, 'if it's in C and we take it slowly.'

Sometimes the offer is accepted, but naturally assemblies need a change of hymn quite often, and I am the first to admit that there is something a trifle lugubrious about 'Hushed was the Evening Hymn' when it is played at my pace. Usually, the next morning, the headmaster brings along a tuning fork, and everyone is happy.

Yet, when one looks back, what an enormous amount of time and care went into the musical education of my generation when they were small. My earliest memories are of the family gramophone which had a green fluted horn, rather like a curled-up rhubarb leaf, from which all sorts of delights emerged, from 'Barcarolle' to 'Oh, You Beautiful Doll'.

Both our parents could play the piano and also 'sang like steam engines', to quote Beatrix Potter. Now and again, musical friends would be invited to spend an evening at our home and we children listened to them trilling sentimental ballads such as:

> *Come, come away*
> *At the break of day*

and 'Sympathy' and 'Absent'. One which seemed to affect the company deeply began:

> *Dearest, the night is lonely,*
> *Waneth the trembling moon,*

but, mercifully perhaps, the rest escapes me.

It was about this time that my own musical talents began to burgeon. I began to pick out tunes with one finger. Naturally, I chose my favourites. Trembling moons, ends of perfect days, and pale hands that other people loved beside the Shalimar had no place in my repertoire, but I thumped out 'There is a Happy Land' (all on the black notes) and such gems as 'K-K-K-Katie' and 'We are the Robbers' from *Chu Chin Chow*.

To my dismay, this accomplishment was greeted with considerable head-shaking by my parents and their musical friends. 'Playing by ear!' they murmured sadly. If I had been caught robbing the poor-box they could not have sounded more shocked. 'Of course, it will ruin her chances of playing from music later. She should start lessons at once.'

And so, at the tender age of six, music lessons began, and all the misery of daily practices. My tears were of no avail but when we moved to the country, my spirits rose. Surely, music teachers could have no part in this Garden of Eden? But one was found, and together we battled on once a week after school.

There was a lot that I liked about Miss Mount. In the first place, she was very small, not much bigger than I was, in fact, and this made me feel kindly and protective. Then she lived in a beautiful old house which stood in a garden high above the lane.

There must have been a drop of eight feet or so from the garden level to the road.

One toiled up six steep steps to reach the gate but, once inside, the garden was welcoming. There were rustic arches across the paths bearing American Pillar and Dorothy Perkins roses, and little box hedges, no more than six inches high, bordered the flower beds.

Another thing which pleased me about Miss Mount was her thoughtfulness for flies. Against the ceiling of her drawing room dangled a red and yellow paper ball.

'It's the flies' playground,' she explained, following my gaze, and there were certainly quite a number waltzing dizzily about it. In an age of glutinous fly-papers, swarming with the dead and dying, I approved of such humanity. Not that I counted myself a great fly-lover. I knew of their disadvantages, but with ghastly fly-papers and messy fly-swats in every home I considered the dice loaded too heavily against the poor things, and was glad to find someone less murderously inclined than most.

She was kind to me, too, as well as to the flies, and after my lesson always gave me tea. This I looked forward to eagerly, partly because I was terribly hungry after school, but also because I enjoyed the ceremony which attached to this light repast.

The kettle, I knew, had been humming over the low flame of the Beatrice stove in the kitchen, all through the music lesson. As soon as I was released from my bondage and had unstuck the backs of my knees from the oilcloth top of the music stool, Miss Mount would vanish kitchenwards.

'Can I help?' I used to call politely, but I was never allowed to. No doubt Miss Mount valued her china.

Soon she would reappear bearing a tray. It was always spread with a beautifully starched white tray cloth which had a crotchet edging very similar to that which adorned the legs of my cotton drawers. I should have liked to point out the similarity to my music teacher, but delicacy forbade.

She poured our tea from a fluted silver teapot which had a knob on its lid like a blanched almond, and we invariably had squares of home-made gingerbread to eat. Sometimes there was seed cake as well which Miss Mount enjoyed while I averted my gaze. The very sight of it made me shudder.

We drank two cups apiece, chatting lightly of this and that, Miss Mount's new pansies, perhaps, or the amazing way her redcurrant jelly had set after only five minutes' boiling that morning. I held my own by giving her interesting details of my rabbit's latest confinement while, high above us, the flies hovered happily round their playground. It was a blissful half-hour when, for once, I felt quite grown-up.

When the tray had been taken into the kitchen again, Miss Mount lifted down a tartan box from the mantel shelf and I was allowed to choose a piece of Edinburgh rock. There was certainly a great deal to like about kind Miss Mount.

That is, before and after the lesson. During that dread half-hour, I quailed under her stern discipline. While I clove, sweating, to the music stool, Miss Mount sat beside me on a chair holding a ruler. It was a cylindrical black one, with an end looking like a draught. She used it to point out the notes and also to correct my fingering. It hurt horribly, more, I am sure, than kind Miss Mount ever knew.

She was a glutton for work, too, and did her best to press me through the pages of Ezra Read's *Easy Pianoforte Tutor* at a brisk pace. I toiled on, but my heart was not in it. Dear Ezra Read I could manage without too much attention from the ruler, but new pieces were apt to bring up the bruises.

I grew cunning, and used to postpone the advent of these new masters by pleading an inability to understand something called Continental Fingering. This meant that the notes were numbered from one to five, in contrast to English Fingering which gave a stout cross for the thumb and one, two, three and four for the fingers. I early discovered that it took longer to procure a piece with English Fingering – the only sort, I assured Miss Mount earnestly, which meant anything to me.

'It should have been here by this morning's post,' Miss Mount used to say anxiously. I think she thought I would be disappointed. 'But never mind. Let's run through Ezra Read's "Sweet Memories" again.' And safe from the ruler's assistance, I would gladly oblige.

Thanks to Miss Mount's tireless efforts, so long ago, I can still render 'Sweet Memories' with speed and accuracy. It is much admired by other teachers who overhear me taking a music-and-movement lesson based almost entirely on 'Sweet Memories with Variations'.

'But I thought you couldn't play!' they cry.

'Only Ezra Read,' I tell them firmly. 'Anything more advanced makes my knuckles ache!'

Return to Arcady

As is evident from her memoirs, Time Remembered, *Dora recalled her village school at Chelsfield in Kent with great affection, and stayed in touch with Norah, her childhood friend, for the rest of their lives.*

In the early 1970s, the Sunday Telegraph *asked her to revisit the school and to write an article on her impressions*

*of how things had changed over the intervening half-century.
She took Norah's daughter and granddaughter with her.*

It's clear that they all enjoyed the day, as did the photographer.

We were eight years old when we first met, Norah and I, at the village school. And now, over half a century on, I was driving with her daughter and her granddaughter, aged six, for a return visit.

What should I find? All my life I have looked back on those three school years as idyllic, always afternoon, always sunny.

This morning might well start a day of disillusionment. For one thing, it pelted with rain. We splashed after the school bus, and drew up behind it at the old familiar steps up to the high playground. Other cars were disgorging tidy dry children with glossy shoes. Little girls rushed to greet their friends as I used to rush to meet Norah. But on such a morning we should have been in dripping mackintoshes, wet-faced, mud-spattered after our mile-long walks. On the other hand, we should have been carrying wet

violets or dog roses, souvenirs of our adventurous journey denied to these non-pedestrians.

The children went up the steps, but the young headmaster, elegant and welcoming, bade me enter by my old headmaster's front door, his house having been incorporated into the school. It seemed positively sacrilegious to walk so boldly into Mr Clarke's hall. Ahead lay his sitting-room, once subfusc and holy but now filled with gleaming stoves and enormous saucepans and a vast basin full of sage and onion stuffing.

'It's roast pork today,' said the lively cook. 'You're lucky!'

And it was, and we were.

The headmaster led the photographer, Michael, and me into assembly, held in the long classroom divided by a glass and wood partition as in my day. It was amazing how little the early Victorian architecture had been altered. I had feared a plethora of reeded glass and chrome. Apart from bright paint and pictures, it was easily recognisable.

The children were singing 'O Jesus, I have promised', followed by 'Kum Ba Yah'. They sang much more melodiously than we did, and the soloists lacked shyness. We might have tittered to see our friends in the limelight. All that was missing was Mr Clarke's magnificent bass – long-stilled – to lead us.

Then came an innovation. About ten children each read a short safety hint. The first advised us to wear our hard hats when riding our ponies. (Ponies! I was the luckiest child in the school because I owned a battered scooter.) The sensible warnings about plastic bags and petrol and playing barefoot went on, and I surveyed the new floor of polished tiles. You could not have gone barefoot on our old floor of splintery boards, scuffed with boys' steel-tipped boots, with here and there a knot of wood as hard and bright as a buttered brazil nut.

The children settled to their lessons, and the headmaster took

Michael and me to view the playground. The shed was in the same corner with, I swear, the same iron girder along which we used to swing hand over hand like monkeys.

'Have a go now!' urged Michael. But my feet would have trailed on the ground. There were hieroglyphics painted on the asphalt for some up-to-date games which had superseded our drill in four lines. But the old lime trees still flourished.

'We're going to try to put back the seats under them,' said the headmaster. 'We've got some marvellously helpful parents!'

The four classrooms hummed gently. The infants were clustered chummily at round tables. Norah's grandchild smiled at me against a dazzling background of wall pictures. In the next room, two goldfish sported in a tank.

'What do you call them?' I asked. (Morecambe and Wise? Janet and John?)

'Goldfish,' said a boy politely.

In the top class, Arithmetic was in progress, a bustle of busy set-squares and frowning concentration, far removed from our inky exercise books and bored sighs. This was the better modern way, I see. They were working from within. Our work was imposed upon us.

The oldest child here was eleven. We had fourteen-year-olds in this room when I sat here. They were known as Standard Seven and reckoned to be practically grown up. The school then was roughly one hundred strong. It was now nearer a hundred and twenty, but I found it more tranquil. The teachers were quieter. The children worked because they were interested. They were amazed when I showed them the cane which was occasionally used by Mr Clarke. It had to be unearthed from some hidden nook in Mr Clarke's bedroom, now the headmaster's office.

School dinner was eaten at the desks. Michael and I sat at the headmaster's table and examined the plates displayed for our inspection as they were returned. Greens, I observed, still got left, the rest went.

'Like to ring the bell?' I was asked.

Like to! Heady stuff, this wielding of power in the shape of five pounds of solid wood and brass.

Painting was on the timetable that afternoon. Entranced, they dipped paper into trays of liquid and paint blobs.

'We're *marbling*!' they said, proudly. I was envious. Most of my afternoons had been spent unpicking some loathsome hem on a blood-spotted oblong of calico smelling of dog biscuits. The boys did Mechanical Drawing, carefully shading cubes and cones on very small pieces of paper. No doubt about it, things had improved.

I surveyed the room. Books and pictures were everywhere, bright, beguiling, an invitation to read, to learn, to discover more. One ginger-coloured bookcase housed our library against the further wall. Battered copies of Henty, Robert Louis Stevenson and some Nelson's classics occupied most of the space, apart from a row of identical grey paperbacks entitled *Thrift*, given, one supposes, by some Victorian society interested in the native poor, and of no interest to any child.

In the lobby, between the warm stove and the row of wash basins, some boys knelt on the floor making boats with their boy-size carpentering sets. There was a snugness about the scene as they chattered and hammered. It might have been an orderly Victorian nursery on a wet afternoon.

It was this domestic atmosphere, which I so clearly remembered – and so feared to find gone – which impressed me most during this return visit. The well-preserved building contributes greatly to this homely aura. The serenity of the staff and the courtesy of the children add to it. It was not ever thus. An entry in an old log book states:

'June 18th, 1883. Obliged to expel Thos. Hills from this school for carrying stones in his pocket and threatening to throw them at the teachers' heads. He has been very tiresome lately.'

We were only threatened with autograph books. Michael watched me at work until one boy said to his friend, 'Shall we ask the bloke?'

Then he was set to scribbling, too.

The school bus was due. We said our farewells, and I took a last fond look at those picture-decked walls. What happened to George V, ablaze with orders below his trim beard, I suddenly wondered? And Queen Mary, wasp-waisted in white lace? Vanished, like Empire Day, and the children I played with here so long ago.

Their descendants waved goodbye enthusiastically.

'Smashing kids!' said Michael, as we drove away. 'Smashing school!'

'It always was!' I told him.

Children of the Trees

Three little girls hung upside down on the bar. Their skirts fell from their sturdy waists like opening umbrellas. Their faces were scarlet, their mops of hair brushed the stony playground. You might think that gripping a cold iron bar with the backs of bare knees and the tender palms of your hands would be a fairly dispiriting exercise, but obviously these three were finding it highly exhilarating. They hung there, smiling, surveying their upside-down world in mute bliss.

The parallel bars were a new feature in the school playground. It was apparent that they were going to give great pleasure. I was glad to see that a pair of boys still swung energetically along the branch of the ancient oak tree which has supplied a natural gymnasium for generations of village schoolchildren. The branch is shiny with honourable use. Strategically growing about six or seven feet above the gravelled surface of the ground, it invites determined leapers to jump to it. Once there, palms tingling against the bark, the children find it delicious to swing along sideways like a human pendulum, hands moving rhythmically all the way from the stout trunk until the branch swoops abruptly skyward and they have to drop off.

This is not the only joy which this noble tree provides. Some years ago, an enlightened headmaster fixed a massive rope ladder from a central branch. It dangles to within arm's reach and offers an exciting path to a leafy paradise. I have passed through that empty playground on a hot day and heard chattering above me, and glimpsed figures among the thick foliage. There they sit, enjoying a secret world, airy and remote, with birds, winged insects and busy green caterpillars swinging on gossamer thread, for company.

What varied joys trees give to children! They can become houses, fortresses, ship's rigging, club rooms for those secret societies essential to growing up, or simply a refuge from the pressure of adult demands. Their branches provide peace and beauty in every season, from spring's shimmering green to winter's dark lace and, perched among them, above the dull world of everyday happenings, a child can look down and catch a rare feeling of superiority.

When I was a child, we had several trees to which we could escape. One was nearby, overlooking a small pond and a fine slope of cornfields. It had the added attraction of being close to the road, so that one could sit hidden, but hear the fascinating conversation of passers-by. The glimmer of dark water below added to the pleasure. Birds splashed at the shallow edge and then returned to perch close by, shaking their feathers and preening themselves quite unperturbed by their young intruder.

A row of fine elm trees near the church offered a challenge to the boys but were too high for us to attempt. The boys scrambled nimbly aloft to collect rooks' eggs from the untidy nests which swayed sickeningly in the topmost boughs. They came down from these raids very gingerly, holding one or two eggs in their mouths. We always hoped that the eggs would break and, better still, turn out to be addled. We were passionately on the side of the birds, and if the boys thought that we should be dazzled by their prowess they were soon disillusioned by our scathing indignation.

There were some beautiful beech trees in a wood half a mile away, with long branches trailing obligingly close to the ground. These made splendid horses, and we bounced up and down until

we were dizzy. Unfortunately, it was impossible to climb into the tree. The long branches were too slippery for a staircase, and the massive trunk, with bark as grey and wrinkled as an elephant's hide, soared like a cathedral pillar a good twenty feet or more before producing the branches which provided our stable. Earthbound, we gazed in envy at the squirrels which leapt airily above us.

Our favourite tree was a well-grown yew, which started its living stairway a mere two feet above the thick carpet of dark needles which squeaked as you walked upon them. It was essential to begin the climb with the left foot, for there was an awkward corner about five feet farther up. After that the going was easy, and the branches fanned out to supply several comfortable perches. Here we talked, sang, had picnics, planned a magazine, discussed the foibles of our families and heartily deplored the wicked waste of time spent on compulsory schooling. Here we pined for such impossible things as an inexhaustible supply of fudge, naturally curly hair and new bicycles.

An added pleasure was to pick at the bark of the branches on which we reclined. The top brown scale, brittle and thin as paper, peeled away to disclose a warmer brown layer. This in turn gave way to softer skins growing ever pinker in hue, until the final soft tissue was exposed – a gentle rosy flesh giving off a resinous scent matched by the fragrance of the glossy foliage around us.

We knew better than to eat the bright soft berries on the tree. Swallow just one, we warned each other, and you will fall down as dead as a doornail! (Years later, in the course of writing a script to be broadcast to schools, I warned the children about yew berries. The result was an irascible note from an old lady in her eighties who assured us that she had enjoyed them all her life!)

Our constant companion, a near-terrier dog called Tony,

snuffled about at the foot of the tree on these occasions, or sometimes lumbered off after a rabbit. One tranquil afternoon, the peace of our siesta was shattered by a gunshot and the ear-splitting yelping of the dog. Shouting and screaming, we crashed earthward through the branches, ignoring the ripping of skirts and bloomers and the immodest display of our liberty bodices.

The man who held the gun stood rooted to the spot, jaw dropped, eyes starting from his head. He was shaken to the core. As we pointed out to him, in passionate unison, he might jolly well have killed us as well as poor Tony. The latter sat shivering with self-pity, but apparently unhurt. We scooped him up tenderly, uttering endearments. With a final sharp warning to the man about the danger of firearms, we set off home.

Lying back in our aching arms, his legs stuck stiffly in the air, Tony enjoyed every minute of his journey.

But it was not only drama, refuge and exercise which trees gave us. They also provided us with many playthings. We collected conkers and made chairs for the dolls' house. We made whole armies of acorn men. We soaked all kinds of leaves and made spectacular skeletons to mount on brown paper. We

stripped the soft part between the ribs of horse chestnut leaves and turned them into kipper bones. Oak apples were a fine substitute for marbles. Hips and haws made splendid necklaces. Hazel, walnut and beech trees provided welcome snacks, and the young leaves of hawthorn proved quite appetising when really hungry. A hollow damson tree made a useful safe for private treasures.

Children and trees go well together. I like to see the climbing frames sprouting in the playgrounds, supporting scores of blissfully up-ended children. But where are the by-products? Where is the bark to pick, the nuts to eat, the nests to discover? And then . . . it's all so clean. *Real* climbing means hands grimy with good bark dust, twigs down necks, splinters in knees, and torn clothes smelling deliciously of bruised leaves and the glorious out-of-doors.

If I could have my way, every playground should have a yew tree as climbable, as consoling and as companionable as my childhood friend. Long may it flourish!

Three Ponds

The dwindling of ponds in our countryside is a sorry business. Not many years ago most country children had the pleasure of dawdling by or, better still, squelching through a pool of muddy water by the roadside as they made their way to school. The pond was a joy in any weather and at any season.

We were particularly lucky in our village because we had three ponds. The one in the centre of the village, though tamely hemmed in by white railings, attracted most of the schoolchildren's attention. Like all ponds, it had sinister legends attached to it.

'Two people bin drowned here,' a big boy told me. I was eight at the time, a newcomer, and ripe to be impressed. On the day that he imparted this false piece of information there was ice on the pond and a bevy of us had congregated to see 'if it would bear'.

The usual procedure was being carried out. The bigger boys were urging the smaller ones to walk across to the further shore where black elm roots writhed snakelike under the ice. Understandably, the small boys were loth to attempt this perilous journey, and taunts and jeers rent the air.

'Who's yeller? Who's a cowardy-custard? Who's afeard of his mum?'

Stubbornly, the little boys hung back, protesting, or broke free and ran home. It was the big boy, I recall, who solved the problem by scooping a massive knobbly flint from the bank and staggering with it to the edge of the pond.

'Git back, you lot!' he yelled. 'I'm going to heave this out the middle!'

We hastened back respectfully. We did not want the thing dropped on our feet anyway and, from the contortions of the carrier, it was obvious that he would not be able to support its weight much longer. He gave a mighty heave over the railings. The stone landed with a crack plumb in the middle of the ice, and remained there.

We all cheered madly and surged on to the ice. The big boy wiped his nose on the back of his knitted glove and grinned proudly. As far as I can remember, it was the only occasion on which he distinguished himself inside or outside school.

Later in the spring this pond was awash with great glutinous masses of frog-spawn. It drifted gently in the waves made by the children wading at the edge. Barefoot, with cold slime squelching between their toes, the boys tried to find pieces small enough to

go into the jam jars that stood ready on the gritty road. It was a difficult job. The stuff was heavy and unmanageable, and like an iceberg in that only a small portion of its bulk was in sight. But somehow the jam jars were filled, and we all admired the eggs swirling about in muddy water. As days passed, we waited impatiently for the tadpoles to hatch.

But, for some reason, the second pond was supposed to produce better frog-spawn. This was opposite our own house and we looked upon it virtually as family property. It was smaller than the central pond and free from tiresome railings. It lay in a crescent of high banks which were crowned with may trees. It was possible to get to them by leaping to a soggy peninsula which jutted out from the side of the road. Once there, one had to jump for a branch and swing perilously over the water, scrabbling at a crumbling bank with one's feet until it was possible to let go and grasp roots, grass and low branches and haul oneself to the plateau where the trees grew. Naturally, more people had been drowned in our pond than in the village one, and the awful blackness of the water, silted over with dead leaves and silky grey scum, made the whole operation pleasurably terrifying.

After the frog-spawn season, the pond was used for playing ducks and drakes with smooth pebbles or for paddling with or without shoes. The trees around it we used as a retreat from the demands of family life. There was one hawthorn tree which could be climbed easily, and from the vantage point near the summit there was blessed peace and a fine view of the valley. Better still, other children coming to play with the water could be watched unobserved, giving a thrill of secrecy as one sat mouse-still among the leaves.

It was by this pond that I received my first proposal of marriage from another eight-year-old. I was rather busy at the time making a dam from the peninsula to the road, but I remember breaking off for half a minute to consider the proposition and the proposer. I told him, I remember, that I might possibly marry him, but that if Leonard Someone (whose surname now escapes me) should have the good sense to ask me then I should be obliged to reject his offer as I much preferred Leonard. Looking back, I must have seemed a trifle offhand, but the dam building was a full-time job and I disliked being interrupted by these emotional complications. I like to think I thanked the young man for the offer, although I doubt it.

The third pond was in a farmyard. It lay in the middle of a square formed by rosy-red farm buildings and a low brick wall on the roadside. Over this we hung on our way to and from school. It was the most enchanting of the three, for it was a private pond always carrying a flotilla of ducks and geese upon it. Sometimes the geese would waddle out, hissing menacingly, necks outstretched, but they were well below our level, and we could afford to be brave and ignore them while we watched the life that seemed to teem round this pond.

The carthorses drank there, stirring up the mud with their great hairy hooves as they splashed ponderously into the water.

Little eddies swirled round their legs, and the ducks fled squawking to the other side, drops flashing from their orange feet and outstretched wings. We watched fascinated as the horses' muzzles stayed below the pond's surface – for hours it seemed – while only the slow rippling of the long bent necks showed that water was being imbibed.

Water wagtails tittupped to and fro and sparrows bathed in the shallows. In the summer, swallows dipped across the surface and caught the gnats which drifted there, and thirsty bees clung along the wet edges pausing between flights from the lime trees and their hives.

Looking back, I think sometimes that we learnt more from our three village ponds than from our three teachers. We certainly learned a lot of natural history and we learned, too, much more about our fellows as we observed them unselfconsciously playing with this happiest of elements.

I mourn the passing of so many ponds.

Silver Paper and Pieces of String

I met a child in the lane the other day. We both carried large knobbly objects of speckled grey and white. Mine was a newspaper parcel bearing a delectable damp conglomeration of potato peelings, cabbage leaves, and the tops and tails of carrots, all for my neighbour's chickens. When I first saw the boy in the distance, I wondered if he too was bearing his burden chickenward, but from the way he stumbled along it was evident that his parcel was considerably heavier than mine.

When we were quite close I saw that he was carrying a massive flint with a hole in it. It was the sort of thing you see edging cottage flower beds, or balanced on top of garden walls in the north. It must have weighed ten or twelve pounds, and the child was red-faced with his exertions.

'Are you going to make a rockery?' I hazarded.

The child looked scornful. 'It's for my collection,' he puffed, resting his burden for a moment on the bank. 'I collect stones with holes in them. This will be the biggest.'

He levered the monster against his stomach with one dirty knee and staggered on. His face was alight with pride and excitement.

Everyone, it seems, is a collector at some time or other, but from the age of seven until twelve appears to be the most fiercely acquisitive period. It is at this stage that stamp and autograph albums are cherished, cigarette and tea cards amassed, and relatives and friends of young collectors find themselves obliged to consume vast quantities of one particular preserve so that a hopelessly large number of paper golliwogs can be acquired and finally exchanged for a handsome badge. This, too, is the time when private museums are set up on bedroom window-sills, ranging from fossilised sea urchins to a morsel of rusty machinery labelled 'Roman Timepeace' in wobbly capitals.

We had just such a museum when we were children. Our most cherished possession was a glass egg. We could not think what purpose this could have served. I now know that such pretty toys were used by cooks to cool their hands before they made pastry, but to us it was a complete mystery. We asked everyone what it could be. My father told us that it was 'a glasshopper's egg', which we considered the height of subtle humour and repeated to our friends *ad nauseam*.

One of my earliest collections was of coloured glass. For reasons I have forgotten, I stored it at the foot of an ivy-clad tree on the way to school. It seemed very romantic to stop there, seek out my treasures and gloat over their beauty. There was a piece of green liniment bottle (an emerald), a piece of blue camphorated oil bottle (a sapphire), part of a watch glass (a diamond), and a fragment of someone's bicycle reflector (a ruby). It was a very small collection but, as you can see, a very choice one.

The boys in the village collected birds' eggs. We girls might have had one or two common eggs such as thrush's and blackbird's – poor things compared to the boys' rook eggs – but our hearts were not hard enough for this, and we preferred to pick flowers or leaves.

It was during the first year at the grammar school that collecting silver paper became the rage. We did not bother with the plain stuff which was rolled into enormous balls in those days, and adorned many a rural mantelpiece before going on to the Cottage Hospital for some good purpose. We sophisticates collected patterned silver paper, and I can recall now some of the beauties in my own collection. One had a gold background with rows of scarlet strawberries on it. Another was a symphony of silver, mauve and pink. One was embossed with coronets. They were all gorgeous, and we pressed them to a satin smoothness with a fingernail which soon grew hot with loving friction.

It was the custom to house these beauties between the leaves of our Bibles. Somewhere between Ezekiel and Daniel was considered the best spot. There was more pressure there than in the New Testament or in the Genesis to Numbers area. We used to sit cross-legged on the hall floor waiting for our headmistress to enter for prayers and turn the leaves of our Bibles with reverently bent heads. Sometimes we transacted a silent swap with our next-door neighbour, but one soon learnt not to snatch back, for nothing tears with such agonising ease as a piece of silver paper.

Some lucky people remain collectors all their lives, and other lazier souls actually pay to view their splendid rows of pastille houses or Waterford glass or those cream jugs made in the form of cows. (I wonder how many people find holding a beast by the tail, while it spews forth liquid from its mouth, rather distasteful!)

Such collections, of course, cost money, and perhaps the most satisfying collections are those, like my silver paper, which cost nothing at all. How rewarding it is to garner that lovely long piece of string from a parcel, or that unusual square paper clip from a rejected short story – almost a consolation prize – and the beautiful uncreased pieces of brown paper which some generous laundries spread over the washing! These are the prizes which stir our collecting instincts still and, as we store them lovingly away, we are transformed briefly into those young magpies which once we were, so long ago.

Midsummer Madness

Years ago, when I was young, I was an unwilling participant in the celebrations for an Empire Day. The planned festivities let loose no end of misplaced enthusiasm on the part of grown-ups, and I well remember struggling with one end of an arch which was adorned with paper roses and ribbon. Another stout five-year-old, identically tricked out in white with a pink sash, and a garland of yet more roses askew on her brow, fought at the other end of the arch.

It was our painful duty to trip round the playground holding the thing, and occasionally to dance under and round it, in company with the rest of the class. Proud mothers smiled upon us from under their dripping umbrellas as we lurched into each other, and the drenched roses dropped pink dye upon our

starched broderie anglaise. That afternoon, the iron entered my
infant soul, and no doubt those of my fellow sufferers.

Later, our agreeable school celebrated its twenty-first birthday, and again those diabolical outdoor plans were made. For
weeks, we marched, hundreds of us, four abreast, up and down
an enormous field, crossing diagonally, weaving in and out, to
the shrill exhortations of those in charge. The final touch of
horror was to rush, when we heard a piercing blast on the
whistle, to allotted places which then spelt out a massive 21.
Secreted in our bodices or our knicker legs were handkerchiefs in
the school colours, and these we waved frenziedly as we ran,
cheering spontaneously, to our places.

Looking back, I think we did very well. Gay spontaneity, after
five or six weeks' gruelling rehearsal, takes a bit of effort,
especially while running at high speed and simultaneously
extracting a handkerchief from one's knicker leg.

But perhaps the most poignant of my memories is of another
Empire Day, when I was teaching. On this occasion, about five
hundred infants were decked in paper hats of red, white and
blue. At a given signal, they were to run happily together, to

coagulate, as it were, into a Union Jack, finally squatting down so that the onlookers could see the finished result.

The weeks of work leading up to this simple exercise can well be imagined. Getting the flag itself the right way up was only the first of our problems. Wearing the right coloured hat, keeping it on at all in a stiff breeze, overcoming childish fury, laziness, curiosity and a host of other obstacles, confronted us with quite enough hazards, but the last movement was the trickiest. Imagine five hundred tightly packed infants squatting down simultaneously. Of course, they fell over, sometimes genuinely, more often 'accidental-done-a-purpose'. And who can blame them?

There is something at once noble and pathetic in the way the English make exhaustive arrangements for summer festivities in the open air. You would think, after battling along this vale of woe for even, say, ten or twelve years, that a person of ordinary intelligence would have stumbled on the plain fact that the weather is not to be trusted and that the summer is the time when rainfall is heaviest in the British Isles.

Nevertheless, the myth continues that it is a season of roses and wine, of cotton frocks and cucumber sandwiches, and that it is a perfect time for outdoor junketings of every description, against a background of mown grass and heavy foliage lit by a brilliant and benevolent sun.

As early as January, in the bleak of the year, committees meet in village schools, church halls and the like and begin to hatch their plans for mammoth fêtes, tennis tournaments, bazaars, concerts and plays – all to be held in some windswept field or garden in the locality. Blowing on their fingers, adjusting their winter mufflers against the winter blasts in their ears, the planners can see it all in their mind's eye – the shimmering heat waves above the greensward, the gallons of lemonade, the stacks of ice-cream bricks, the happy throng in shady hats spilling gold into the needy coffers as generously as the sun above.

Teachers, who are normally dourly realistic as a race, are not immune to this fever, and the summer term can bring some of the most frustrating occasions of the school year. Because of the inability to recognise our climatic shortcomings from the outset, arrangements for outdoor jollities get completely out of hand. The mere fact that it is to be out of doors means that there is no restriction on space. This in itself breeds a dangerous euphoria which is particularly violent in those who are in charge of physical education, cadet forces, dancing and the like.

Visions of marching and counter-marching, four abreast, vast wheeling motions, gigantic formations of perfectly drilled children (all smiling, of course), flicker before those of a martial nature. Even more ambitious are those with actual uniforms, guns and other military paraphernalia at their command. Mock battles, assault parties, heaving guns across ravines, rescue operations under fire, explosions, Very lights – all these delightful and deafening activities can be indulged in, giving unalloyed pleasure to the organisers.

The dancing fanatics waver between large-scale excerpts from various ballets and ten country-dance teams performing 'Gathering Peascods' simultaneously. Infant teachers (who should know better, geared as they are to everyday crises) see their charges weaving accurate and charming patterns round the maypole or enchanting the spectators with a series of those galumphing folk-dances involving a lot of clapping and stamping.

Madness is in the air, and the school calendar has an ominous entry: 'Summer Fête' or 'Country Fair' (perhaps even 'Country Fayre' – it is going to be that sort of occasion) and the die is cast. It is all about to start again, the same crazy hopes and visions – pageants, dancing displays, tattoos, while the organisers live in cloud-cuckoo-land peopled with fragile girls in floppy hats and frills, looking like one of Louis Baumer's delectable pastel illustrations in Ian Hay's *The Lighter Side of School Life*.

Meanwhile, my more sober friends, get out your wellingtons and umbrellas. Midsummer madness is upon us. It is a chronic disease, and there is no hope of coming through unscathed. But we may as well go down fighting.

THE JOYS & PERILS
OF TEACHING

Infants Long Ago

For one term only I had the pleasure of taking the babies' class . . . but what a term that was! We met first, those forty-odd apprehensive newcomers and I, in a large sunny classroom on the western fringe of London. It was late in August and the year was 1940.

We had settled in comfortably by the end of the week and I was particularly pleased to find that I had a larger proportion of little girls to little boys in the desks in front of me. There were two fat dumplings called Julie and Jill who sat by the door and fought silently and savagely over the door handle whenever anyone went in or out. There was a blue-eyed beauty called Elizabeth, and another called Pauline, with a silky fringe, and a dozen or two more potential heart-breakers.

We had hardly got to know each other before the Blitz began. Most of the classes had to scamper to shelters in the grounds, but the babies and I were allowed to take up our chairs and walk just outside into the corridor which had been reinforced to withstand (we hoped) most of the bomb damage.

The children soon became aware that fighter aircraft from a nearby station went up a few seconds before the siren wailed, and I would watch them stacking their treasures carefully in case the warning was given. Then, as soon as the siren began, they would set off burdened with their belongings and tutting to each other testily, like so many old women disturbed at their knitting.

I had fully expected tears and terror from my charges but I need not have worried. Usually they gave a few long-suffering sighs when the wailing began. Sometimes a few exasperated comments escaped them at these interruptions.

'Just as I'd started cutting out!'

'There now! That thing made me drop my crayon!'

'Can I bring my painting water?'

But there was never a sign of fear as they collected chairs, gas masks and their work and struggled manfully to the door.

In the corridor we did the best we could. Usually we returned after a few minutes to the comparative peace of the classroom, sometimes a whole hour would drag by, and on one occasion we were stuck there from mid-morning until seven at night, and the iron rations had to be doled out to yawning children.

'Not *too much* lemonade, dear,' my headmistress said meaningly. 'Heaven knows how much longer we shall be here.'

Circumstances whisked me from them at the end of that one term and I never saw my favourite class again. But whenever I remember those

> *Old unhappy far-off things*
> *And battles long ago,*

I think of those forty-odd babies who were the best morale boosters I have ever met.

Trafalgar Day

Surprisingly enough, the voice at the other end of the telephone wire had an English intonation. I had been invited to visit the American school at a nearby USAF station, and was making the final arrangements with the principal's secretary.

'Can I come early?' I asked. 'Perhaps I could come up on the school bus?'

There was a gasp at the other end and a shocked pause. When

at last she answered, the secretary spoke doubtfully. 'You could, I suppose,' she said slowly, 'but it would be . . . well . . . quite an experience!'

At 8.30 the next morning, I waited at a bleak corner for the bus to come. I was beginning to wonder if I had picked the wrong place, when a small boy appeared in jeans and a dashing hat with fur ear-flaps.

I plucked up the courage to ask him if the American bus stopped here.

'Yeah,' he said suspiciously, 'but you can't get on it.'

I explained that the principal knew I was coming, and so I hoped that I should be allowed to board the bus. At the principal's magic name, the child thawed a little, contenting himself with a shrug which dismissed the whole unsatisfactory affair. At this moment, the bus arrived and ground to a standstill.

There were about a dozen children of assorted ages inside. They were all very quiet, sitting well down on their shoulder blades, with their knees lodged up against the seat in front, and deeply engrossed in comics. Nobody bothered with me, and we chugged along to another street corner where a knot of children waited.

The bus by now was much more lively. Derisive comments were hurled about, children began to press their way up and down the aisle to exchange comics and sweets; a comic or two even sailed through the air and someone's hat landed in my lap. We began to roar up the long hill that leads to the school but as we swung into the drive, comics and sweets were crammed hastily into satchels and pockets, and seats were resumed.

The bus was unnaturally quiet as we scrunched to a standstill by the front porch. As I descended from the bus, I saw the anxious faces of the principal and his secretary peering from the windows on the ground floor.

'You've arrived safely then?' asked the principal. His warm American voice breathed relief. I might just have emerged from a cageful of man-eating tigers. His secretary was scrutinising me closely, presumably for flesh wounds. Seeing none, she spoke with quiet pride.

'We still breed 'em tough in England,' she said.

The last classroom which I visited before catching my bus back from the American school housed the top grade – twenty or so boys and girls of about fourteen years of age who worked quietly at their desks while their master showed me round.

At length, his gaze wandered to his table where a clock stood side by side with a calendar. The clock said 2.15. Suspecting that I had kept him too long with my questions, I began to gather my things together and to make my farewells.

He put forth a detaining hand. 'I wasn't looking at the clock,' he protested, 'but at the calendar. It's Trafalgar Day, I believe?'

'So it is,' I said, 'I'd forgotten.' I picked up my umbrella.

'And Lord Nelson? He was killed at the battle, surely?' His voice was uneasy, his eyes troubled.

'Yes. The Battle of Trafalgar, 1805,' I recited glibly, reaching for a glove.

'I feel these children should know something about it,' confided their teacher, with a distracted air, 'but, to tell you the truth, I know mighty little about it. I daresay it seems a shocking thing to you . . . but being an American . . . well, somehow . . .' His voice trailed away apologetically.

'Not at all,' I began politely. And then the full horror of the situation broke upon me. This was an appeal for help and, to tell the truth, I knew mighty little about the battle, too. However, this *was* Trafalgar Day, and across a century and a half came the call. 'England expects . . .'

The master had very expressive, pleading eyes. I put down my umbrella and bag and took a deep breath.

'I'll tell them,' I said.

With twenty pairs of American eyes turned upon me, I found I knew even less than I had at first thought. I had no clear idea of the location of this battle, what were the issues at stake, what were the relative sizes of the opposing forces, nor – apart from Hardy of Kiss-Me-and-Or-Kismet fame – who were the other characters in this great scene.

I had vague memories of a picture of this admiral planting acorns to replace the wooden ships of England. It had been in a copy of Arthur Mee's *My Magazine* which our parents bought in the fond hope that we would improve what little mind we had between us. Monthly, we flung ourselves upon this excellent journal, devoured 'The Hippo Boys' avidly, and tossed it to one side. If only I could have foreseen this present predicament, I told myself sadly, how differently would I have treated those pearls.

Luckily I remembered that HMS *Victory* lay at Portsmouth, a mere hour's run from the school and, leading off with this fact, I launched into an account of Nelson's last battle, hoping that dramatic detail would make up for shaky data.

There was a boy I did not much care for in a desk near the front. He looked a knowing sort of child, who had summed up exactly my meagre hold on my subject. It was he, alone among the other attentive children, who interjected occasional queries, of a carefully careless nature.

'Fought Napoleon, didn't he, ma'am? Saw Marlon Brando as Napoleon. Was he good!'

I said Nelson was fighting the French. Yes. I continued with my narrative.

'Nelson,' said the child reflectively, 'there was a Nelson Sump'n somewhere used to sing.'

'Nelson Eddy,' I said shortly. 'Nothing to do with it.'

The rest of the class listened closely, and I began to feel that they were warming to Nelson, that slight, pale figure, maimed and half-blind, but indomitable, moving in the heat of battle. They sat forward in their desks as I swept them on, adding a few lurid asides about ship's surgery and buckets of boiling tar.

'Tar?' exclaimed my thorn.

'To cauterise the stumps,' I told him.

'Cauterise, ma'am?' came the echo.

His companions moved impatiently, rounding upon him. 'Stops the blood!'

'Heck! Never heard of that before? Cauterise?'

They turned away from him impatiently, and fixed their thirsty gaze once more upon me. I felt that I could not fail such trust. Tapping hidden springs of submerged knowledge, I poured forth all that I could to quench that thirst. What if it was slightly inaccurate, and decidedly over-coloured? It was the best that a hard-pressed Englishwoman could conjure up at a moment's notice.

Smoke poured through the rigging, spars splintered, powder flashed, men rolled over and were still, and the guns boomed. Hardy (dear, remembered Hardy) and other great men (names unknown) clustered round the small, broken figure on the deck. The star on his breast glittered in the flickering lamplight as they carried him below . . .

When I stopped, the children were very still. Then suddenly they began to clap. Their faces were solemn as their hands beat steadily together. For a moment, I was nonplussed until sharp realisation pricked me into proper humility. Gratefully I recognised that it was the small pale ghost of Nelson they applauded.

Restless Young Disciples

The difficulties of imparting religious knowledge are manifold, as everyone knows. It is hard enough for an experienced parson to explain one of St Paul's messages on Sunday morning to an adult congregation which is listening, or at least appears to be listening, with respectful attention. How much harder it is for those who try to instruct fidgety young children!

For one thing, the period allotted to religious instruction, in most primary schools, is the first of the day, coming hard on the heels of school assembly. Back in the classroom, the teacher confronts her forty-odd souls amidst the noise of hymn books being thrust into desks, the slamming of desk lids, ubiquitous chatter, the sniffling of those who have left handkerchiefs in the cloakroom, the jingling of money brought for school dinners, school photographs, school outings, school needlework or even a contribution to a school present for some member of staff whose school duties have finished for ever.

A queue, or a mob, according to the disciplinary skill of the teacher, waits by her table. Each member of it is in urgent need of attention. This one has toothache, that one has an aunt coming to stay, a third is due at the doctor and intends to be in good time. Someone has found a revoltingly dirty pink comb. Someone else wants to take charge of the tadpoles. And half a dozen are there, milling about aimlessly, simply because they want to be noticed.

By the time things have been sorted out, and the class is once more desk-bound, a good five or ten minutes have vanished.

Even then danger lurks outside. It is useless to imagine that once embarked on the story of Moses in the bulrushes, one is going to steer an uninterrupted course to his adoption by

Pharaoh's daughter. Scarcely has Pharaoh's edict on the Hebrew male children been explained when the first knock comes at the door, and in bounces a self-important child bearing anything from a stuffed squirrel to a pair of plastic sunglasses.

The number of child-hours wasted, up and down the country, on roaming school corridors with lost property must be phenomenal, and most of this perambulation takes place during the R.I. period.

By the time the construction of Moses' cradle has been explained and the mud is still wet, the classroom door will no doubt have been opened and shut a dozen times. It is useless to give way to exasperation and to shout, 'Go away!' to the thirteenth interrupter. It is bound to be the headmistress bringing the book one particularly wanted, and one will appear ungrateful as well as downright rude. It is simpler to face the fact that the period will end with Miriam's return to fetch the baby's mother, instead of the education of a boy at Pharaoh's court, as set out in this week's lesson plan.

But these difficulties, thrust upon one by circumstances, are nothing to those which exist, unsuspected by the teacher, in the minds of the children sitting in front of her. Only now and again does one get a glimpse of the thinking processes of the young upon the religious matters so carefully inserted.

It is rather like the fleeting view seen through the window of a washing machine. There goes the familiar bath towel, churning round and round, tossed this way and that, wound up with pillow slips and petticoats, curtains and coverlets. It is no longer flat, fluffy and oblong. It is a shapeless, sodden serpent of a bath towel, completely metamorphosed. Just so does a simple, straightforward question become mangled into chaos by the machinery of the child mind.

'Of course God's name is Harold!' asserted a five-year-old

having intoned 'Harold be Thy Name' during the Lord's Prayer. Another said that it seemed a pity that John the Baptist wasn't well and, on being asked how she had arrived at this conclusion, replied, 'He said he wasn't fit to stoop down.' The children's pictures illustrating Bible stories are equally matter of fact. God has three buttons down the middle and rake hands, just like any other male figure has when drawn by a small child.

This sort of sublime madness only comes to the surface occasionally to baffle the adult. It is sobering to think of the scale of secret misunderstanding which seethes in children's minds, perhaps for years. If any subject can bewilder more than another then that one is religious knowledge. The very nature of things spiritual leads to confusion, and the language of hymns and prayers is often obscure.

Naturally a child relates all his new knowledge to his experience and comes to terms with it, as in the two cases quoted. It is not the teaching which is at fault; it is the ruthless logic of the young savage working upon material as relentlessly as the washing machine.

As teachers, we do our best to put forward the stories, the ancient history, the geographical details, the drama and, above all, the moral teaching to be found in the Old and New Testaments. Sometimes we think we have been successful. The children have sat rapt. One or two have asked intelligent questions. We ask a few ourselves and get satisfactory replies.

But we know from past experience that many of the children have already started working silently on this morning's food for thought, hashing it up, chopping it this way and that, rendering it digestible for themselves according to individual needs and in the light of their own limited experience.

One of the best stories illustrating this comes from Norfolk. The incident happened at the beginning of the twentieth century.

A schools inspector had given an inspiring account of the Children of Israel in the desert. He had worked particularly hard in explaining to these rural children the usefulness of the camel. The camel's large feet gripped the sand easily, he explained. Its hump was its water supply. It provided transport, and shelter from the wind and sun for its master. It was long lived. Why, he asked the children, didn't we have such useful animals in Norfolk?

A gamekeeper's son rose to tell him. 'With them great feet,' he said witheringly, 'they'd crush the young pheasants.'

Truth is revealed in many ways. After a dozen or so interrupted lessons on Moses, we may at last come to the time when we watch the class busily drawing a picture of Moses talking to God. Both will have, of course, rake hands, large teeth and three buttons equally spaced down their fronts. But amusement is not the only emotion an honest teacher of R.I. will feel as she observes these efforts.

How would she set about such a task herself, she wonders? For, to be frank, in spite of those years of study, of giving and receiving religious instruction, is she really much farther advanced than the child when it comes to the heart of the matter?

Scriptural Matters

It is a fact, undisputed among teachers of young children, that of all the subjects on the timetable, Scripture or Religious Instruction provides the largest amount of innocent entertainment.

This is understandable. A subject so vast, so deep, having to do with things intangible and mysterious, bristles with problems for both teacher and pupil, and young children – ruthlessly logical – will relate spiritual matters to their own everyday experience, often with bizarre results.

A six-year-old, it was reported recently, could not accept that God and Jesus were one and the same. 'If God's the Father, then he's boss,' he asserted.

'Why didn't God make us knowing everything? It would have saved a lot of trouble,' observed another.

Teachers and parents get accustomed to this direct approach, but I often wonder how clergymen feel when confronted by such questions. In many church schools, of course, the vicar is a regular visitor and has a ready answer for the sort of questions which would floor many reverend gentlemen who are not in touch with the child mind. There must be many occasions, such as Scripture examinations, when they are somewhat shocked not only by the pupils' ignorance but by their interpretation of the little that has penetrated.

In this part of the country, the annual Scripture examination takes place in the summer term and is under the auspices of the local diocese. A visiting clergyman comes to examine the children orally in the morning and a half-holiday is decreed for the afternoon. It is a pleasant occasion, usually in June, and by some divine dispensation always seems to be blessed with sizzling hot weather.

It was on such a day of splendid heat that our visiting examiner arrived at our downland school. There was a full attendance, all sixteen pupils being present, clad in their best with hair unusually well kempt. They ranged in age from five to ten and each hoped to be the lucky child who did well enough to gain the prize of the Bishop's Bible.

Outside, the world shimmered in a blue haze. Larks sang and bees droned. Inside, the air was heavy with the mingled scent of mignonette and hair oil. The clergyman was silver-haired and soft-voiced. It was obvious from the outset that he wanted to give us a favourable report and our hearts warmed towards him. Even the five-year-olds, usually over-awed, were emboldened by his easy manner to suggest some of the colours which might have occurred in Joseph's coat, and the story unwound as quietly as a skein of wool with only a minor tangle here and there to hold up the progress.

'And so Joseph saw seven fat kine and seven thin kine, you remember. Of course, you know what "kine" means?'

A heavy silence fell. A large proportion of the sixteen souls present obviously did not know what kine were. Some, succumbing to the heat, had slid down in their seats in a state of extreme languor. The two or three ten-year-olds, vying with each other for the coveted Bible, were chary of giving the wrong answer and remained silent.

'Come along now,' persisted the vicar. 'Kine! Think! What does it mean?'

His blue gaze lit upon seven-year-old John, nearly asleep in the front desk.

John jerked himself back to reality. 'Not being cruel,' he suggested. 'Not hurting no one.'

'That,' replied the vicar with a touch of frost in his tone, 'is "kind"! I said "*kine*"!'

There was an uncomfortable pause. A bluebottle whizzed in at the open door, scented the chill in the air, and whizzed out again.

'Oh *kine*!' said one of the ten-year olds suddenly. 'That's cows and that!'

'Quite right,' said the vicar, thawing immediately. The assembled company relaxed thankfully.

Question and answer continued, the air grew warmer. John rolled down his socks and scratched the pink garter marks encircling his stout legs. A light dew of perspiration appeared on the examiner's venerable forehead.

'And Joseph went to work for a good Egyptian. Who remembers his name?'

'Jesus,' said someone hopefully.

'Jesus was not born then,' replied the vicar with commendable patience.

'Pharaoh,' said another voice, listless with the heat.

'Not Pharaoh, although his name begins with P,' said the vicar helpfully.

A perplexed silence fell. No doubt those who had any idea at all of spelling sensibly supposed that Pharaoh began with F. There was a lull while a few scholarly souls contemplated this enigma. The vicar glanced at the clock on the wall.

'P-p-p-p-p,' he said softly. A few children sat up.

'P-o-t, P-o-t . . .' continued the vicar, turning hopefully from one side of the class to the other. The children looked troubled.

'P-o-t-i, P-o-t-i, P-o-t-i,' prodded the vicar.

'*Potiphar!*' shouted five-year-old Timmy triumphantly.

'Very good,' beamed the examiner. 'You see, you've beaten the bigger children this time.'

Timmy, pink and smug, glowed like a rose. His elders looked sourly at this display of infant erudition. He'd have plenty more chances to win the Bishop's Bible. Their own time was running short.

The examination wore on. The dreams, the years of plenty, the years of famine were behind us. Joseph was reunited with his brethren, and Jacob their father had been told the joyful news of his favourite son's survival. The hands of the clock crept towards twelve and the half-holiday was almost within grasp. It was now that the subject of Jacob's grey hair cropped up.

'An easy one for the last question,' said the examiner. 'Why was Jacob's hair grey?'

There was a little pause. It seemed almost too easy to answer. 'Because he was old.' While the bigger children, Bible bent, hesitated, young Timmy, flown with earlier success, chirped up again.

'Because he'd got twelve children to worry him.'

The vicar surveyed his own flock of sixteen with amusement, passing a tired hand over his own silvery thatch.

'I think that might well be the right answer,' he said gravely.

Joys on Supply

After the Second World War, the family returned from Witney to Newbury, where Doug's teaching job had been kept open for him while he was in the RAF. Dora did not take a full-time job but became a supply teacher, in theory for any school in Berkshire that might need her.

She did this for a number of years, gradually accepting fewer jobs as the writing took more of her time. They were usually in rural schools, and furnished her with a good deal of varied material for her subsequent novels.

With the onset of winter, I become increasingly solicitous for the health of the teachers at four nearby schools. As a supply teacher, I may be called to any one of them, and experience of all four during bad weather has made me a sadder and wiser woman.

At School A, for instance, a long dark corridor, rather like a claustrophobic cloister, runs from one end of the building to the other. Heavy double doors clang dismally at each end of this wind-tunnel, and the force of the gale which whistles down it has to be endured to be believed.

Five classrooms open from one side of it, and on windy days children fight their way from them, against enormous pressure, and can only gain admittance again by beating on the door and wailing for help from inside.

School A has one excellent advantage, though. A fine, roaring stove is housed in the end classroom, complete with a square oven door, which opens just wide enough to admit a squat, black kettle, which is thrust in among the hot coals at 10.30 a.m. and 2.30 p.m. regularly. Unfortunately for me, the teacher in this delectable room enjoys excellent health, and I usually find that I am in the room furthest from the stove, where the pipes are tepid, and the partition rattles like a wheelbarrow over cobblestones.

School B is small and snug, with two rooms only, and comfortably tucked into the side of a hill, but if the wind veers to the east, both open fires smoke appallingly. One's class is seen as in a glass darkly. Coughs and sneezes rend the blue veil around us, and smuts are wiped diagonally across the page with coat sleeves, while our complexions take on a kippered appearance. It must be said in School B's favour that it is always delightfully warm.

School C has a window, directly behind the teacher's desk, which lets in a draught that has defied generations of local builders. A woollen scarf, if only one can remember to take it, helps here. A mysterious, damp draught which blows upwards from ill-fitting floorboards is uncommonly sinister. On dank, dim, winter afternoons, dispiriting gossip about how far the vaults of the adjacent church extend, is best forgotten.

The last school, D, is also built on the side of a hill, and the playground descends so steeply that water drains down to the back door. A soak-away nearby is quite inadequate during a downpour, and a slow, dark trickle appears under the edge of the door, much to the delight of the children. A stiff broom is kept in this room, and, like Mrs Partington attempting to sweep back the sea, one attacks the invading force, to the accompaniment of such cries as:

'Mind that worm!'

'It's all over the top of your shoes, Miss!'

'Can I have a go?'

'Once we had a frog in!' and so on.

Yes, I think that room at School D is the worst of the lot, for as well as the outside door, there are two others, and the permutations and combinations of cross-draughts must run into hundreds. The only person on School D's staff who is ever ill is the one who has reigned in this room for years. Can this be cause and effect?

Of course, all four schools are elderly specimens, and are the victims of gentle decay. One forgives as one suffers. Less tolerance can be felt for some modern buildings. Surely, among all professions of men, school architects must be the most sanguine. What buoyant, happy-hearted optimists they must be to design some of the structures one sees, airy masses of glass and steel, riding out the gales on windswept plains. I remember, painfully well, one particular school.

The entrance hall, staff-rooms, cloakrooms and so on were in a central block, compact and sensible. But from this comfortable nucleus, three long arms radiated, each housing a row of four or five classrooms. Both sides of the rooms were of glass, and an open verandah took the place of the corridor which ran along the side of the row.

Many a time, with the maxim 'A teacher must set an example of neatness to the class' ringing in my ears, I have combed my hair, and set off – a model of tidiness – to run the gauntlet of that open verandah, only to arrive in front of the class looking like a Yorkshire terrier. On any day when there was the slightest wind, the opening of the door set papers whirling and cupboard doors swinging.

Ironically enough, the other side of the row of classrooms was fitted with sunblinds that pulled out like those of a shop. As far as I can remember, I only had occasion to use them once, and then they were firmly rusted in – a salutary comment on the English climate.

The school building on which I look back with the most affection was a one-storey affair of solid red brick, built round a quadrangle. This meant that the corridors, which ran inside the building round the quadrangle, were sheltered, and as the building was a low one we did not catch the wind too badly. The classrooms were placed on the south and the east sides, the hall took up the west, and staff-room and cloakrooms the north. The staff-room has a big open fire, well-fitting windows and – crowning mercy – a quick-boiling kettle. A first-class heating system and an ex-naval caretaker made that school as warm and weatherproof as its sagacious architect had intended.

There is a gale lashing at the windows as I write, and the rain is torrential. Someone will be wielding that broom at School D tomorrow. The weather forecast was that 'Continuous rain, heavy at times, is to be expected for the next twenty-four hours.'

The telephone has just rung and, as I felt in my bones, School D's frailest member is absent with a chill. I must go and look out my wellington boots.

One Afternoon

The SOS had come while I was making pastry. The head-master of the next village sounded agitated on the telephone. Could I possibly come over – just for the afternoon? It was the day that he took the bigger children swimming, and his only assistant was ill. Could I hold the fort from 1.20 to 3.30 p.m.?

His fervent thanks, when I said that I could, were enough to turn me into a female Walter Mitty – the-woman-who-saved-the-school.

The children had had their dinner and were playing in the dazzling sunshine as the bus drew up outside the gate. I descended in solitary glory and the children rushed to the railings and beamed upon me.

'She's come!' shouted one excitedly, to somebody in the background. 'Come here, quick! She's come!' The Walter Mitty feeling was intensified at this flattering welcome and I wondered if I should bow graciously, to right and left, as I walked through their ranks. I was spared further embarrassment by the arrival of the headmaster who, after greeting me as warmly as if I were the relieving force to the beseiged garrison, bore me off to the school-house to be fortified with cups of tea, before the two-hour ordeal in front of me.

While I drank I thought, not for the first time, how extraordinarily pleasant it is to be a supply teacher; for, if you have to refuse a head teacher's sudden appeal – why, that is all that is to be expected, and the whole affair is taken philosophically – but if you can go and help, why then, what a heroine you are! Whereas, if you are a down-to-earth, five-days-a-week, permanent slogger in the teaching world, what thanks do you get for turning up regularly at the job? Alas for justice! There is none.

Refreshed, we walked across to the school. The playground shimmered in the heat, and now most of the children had settled in the shade of a clump of horse chestnut trees that towered, dark and cavernous, above them. A froth of cows' parsley bordered the playground, and beyond the Downs rose veiled in a blue heat haze, to meet the bluer sky above. Somewhere, far away, whirred a hay-cutter and, near at hand, a row of late-flowering broad beans in the trim school garden wafted such soporific waves of scent that I was reminded of the Flopsy Bunnies who succumbed to lettuce on just such a drowsy afternoon, and wondered, with some alarm, if I too might not drown in sleep, here and now, at my post.

The register was marked, the swimmers departed, and I was left alone to survey my flock. There they sat, in every position of sticky heat, aged from five to nine. Remembering Napoleon's maxim that an army progresses at the rate of its slowest unit, I had decided to tell them an old German folk tale, suitable for the younger children rather than the older ones.

'Just for this afternoon,' I began diplomatically, fearful of creating a precedent for their absent headmaster, 'you may put your heads down on the desks to listen to the story.'

The older children looked slightly affronted at this suggestion, and drew themselves up into more decorous attitudes, but the young ones drooped thankfully. A thumb crept into one mouth, eyes assumed a glazed expression, and I wondered how soon sleep would close them altogether.

The story unfolded, and the room was very quiet. A small blue butterfly from the Downs outside fluttered inside the high window, and on my desk a full-blown rose dropped a shell-like petal with a pattering sound – then another, and another. By the time the story had ended and 'happy ever after' had drawn its customary satisfied sighs, only a ring of golden stamens trembled on the rose head, while on the desk lay a fragrant drift of fleshy pink petals.

As the children lolled, still bemused by the story and the heat, I thought of how much one hears about learning by doing, and how little about learning by non-doing. If the assimilation of atmosphere, that subtle but strong awareness of surroundings that makes the very stuff of personal memories, is to play any part in our make-up, it is in the inactive times that we store up, our treasure for the future. Here before me, rosy with heat and sleep, glassy-eyed and somnolent, were twenty children whose appearance might well raise sarcastic comments from an observing ratepayer. But, as they lay there, quiescent and receptive, who knows what priceless summer sights and smells were being savoured? Around them was a glorious hotch-potch of blue butterflies and pink roses. The drone of the distant hay-cutter mingled with the mixed scents of the neighbouring bean flowers, and the delicious biscuity tang given off by their own sun-scorched arms.

The clock ticked on. We learnt 'Bread and Cherries' by Walter de la Mare. They returned from play, tousled and hotter than ever, and drew, busily, pictures to illustrate the story and poem they had heard. They sang grace, wished me a polite 'good afternoon', then vanished from my sight, waving to the last, round the bend of the lane. I returned to the empty schoolroom and looked again at the drawings. Emaciated children, with rake hands and every conceivable deformity, were buying cherries as large as tennis balls, but to make up for the deficiencies of drawing, the pictures were as rainbow-hued as the twelve colours of a scholar's fine art crayon box could possibly make them.

It had been a lovely afternoon, I thought, as I waited for the bus in the sun-throbbing lane. At once, a stern accusing voice spoke within me. I recognised it as the inescapable call of conscience.

'But you,' it said with horrid truth, 'don't have to go tomorrow!'

Foot it Featly

One of the nicest things about being a supply teacher is the welcome one receives from the relieved headmaster or mistress. Equally warming is the unconfined joy of the members of staff who have been facing three-in-a-desk and absolute chaos among milk allotment at playtime.

After introductions, one is borne away to the temporarily bereaved classroom, and I sometimes wonder, as we make our way between knots of curious children, about the touching faith that head teachers have in my ability. For all they know, I may be quite incapable of teaching even the three times table (the multiplication tables are always drawn to my notice as in dire need of constant revision at every school). Or I may be wickedly cruel, and keep order by standing small children in corners with piles of slates on their heads. Or I might thrust my political opinions, if any, down their innocent throats. In fact, I might be a thoroughly bad lot, but on the very sound principle that a man is innocent until he is proved guilty, I am cheerfully accepted, and before long we are poring over the day's timetable.

Joseph for Scripture . . . then PT (apparatus next to the broom cupboard and please, please, check balls!) . . . Arithmetic – table practice essential, then carry on with Larcombe's textbook . . . But my eye is running ahead to the end of the day where I see 'RHYTHMIC WORK', and I have flashed back twenty-odd years.

*

'As you know nothing about Rhythmic Work,' my headmistress had said, 'you'd better watch Miss X taking her class a few times. She is most competent, and you can take notes.'

Secretly, at twenty, I was a little afraid of Miss X, a middle-aged woman of nearly thirty, sandy-haired, and with the extensive wardrobe to be expected from one with so many increments. Miss X also made up her record book a fortnight in advance, which I found intimidatingly efficient. I sat in a corner of the hall, notebook ready, and nervously acknowledged Miss X's brusque nod as she strode to the piano.

'Find a space! Don't huddle! Spread out, children!' she directed. There was a sluggish redistribution of knots of friends, Miss X crashed out a chord, and called loudly, 'Trees! Remember? Trees, then!'

The children began to wave their hands vaguely above their heads. As might have been foreseen, several naughty little boys very soon had branches interlocked in the most pleasurable way. Miss X, I noticed, did not sit on the stool provided, as this would have meant that half the class were out of her sight. She half-stood, therefore, with her knees bent at an unlovely angle, and peered at her charges over the top, her hands dashing up and down the keyboard with great gusto. I thought of the only two tunes I could play – both from Ezra Read's *Tutor*, and learnt, with tears, at the age of seven – and wondered if I should ever make the grade.

The lesson progressed. The children were butterflies, snow-flakes, frogs, fairies, giants and mettlesome horses. They fell asleep (to lullaby music), they woke up (to music which would have successfully aroused the dead), they swept floors, they plucked apples, they blew feathers from their hands up into the air, they watched them mount ('Up . . . up . . . up! Don't be idiotic, John Potts! Uncross your eyes!') and sank gracefully to the ground to collect them again. ('There is no need to crash like a sack of coal, Billy Bates!')

There was no doubt about it, Miss X knew her job, and I made feverish notes. The only snag was that Miss X was impatient by nature. She found that the children's ardour did not match her own, and their halting efforts annoyed her.

'Skip happily along the sea shore! Happily! Happily!' she intoned rhythmically. 'Feel the sun, and smell the sea! Happily skip! Happily skip!'

She left the piano and tripped among the stumbling, perspiring forms. Gracefully she bent from side to side, pointing her toes, and steadily her temper rose as she capered past her leaden-footed companions. 'Happily skip! Happily skip!' she panted, a trifle menacingly, and catching some breathless child by the hand she jumped the luckless infant ruthlessly along with her, doing her best to instil some of her own vitality into its sluggish movements. Her face was red and her eye was wild, but on she skipped.

'Smell the sea, happily skip!' she chanted. And then she saw the little boy. He was STANDING STILL. Dropping her bouncing partner like a hot cake, she flew to the unsuspecting child, and gave him one sharp slap on his plump leg.

'*Now* will you happily skip!' she said wrathfully.

The headmaster's forefinger had by now reached the last lesson.

'Rhythmic Work?' he asked anxiously.

'I can do that!' I assured him.

Love and Pea Tea

The great clock gazed from the schoolroom wall, its yellowing old face contrasting strangely with the children's drawings, bright and bizarre, which hemmed it closely on all sides.

Twenty to eleven, it said blandly. My watch said a quarter past ten. Full of doubt, I lifted it to my ear and compared its fussy ticking with the measured tread of the lying old gentleman on the wall. I had carefully put my watch right the night before. It was one of the preparations I had made as soon as I had been asked to go to the school to take the place of a stricken teacher. Other preparations had included sharpening my penknife (for automatic pencil-sharpeners in my temporary charge have an unnerving way of collapsing altogether or making such an ear-splitting din that I prefer to fall back on humbler methods), and looking out an ancient whistle for drill lessons.

'Drill?' my family said derisively. 'It hasn't been called drill for years. You're thinking of the black-stocking-and-Indian-club era.' I made a mental note to find out the prevailing title for the lesson at our school.

And, now, according to my watch, the time for that lesson had arrived. Or, horrid thought, if the wall-clock was right then we had missed it altogether.

The children, who had been flatteringly welcoming, were now busy with their work-books.

I addressed their glossy downbent heads. 'That clock is fast, isn't it?'

They came to garrulous life at once.

'Yes, Miss!'

'Been fast for a week, Miss.'

'That's why Mrs Dibbin hurt herself. She was standing on the desk, see, to put the hands back and she fell off.'

Encouraged by my interest, work stopped and tongues wagged.

'I could see she was on the edge, sort of, and I hollered out . . .'

'So did I. "Miss," I said, "Miss, look out! You're a-tippin up!" But it were too late.'

'She fell all up against these other desks. It must've hurt, but she never said much.'

They were obviously greatly impressed by their teacher's stoicism. They continued to praise her bravery as we clattered over the door-scraper to have our belated lesson.

I heard more later in the staff-room as we drank tea. Mrs Dibbin had continued through the day and went home, as usual, on the school bus to the neighbouring village. A boy and a girl had insisted on helping her to her house. The girl had made tea while the boy lit her fire.

'They're all very fond of Mrs Dibbin,' said the infants' teacher, collecting the cups. This was to be proved yet again within the next hour.

My suggestion that the class might like to write letters to their absent teacher was received with rapture. The children applied themselves diligently to their papers and I was kept busy putting awkward words like 'Brought' and 'Yesterday' on the blackboard.

The dinner-bell rang, the letters were piled on my desk, and the children streamed out.

In the quiet classroom, the wall-clock ticked steadily. By now, it was a triumphant half-hour ahead. I picked up the first letter.

Dear Mrs Dibbin
I hope you are better now. We all miss you very much. Mrs

*Saint has come to teach us and I wish you were back. Will you
have to be away for long? Please come back SOON.*
With love from,
Elizabeth.
P.S. We had pea tea today.

This letter, I discovered as I glanced through the pile, was
typical, for all breathed affection, bereavement and earnest hope
for Mrs Dibbin's early return to her own. All too often, I noticed
wryly, the plaintive cry for speedy reunion followed hard on the
heels of news about their temporary teacher.

Ah well, I thought, as I made my way towards my own dinner
in a suitably chastened frame of mind, at least I know what they
call 'drill' these days.

Distant Revelry

Well before halfway through the autumn term, some misguided enthusiast in the staff-room will have said, 'What
about a Christmas concert?'

It is an ugly moment for those quiet souls who ask for no more
excitement than getting the slower children safely from the com-
ponent parts of ten to the dizzy heights of carrying figures, and
who are content to jog along comfortably with Old Lob in his
farmyard, for a few weeks more, before abandoning work for the
inevitable orgy of paper-chains and slit wallpaper lanterns.

But they can count themselves as lost from the moment those
words are uttered. The very young members of staff – still trailing
clouds of psychology notes from college and eager to tackle
anything that gets them out of the classroom – look up from
their tea cups with a glad cry. Some older, but still vivacious,

members are equally enthusiastic, and a look comes over the headmistress's face which the faint-hearted recognise all too well. She is thinking:

(a) that the parents will love it;
(b) that it will swell the school funds;
(c) that it will cheer up the staff; and
(d) that the children will be able to let off pre-Christmas steam through this well-organised safety valve.

No one disputes the first two, although the last two assumptions are debatable, but no prudent assistant will join issue with her headmistress over points like these.

Headmistresses of larger primary schools have, on the whole, a kindlier attitude to life than their assistants have. Possibly it is because they are one degree removed from the rigours of the classroom. Their well-polished rooms, the rug on the floor, the desk calendar, the box of cigarettes for visitors, the paperwhite narcissi already in bud and standing squarely on a hand-woven mat, the tidy cupboard filled with new specimen readers and, above all, the ineffable, blissful quiet which pervades their havens, give headteachers a sedate mellowness which places them apart from those nearer the heat of battle. When they emerge into the scurrying corridors to be butted brutally by some bullet-headed child, they do not respond with a fierce '*Look* where you're going, silly!' as do their harassed assistants, but with a forgiving 'Steady, dear!' and, as like as not, a serene smile thrown in. They draw in great draughts of spiritual refreshment from the decent chintzes at their windows, their private matching cups and saucers – so different from the motley collection that stands, chipped and sketchily washed, on the tin tray in the staff-room – and from the pictures on their cream walls, Greuze, Constable, Reynolds, or a carefully selected corner from one of Breughel's scenes. Thus refreshed, they can face the hurly-burly of school life, and rise, strong and well-armoured, to meet the challenge of a Christmas concert.

A staff meeting is speedily arranged. Here the lukewarm teacher finds cold comfort since the babies, by right and ancient custom, are to be given the percussion band, the top-class master has plumped swiftly for a gymnastic display, 'The Mad Hatter's Tea Party' has been filched shamelessly by young Miss Smith, and ball throwing and bouncing to music will be performed, as always, by dear old Miss Jones's children. Not that anybody minds the last item. On the contrary, parents, teachers, managers and all old friends of the school would feel slighted if they could not expect ball games to music as soon as they saw Miss Jones approach the piano.

But the slower-witted teacher at the staff meeting faces the fact that it will have to be 'The King's Breakfast' all over again, and hopes that she can put her hand on that rather charming cow-mask, which she concocted from a chalk-box four years ago, and which she earnestly trusts is somewhere on top of the raffia cupboard, behind all those cereal cartons that may come in useful for a shop project if ever the inspectors come round again.

Excited chatter flows round her, as she sits bemused. Would that old dormouse costume be big enough for Tubby Bates? No, it would not be wise to borrow the canteen teapot. There were words last time. Not nice words. There was no earthly reason why tennis balls could not be dipped in carpet dye if the school sorbos bounced too high. Of course, *all* the babies must appear with the band! The mothers would be frantic if any were left out. Some must sit on the floor. Cross-legged babies could be packed up like sardines.

The battle is on. For the rest of the term the staff-room table will be littered with crêpe paper, as outfits for dairymaids, kings, hatters and dormice are hacked out with somebody's best needle-work scissors. Crowns and buckets, egg cups and teapots will jostle in the classrooms, and the strains of 'The Grand Old Duke of York' – with an irregular clashing of cymbals as accompaniment – will be heard from the babies' room.

And yet, funnily enough, when the curtain jerks down for the last time, at the very end of term, it will seem well worth it.

Friday Afternoon

It is worth remembering that many of these articles – including this one – were written in the 1950s. So when 'present-day' toys are mentioned, we should be thinking of mid twentieth-century toys, and those of Dora's childhood would have been Edwardian.

There is no doubt about it – Friday afternoon is, for most teachers, the happiest period of the week. Just as William Wordsworth's heart leapt up when he beheld a rainbow in the sky, so does a teacher's when he hears those comforting words 'Friday afternoon'. They are as much a symbol of hope to him as the rainbow is to all mankind.

Even those poor misguided fellows who have to teach on Saturday morning see the gleam of light at the end of the tunnel during the afternoon before. The weekend is at hand! Soon the classroom will be left to the activities of the cleaner, the goldfish in the tank and the mouse in the handwork cupboard.

But, of course, it is in the classrooms of the younger children that Friday afternoon blossoms most profusely. For generations it has been recognised as the fitting time for toys to be brought from home to be displayed to, and shared with, admiring friends. Friday afternoon, in the infants' room, would not be right without a worn teddy bear, dressed in its owner's outgrown baby frock, slumping against the wall on top of a cupboard in company with a motley selection of dolls. There will be stacks of bright cardboard boxes, too, containing anything from miniature spectacles, hats and moustaches for the adornment of potato men to a great jangling monster housing a railway system.

Thick short knitting needles proudly displaying two inches of desperately tight knitting – for what is presumably going to be a bright red lamp wick – jostle with glass-topped puzzles, boxes of crayons and a grubby card with the outline of a swan upon it in punched holes. Some erratic stitches executed in green wool show that work is in progress upon this masterpiece. Sometimes a tea set appears, and then the teacher resigns herself to the puddles which will surely dribble from the teapot spout.

A certain amount of modern armour – pistols in garish holsters, space guns, rockets and the like – denotes the boys' contribution. Some boys lie in varying postures on the floor, manoeuvring trains, lorries, vans and every other known wheeled vehicle, and making that horrid whining noise which seems inseparable from such tasks. The slide is besieged, the Wendy house packed to suffocation, the sand-pit jammed with occupants, and the noise indescribable as the children dash from one pleasure to the next.

Small wonder then that one hears such wails of despair from one's friends as Christmas or birthday times loom up. 'What on earth can I give the children?' they cry. 'He's got absolutely *everything*!' And, more's the pity, he usually has – and the fault is ours.

All around me on one such Friday afternoon are jigsaw puzzles, balls, beads, plasticine, weaving sets, peg frames, bricks and a hundred other games jostled together while, nearby, two tiny enraged girls squabble over a heap of treasures.

Beside them, alone at his table, sits a thin, quiet little boy, holding in his bony fingers a small plastic top, the sort of trinket that falls from a Christmas cracker. He sets it spinning across the bare table-top and watches it with absorption. It spirals delicately this way and that across the polished surface, dipping and hovering as it meets a crack and gradually totters to its last dizzy swoop.

The child's eyes are fixed upon it, and no sooner has it settled than he picks it up again and sets it spinning. He is completely engrossed, a silent, lonely figure in the midst of the hurly-burly around him – the calm spot at the heart of the tornado.

Intrigued, I break in upon his privacy. 'Wouldn't you like to play with something different now?' I ask, indicating the wealth around him.

He looks about him with vague distaste. 'Don't want anything else. Just this,' he replies, turning to his top again.

I stand back respectfully, thinking how uncommonly refreshing it is to meet someone content with something so simple.

Roaming among this paraphernalia, the middle-aged observer is interested to note the differences between present-day playthings and those of her own childhood. It is, perhaps, the dolls that differ most. The majority on top of the cupboard are sophisticated young women with nylon hair and immaculate plastic faces and bodies. Their tiny fingers sprout morsels of rubbery fringe where the mould has not been quite exact. Their expressions are sometimes arch, sometimes vacant. They are dressed in the kind of clothes that those in their teens wear today – Dolly-Rocker frocks, or tapering trousers, with a dashing shirt-blouse atop with a bow tie. There is something faintly repugnant about such svelte worldliness to those of us who remember their own china-headed beauties.

I have one before me now, as I write. She looks like a six-year-old child (which is surely the right idea) and she wears a pale green cotton frock and a floppy sun-bonnet to match. Round her waist is a narrow sash of pink velvet ribbon, and from it dangles a miniature dorothy bag – her pocket – complete with a lace-edged handkerchief one inch square. Her underclothes are miracles of scalloping, feather-stitching and tucks, and her pretty little feet are encased in white lace socks and white buckskin shoes.

But it is her face which affords the greatest contrast with her modern counterpart. It has an expression of innocence and gentleness not seen today. Her mouth is slightly open, showing three tiny teeth, and her eyes of grey glass gaze upon the world with child-like wonder.

But it would be churlish to dismiss all modern dolls as gimmicky and cute. Some of today's baby dolls have a pudgy attraction of look and texture which is irresistible. Square-headed, slit-eyed, lacking any sort of neck, with a cock's-comb of unruly hair, they are every little girl's idea of a perfect baby and fully worthy of the devotion given them.

Sadly enough, there seem to be few really small dolls these days – the type that lived in the dolls' house in our youth. There were inch-long china ones with shiny black heads, which came out of the Christmas puddings, I remember. They lived the rest of their lives standing to attention in the drawing room of Eva Villa, named in honour of the aunt who first owned this well-appointed establishment, complete with green baize lawns in front. There were other little dolls with scarlet cotton bodies stuffed with sawdust. They had china heads, arms and feet, and were obliging in the way they sat on dolls' chairs. When dressed in scraps of voile or muslin, they had an air of delicate fragility but in fact stood up to years of handling.

Some toys, of course, are not to be found anywhere on top of the cupboard. Where, for instance, are the tops which were whipped so anxiously across the playground amidst a hundred careless feet? Some owners enhanced the beauty of their tops with a chalk pattern which gave added glory as it spun round and round. Others were extremely fussy about their whips, choosing especially smooth string or making a knot at the end. Others voted a leather thong the best whipper. The boys had heavy peg tops, as large as a good-sized pear and much the same shape.

There was considerable skill needed in winding the string round the base and sending it whizzing across the playground.

The boys came off best, too, with their hoops. They trundled their iron monsters along making brave music, while we girls had to make do with wooden ones and sticks. The menace of traffic today has killed the hoop stone-dead and I, for one, mourn its passing. A hoop was excellent company on a solitary walk.

Beads are another toy which has altered over the years. Today's collections are bold, bright affairs of painted wood, spherical, tubular or square in shape. They are usually large, and a tagged cord is supplied for threading them. It all seems rather too easy. A necklace is made in the twinkling of an eye.

We enjoyed boxes of small china beads which first arrived in a glass-topped box. They had been packed with exquisite precision to form a pattern which, once shattered, could never be made again by five-year-old fingers. In fact, the beads never would go back again, in entirety, into the box after the first delicious threading. These were strung with a needle and double cotton, or with a fine piece of string, and part of the ritual of bead-threading was sucking the end of the string to a workable point. It is amazing how many different flavours can be extracted from an assortment of string.

Better still were the minute glass beads, not much bigger than hundreds and thousands, and greatly resembling them in their diversity of colour. We threaded these on fine wire. They made excellent rings, and if one had the patience to thread four or five hundred the result could be a charming bracelet wound several times round the wrist. The best way to pick up these minute beads was to wet a finger and press it into the saucer holding them. If any were inadvertently swallowed, it was comforting to think that they were so tiny that it really did not seem worth reporting to those in authority. Who knows? They might become over-anxious and stop the pastime.

But nostalgia must not be allowed to blind the middle-aged completely. Among today's treasures on the cupboard top will be found many delightful attractions too good to ignore. Look at that kitten knitting, and the bear drinking a glass of milk! Look at this doll's wellington boots and elegant mackintosh! And what a superb crane that small boy is operating in the corner! Perhaps he needs a little help. Surely it's just a case of pulling this lever . . .

Let's get right down on the floor and enjoy it. Dash it all, it's Friday afternoon, isn't it?

THE HEART OF THE VILLAGE

Beyond the Road Sign

To the average motorist nosing cautiously along country lanes, the road sign announcing 'School' on the grassy verge merely spells the added hazard of running children.

The school is quite likely to be a building of sixty or eighty years of age, faintly ecclesiastical perhaps – a lesser image of the church nearby. It may be of Cotswold stone with mullioned windows, or warm red brick, or a mass of grey flints, pock-marked with fossils.

Its exterior may be charming, but only those who work inside can tell of the defects of its interior. The high-pitched roof makes for a very lofty room which takes an enormous amount of fuel to heat, and worn lintels and ancient doors and floorboards can let in the cruellest draughts. The narrow windows, of Gothic design, placed high in the wall, so that Queen Victoria's small subjects could not waste their time in idle gazing, tend to make the room dark, while the persistence of local decorators in using chocolate or, at their most frivolous, a morbid dark green paint for the lower half of the walls, adds to the general dimness.

The playground, all too often, is small and badly surfaced with scanty gravel. In many cases, it is only through the kind offices of a local farmer that a nearby field can be used by these country children for their school games.

Since the war, most villages have had water piped to them, but some still remain without. Here, the village schoolteacher has a formidable daily problem. At one school of this description, at which I once taught, we relied on the kindness of a neighbour for two buckets of drinking water daily. For washing-up, washing hands and faces, for flowers, aquarium, painting and general use, we used rainwater which was collected from the roof into a galvanised iron tank. As there was no drainage, all dirty water had to be carried some distance to the school garden to be thrown away. Naturally, in schools of this type, the sanitation is necessarily primitive, and heroes indeed are the men who make themselves responsible for emptying buckets after school hours.

Yet in spite of these problems, which are the daily lot of more schoolteachers than one realises, there is something very endearing about these inconvenient backwaters. 'They ought to be closed!' someone says indignantly. Thinking of the sanitation, the damp corner cupboard, the adjacent churchyard, the lack of money and the colossal sum of money needed to keep the whole creaking machinery going, one agrees wholeheartedly. But, illogically, the closing of these little village schools – happy anachronisms as they are in this horribly well-ordered life – fills one with secret regret.

The Village School

When reading Dora's references to 'modern' textbooks or toys or teaching methods, it should be remembered that this was written about sixty years ago.

The traveller in Britain, pausing to cast an appraising or critical look at our villages, cannot fail to notice the local school, usually located in a central position.

Sometimes it lies in the shadow of the parish church, and frequently echoes its architectural style in modest form. Occasionally, it is an integral part of the village street, blending in with the cottages and small shops that flank it. Often these buildings

were built with the local stone, and designed by a sympathetic architect, and the result is harmonious.

But all too frequently the village schools were built in the late Victorian times, after William Edward Forster's Education Act of 1870 was passed. This was the Act which set up locally elected school boards with power to build schools, appoint staff and supervise attendance. It made sure that no part of the country would be without a school, and that no child, however poor, would grow up uneducated.

It was a great step forward, but it was an unfortunate time for building, and not even the most ardent follower of Sir John

Betjeman could admire some of the semi-ecclesiastical design, often executed in a harsh red brick quite alien to their ancient surroundings, and embellished with bands of stonework which, however skilfully incorporated, present a certain fussiness to the eye.

And yet they have their charm. If the traveller stops to talk in the village, he will soon discover that our village schools are regarded with deep affection, sincere admiration and by a surprisingly large and varied number of people.

Naturally, those in the village are – or have been – directly involved with the school as scholars, parents, teachers, helpers or managers. They have worked at those desks, played hopscotch in that playground, and popped the paint blisters on the sun-baked school door. As grown-ups, they have squeezed into too-small chairs at school meetings, sat through their children's Christmas plays, dutifully attended talks by the headteacher about New Mathematics, and gone home none the wiser. The village school remains part of their lives.

But there are others, often town dwellers, who feel the same affection for some particular village school. Many men and women were evacuees in war-time Britain, and exchanged the city streets for life in the country. They spent a number of their most impressionable years as pupils in these foreign parts, and a great many never broke the ties they made then with their adopted school. Others were sent to stay with grandparents or other relatives if illness cropped up in their town-based family or any other crisis occurred. Usually the schoolmaster would be willing to take in these temporary scholars, and another lasting link would be forged.

But it is the older villagers who give the clearest picture of how much the village school contributes to the community it serves. They remember when the school leaving age was fourteen, although many left before that time. This meant that from the age of five – sometimes four – until fourteen, the child stayed in the same school. A good thing? That is debatable, but it certainly made a strong bond between the pupils themselves, and the grown-ups who lived around them.

It made for continuity, for tolerance of others' foibles, for time to watch the growth, not only of physique but of the formation of character.

A good village school teacher can be of enormous benefit to a small community. By the very nature of his position, he is expected to set the same sort of standards of behaviour as the local vicar, the doctor or the squire. If his school is a church school, then he may well find himself actively involved in the choir or a churchwarden's duties.

The older generation remembers well the vital part that the school-master or -mistress played in the parish. The school-house, adjoining the school, was lived in then by the school-master, and parents who wanted advice about their children knew where to find him. Today, more often than not, the house has been sold to strangers, or is used as part of the school premises for the school dining-room and kitchen, or a place for stores, and the headteacher comes to school by car, from a home miles away.

Better transport is one of the reasons for the sad decline of the village school. In earlier times, the children walked in from their homes, walked home for their midday dinner, and back again for afternoon school. (I did it myself, thinking nothing of a mile and half's trot four times a day in all weather, and learning more about Kentish flowers and birds in that short time than ever I learnt since.)

Now parents can take their children farther afield if they prefer to. They too have no need to look for work in their immediate environs.

The little school of sixteen pupils in which I once taught used to have a roll of over a hundred early in the century. Then the fathers were needed in great numbers as ploughmen, carters, carpenters, foresters, gamekeepers, and the mothers as domestic workers on the big farms and estates. The families stayed put, and the school thrived.

Now a thousand-acre farm can operate with only a handful of men, and those who want to drive miles to different employment do so.

Transport is not the only nail in the coffin of the village school. Families are smaller. Some of those earlier families had ten or twelve children. Now mothers need to go to work, usually farther afield, setting off as soon as their one or two children are of school age. They know that school dinner will be provided. Their houses are compact and easily cleaned. They have time to return to their careers and to earn something towards the family income. But it means fewer children at the local school.

The obvious answer is closure of the school when numbers become really small. The traveller, looking for the village school, may well find the building, but no children playing round it, and no sound of youthful singing coming from it. It has probably been transformed into an attractive dwelling. The playground has been overlaid with lawns, the shaky bell tower has been removed. Only the Gothic windows and the basic ecclesiastical architecture reveal the building's origin, although an elegant wooden name plate, swinging from a wrought-iron support, may state unequivocally 'The Old School' and save the traveller any detective work.

There are very few schools which have closed without a stout battle. It is that affection, loyalty and strong sense of the need for continuity which unites a village when its old school is threatened. That indignation is justified. The first reason for parents' wrath is the removal of young children farther afield, away from their familiar background.

There are plenty of other good reasons. Let's say the schooling has been efficient. The small classes have meant individual attention which may not be the case when the child goes to a larger establishment. Then there is the loss of the headteacher and any other staff who may have played a great part in the life of the village. Why should they be uprooted?

And, above all, is the sense of loss. If the church represents the soul of the village, then the school is its heart. The school has served the people well, their parents and probably their grandparents. They like to see their own young blood there, learning these new-fangled metric tables where once they wrote £ s d in their best copperplate.

They like to see them screaming around the playground, or hanging over the railings to shout at their mothers as they make their way to the shop. They like to hear the whistle which obtains partial – if not the desired complete – silence, as playtime ends. It happened in their own day. It is as unchanging as the seasons, they feel, and rightly so. Memories forge strong bonds, and local authorities ignore this fact at their peril.

But one can see the local authorities' point of view. Financial advantages aside, there are real problems in these small schools. Staffing is difficult. The more remote the village, the shorter is the list of applicants for any post advertised. With railway branch lines closed, and buses few and far between, teachers need to have a car. In the old days, there were usually one or two of the houses in the village whose owners would be willing to accommodate a teacher. Now the landladies of yore are out at work, and even if they wanted to take in a lodger there are few teachers who would want to spend their evenings, as well as their days, among their pupils. The nearest town is where they want to live, and who can blame them now that village activities, which once offered scope for talent and initiative, have declined as sadly as the small schools themselves? It is an uphill job, as any villager will tell you, to keep the football and cricket clubs going, the Women's Institute, the choir, and the upkeep of the village hall itself. Small wonder that teachers, particularly young ones, look to the town schools for their livelihood and their recreation.

Getting staff is not the only difficulty. *Keeping* staff is another. A two-teacher school needs a greater degree of compatibility between the staff members than is usual. It is easy enough if you are Mr Perrin, in a comprehensive school of a thousand children, to dodge Mr Traill, your *bête noire*, among the labyrinthine corridors. It is less simple when only a frail partition of glass and marmalade-coloured pitch-pine separates you from your sole colleague, and you share every playtime and dinnertime in his company.

Of course, it can be even worse if there are three on the staff. Some very ugly triangles can be formed. But worse still, perhaps, is the plight of the teacher who is in sole charge, and it is right, I think, that the one-teacher school is on its way out. As I have mentioned, I taught by myself in a tiny school for about two months until a new head could be appointed. I count that period as one of the happiest times of my teaching career, but it opened my eyes to the problems faced by one-teacher schools.

With an age range from five years to eleven, it is virtually impossible to find a story or music which all can enjoy at the same time. All work has to be individual, and there is no hardship in that when numbers are small. But there are things which the eight- and nine-year-olds miss. At that competitive stage they love, and need, team games which are impossible with sixteen children, and the everyday stimulation of pitting their wits against others.

The sole teacher too is dangerously vulnerable when accidents or sudden illness arise. She must guard too against becoming neurotic or taking an unreasonable dislike to one of her number. It is a lonely life, particularly for a single woman who returns to her own solitary life after school hours.

Nevertheless, I was as sad as the rest when that little school closed. It seemed to me that the heart of that village had stopped beating, and the knowledge that this is happening all over the country only makes the whole business more piteous.

But one wonders if there is not some change of heart about rural communities. Anything affecting our children makes a swift impact on people, and the closing of village schools and all it implies may have given the impetus to a good deal of thought about living in the country.

For, more than ever, people are rebelling against the congestion of town life. If they have children they want a garden, somewhere for them to play, somewhere to hang out the washing, somewhere to rest in a deck chair, somewhere to put the pram. A garden is a rare commodity in a town centre, and whereas suburbia offers space, pleasant surroundings, shops, company and usually decent modern schools, there is the disadvantage for the wage earners of travelling to work. The cost of fares or the frustration of trying to park a car make this business of commuting a hazardous affair.

With the coming of the motorways, many young people have decided that it is probably more sensible to buy a house in a village within striking distance of a motorway junction and to rely entirely on a car to get to work. In the old days, they might have been in a position to pay for private education for their children – some still are – but a great many simply cannot afford the fees which these schools are now obliged to ask, especially if there are three or four children to educate. They look to the state schools with increasing interest, and this is a good thing from all points of view.

Village schools today are staffed by teachers as well qualified as their town counterparts. The discrepancy in salaries which tended to concentrate capable teachers in the urban areas years ago has now gone. Parental and staff participation is mutually stimulating and helps to improve the standard of education.

Is it too much to hope that our existing village schools will remain open? They have so much to offer. A great many, up and down the country, have already celebrated their centenary, and the ravages of age may show in crumbling plaster and leaking skylight.

But the spirit within is as lively as ever, and the friendships made and the lessons learnt, in the family atmosphere of a village school, can warm a lifetime, as I am fortunate enough to know.

Evil Genius

What sinister spirit is it that lingers in every stationery cupboard? From among those stacks of crisp exercise books, those rosy piles of blotting-paper, the metal-edged boxes a-rattle with cardboard money, and the towering piles of powder paint, there emanates something more than the heady scent of a year's supplies. There is a hidden force at work here – a mischievous and malicious sprite whose delight it is to work his will upon his unheeding victim, the innocent soul who holds the key of the stationery cupboard.

This poor wretch has the unenviable job of apportioning the stock among those who are fellow members of the staff. To his jaundiced eye, as he stands at bay amidst the alien raffia, they appear to be no better than a ravening pack of wolves. The plain fact that they are as anxious for the welfare of his supplies, are as thrifty with gummed paper and as tender with coloured pencils as the keeper of the stationery cupboard himself, carries no weight with him. He is under the baleful influence of the evil genius of the cupboard the minute that its key is added to the jingling collection in the sagging pocket of his grey flannel trousers.

Up and down the length and breadth of these islands, this evil beast is constantly at work. In infants' schools, it is usually the headmistress who holds the key and who suffers a sea-change on entering the stationery cupboard. Plump, motherly, given to remembering birthdays and to bringing cakes for staff tea at the drop of a hat, let her once get into that bewitched cell, and all is changed.

With what pursing of lips are the sticks of chalk handed over! With what stern frowns are those few – ah! so very few! – sheets of black mounting paper counted out. How sharply the breath is drawn in on hearing that timid request for coloured gummed squares! There is something about coloured gummed squares that makes them particularly dear to headmistresses of infants' schools. The invisible spirit quivers with delight when he hears his victim preparing to give battle. She presses beads, modelling clay and cowrie shells upon her subordinate. (They are parted with comparatively painlessly.)

The bewildered girl, still trailing clouds of college lore ('Never economise on handwork material. Let the children have *large* pieces of paper. Yes, of course, as much as they like!'), bleats again for coloured gummed squares, and the unhappy head-mistress begins to count it out with a miserly hand, admonishments flowing the while. No, she certainly can't have more green.

Grass, you know, and leaves and things. Everyone always wants green. She's very sorry, but purple and this rather shocking pink can easily be used with a little ingenuity. No, that nice bright red will be needed for Father Christmases before long. Someone has to look ahead. It may *look* a lot of stock, she knows, but it has to last a whole year. And behind her, in that cobwebby corner, near the man-sized abacus, there is terrible and secret mirth.

In the homely little country schools, dotted like daisies among the fields of England, this foul fiend has narrow confines, for his cupboard is a very small one, but in spite of his cramped quarters, he does his work well. Here, with possibly only one other person to make demands on the school materials, the headmistress should be more fortunate; but there is always the school cleaner to combine with the hidden force behind the cupboard door. And what battles can be waged for the treasures crowded on the bottom shelf! Here, bars of yellow soap are stacked in aromatic piles. Two dozen glittering canisters of scouring powder stand arrayed like knights in armour, beside blue check dusters and fleecy square-meshed floor cloths. All these beautiful things cling like tendrils round the headmistress's heart. She stands, with her back to the wall, holding the key, and her voice is piteous.

'But only last week, Mrs Briggs . . .' she begins, facing her implacable foe.

'Can't work without tools!' comes the inexorable answer. The key is turned in the lock, the soap is passed over into those red and grasping hands and somewhere, at the back of the cupboard, there is unholy joy.

There is one particular commodity which the evil spirit prizes above all others, no matter where he may be lurking, in Westmorland or Wapping, and that is . . . DRAWING PINS. Let his unhappy victim be asked for these apparently innocent articles, and the fiend curls up in ecstasy for, as any teacher in the kingdom can tell you, there is not a stationery cupboard keeper anywhere to be found who can part painlessly with even the most grudging shake of the box into the suppliant palm. The spell is strongest, the spirit at its most baleful, when a sprinkling of drawing pins changes hands.

Most certainly the time has come for stationery cupboard keepers to throw off their shackles. Knowledge is power. Face, I say, this insidious foe; better still, laugh at him! When your timid colleagues come with their pathetic pleas for graph paper or mapping pens, even when they ask, in their diffident way, for a few drawing pins, do not flinch. Show the waiting fiend your mettle. Hand over an armful of this, a bale of that, a gross of the other, and a whole box – no, be bold – *two* boxes of drawing pins. You will feel all the better for it and, uplifted and sublime, you will be free, for ever, from the tyranny of that evil genius.

You may, of course, find that the keys of the cupboard are taken (somewhat hastily) away from you and given to another. You may be offered, inexplicably, an aspirin and a rest in the staff room. But the glorious fact will remain. You will be free, free, free!

Feeling Poorly

'Got them home again!' comments one disgusted mother to another. 'Just had seven weeks' holiday, hardly had time to get the house straight, and here they are again!' They survey their boisterous broods moodily.

'Wish I were a teacher,' responds the other gloomily.

The conversation turns to the idle leisure enjoyed by the teaching profession – those endless holidays, those laughably short hours, those lovely surroundings and, more especially, the good fortune of those who have the privilege of teaching those gifted children which they themselves are already observing with hearty dislike.

'I wouldn't mind so much if they *were* a bit ill!' shouts one to the other above the din of two joyous families. 'At least they'd be safely in bed.'

Bed! That is the very essence of the whole affair of illness, and for which there is really no substitute, as harassed teachers know when confronted by an ailing child in class. If it happens to be a boarding school, all is relatively easy. The bed is there. Matron or nurse takes the child in tow, the classroom holds one less and the teacher relaxes in the knowledge that the thermometer, light diet, bed-with-curtains-drawn routine is going smoothly forward, with only the scrunch of the gravel under the visiting doctor's tyres to enliven the afternoon session.

But what a different kettle of fish it is at a day school! In the infants' department, it is usually a bustling little girl, full of importance, who brings the first tidings that something is amiss.

'Reggie Smith,' she announces with horrid smugness, 'doesn't feel very well!'

And, sure enough, there is poor Reggie, head on desk, with the tears beginning to gush as soon as he hears those delicious words. The anxious teacher, envisaging typhus, typhoid, scarlet fever, measles – in fact, anything alarmingly infectious – hastens to wrestle with Reggie's tie, his obstinate shirt buttons, and a seething mass of interested spectators who surround the desk, gulping down clouds of Reggie's germs.

Having overcome the obstacle of the shirt-fastenings, the overwrought teacher discovers that little boys are invariably clad in up-to-the-neck woollen vests with a row of pearl buttons, each in the vice-like grip of a very small button-hole, embedded in stiffish material. By the time a small portion of the child's chest is exposed, she herself is in a light perspiration. There may, or may not, be a rash, but in any case something must be done. It is at this point that the teacher yearns, in vain, for a bed for the patient.

Its substitute varies considerably from school to school. In a small country school, the child may be led across the playground to the teacher's school house, ensconced on the sitting-room sofa with a copy of *The Chummey Book for 1930*, and left with the household cat for company. Any patient under eleven responds well to this treatment for to be alone in one's headteacher's premises with the privilege of inspecting the objets d'art undisturbed, and perhaps lifting the lid of the biscuit barrel to see if she has Nice or just Osborne, has a wonderfully stimulating effect.

If there is no school house available, a deck chair by the tortoise stove may be the patient's lot and has, in fact, much to commend it. The sight of his fellows tracing the coastline of Scandinavia, in all its horrid intricacies, while he lies back toying with his bottle of milk, takes him halfway to recovery. After all, it is the attention, the singling-out, the being-an-invalid that matters. Once one's status is established, one can go ahead and enjoy it.

Larger schools may rise to a well-appointed sickroom, a bright stream-lined apartment with blindingly gay curtains. Or it may go to the other extreme and give over to the afflicted some obscure little room of no use otherwise. I well remember one such bower.

It lay at the top of a very tall school, so that the limbs of the sufferer were in an advanced state of palsy by the time they were disposed upon a slippery sofa under a green rug. The patient, on opening his eyes, became conscious that the walls as well were green. The curtains were green. A large bowl, left ostentatiously near at hand, was also green. The patient, by this time, was not surprised, on catching sight of himself in a murky and distorting mirror, to find that he, too, was an unbecoming shade of eau-de-nil. There were no books and no pictures but, hanging in a dim corner, was a passage from Chaucer, which began:

> *Twenty bokes, clad in blak or reed,*
> *Of Aristotle and his philosophye.*

There were fifteen lines of it, illuminated in timid colours all the way round. No patient had ever been known to read the whole thing. Long before line three, he had fallen back, failing, overcome with torture, ennui and greenness.

Of the patients forced to take their uneasy rest in staff-rooms, at the mercy of each member of staff who enters and hands over aspirin, laxative tablets, milk of magnesia, liver salts, cups of tea or half a gingernut in quick and ghastly succession, there is not space to tell. Nor of the others who must do as best they can in the headmistress's room under her eye. The diversity of blankets pressed into the service of the sick-at-school, ranging from a mad assembly of woollen squares to those heavy, grey horrors smelling of wet dog, would provide enough matter for another complete article. But we will end on a happier note.

The teacher may discover, on questioning the invalid in the first place, that his mother is at home and, better still, an older sister is in the school. All sorrow melts away for is there not a bed at home? The big sister is summoned. She surveys her little brother with an unusually kindly eye. She sings as she dresses him in the cloakroom and, taking his feverish hand in hers, she escorts him home, dancing lightly.

'He was feeling poorly!' she announces blithely to her mother.

It's an ill wind that blows nobody any good.

THE VILLAGE YEAR

This came to light after Dora's death. I discovered the material in a rather splendid period envelope from the Newbury Relief Typing Agency – Dora always wrote in longhand, and needed to get her manuscripts professionally typed.

From the correspondence with Michael Joseph Ltd, it appears that, late in 1967, Peter Hebdon, the publisher's Managing Director, wrote enthusiastically to Dora: 'I would like very much to publish a non-fiction book by you giving a rounded picture of life in an English village. Probably some of the material might be drawn from books already published, and it would be produced very much as a gift book.'

There is subsequent correspondence during 1968 when discussion and planning were clearly active, and then nothing. There is no clue as to why this was dropped, or why only four months appear to have been written. The typing agency produced January, February and June but March was still in Dora's longhand. It is a slightly odd mixture of general observations on country matters with some references to Fairacre characters – which made it difficult to know where to place it in this book. March, too, is rather different from the other months, with a long section on moral values.

Undoubtedly a few passages were later re-used in the Fairacre books, but as an excellent portrait of country life in the 1960s, we felt it was worth including it in this book.

January

In the bleak mid-winter
Frosty wind made moan,
Earth stood hard as iron,
Water like a stone.

CHRISTINA ROSSETTI

No matter how cruel the winter, there is something hopeful about New Year's Day. Cold reason may point out that the worst of the weather is to come, that finances are at their lowest ebb, thanks to Christmas, that the income tax is due to be paid and that it is foolhardy to imagine that one can escape influenza for much longer.

Nevertheless, irrationally, cheerfulness breaks in on the first day of the year. It is a fresh start. We will be kinder, patient, more industrious, more efficient. Who knows, we may even start saving!

It was with such good resolutions that I glowed as I dressed on New Year's morning. It was past eight o'clock, late rising for a village schoolmistress, but this was holiday time and it was wonderful to get up at leisure.

The grass was rimed with a hard frost, and the water in the bird bath had turned to stone. A robin, match-stick legs astride, puffed out his orange breast and cocked a beady disapproving eye at the ice.

It was a world of black, white and grey. Snow had fallen thinly the day before, and traces of it clung to the roof tiles and to the black trunks of the trees. Against a pewter-grey sky, the bare branches spread their tracery, and further away still the Downs made a dark streak on the sky line.

Even Mr Roberts' cows, in the field across the lane, were black and white. Twenty or so fine Friesians clustered round the grey metal drinking trough. Two men, huddled in thick ex-Army coats girdled with binder twine, were busy with a bale of straw. Suddenly, in the midst of the bleak black and white, colour blossomed. A great scarlet flower seemed to burst open by the trough. The men had set a match to the straw to melt the frozen water. The flames licked the metal, the cows withdrew a few paces, but appeared unafraid, gazing steadily at the trough. The men flailed themselves with their arms and kicked the straw to the most advantageous point. In all that waste of drear landscape, the fire brought colour, warmth and succour. The cows waited hopefully as the men thrust the straw this way and that. Things would be better now.

The fire, I thought, was a little like New Year's Day – a bright spot of comfort and hope in the midst of winter. It would soon be gone, and the grey ashes would be one with the all-pervading lack of colour in the winter scene, but nothing could take away the memory of that first brief glory, and the gleam of hope renewed.

The blessing of piped water came late to Fairacre. Generations of farmers relied on rainwater or local ponds for watering their stock. Many of the great barns in this area still have water tanks below ground, while a hand pump was in regular use to fill the troughs in days gone by. In times of drought, a water-cart, drawn by a plodding carthorse, made the steep descent to the valley, over two miles away, where the Waybrook, a tributary of the river Cax, wound its way through half a dozen villages. Fairacre farmers can remember days on end when the water-carts climbed up and down the dusty hill road taking river water to the flocks of sheep and herds of cattle on the upland slopes.

The villagers' wells rarely ran dry, but water was used sparingly for domestic purposes. 'A nice drop of sudsy water' was recognised as something valuable. After washing the linen, it would be used for washing the kitchen floor, and even then it still had a further use. It would be the turn of the doorsteps to be scrubbed, and the flagged passages and porches. Finally, the suds would be flung over the brick or tiled paths near the door and energetically swept away with a stiff broom, so that all approaches to the house were as free from dirt as it was humanly possible to make them. When one has to wind up water from a deep well, or pump it up by hand, every bucketful is treated with care.

'Fetching the water' was one of the most back-breaking and time-wasting chores of the day before the coming of piped water. There was no central parish pump here, but several which were shared by groups of cottages. The more sociable villagers enjoyed meeting their neighbours and exchanging gossip as the water gushed from the pump into the buckets. In fine weather, a trip to fetch the water could make an agreeable break in a lonely woman's life. Those with little time to spare, however, or a dislike of gossip, took care to visit the pump when no one else was about. 'Keeping oneself to oneself' was ever considered a virtue in the country.

A sturdy rainwater butt stood by most houses and saved many a step. The rainwater thus collected was always in demand for washing hair and bathing, and even today many of us in Fairacre rely on this source of water for the best shampoo.

It was not until the end of the 1939–45 war that mains water was supplied to the village, and even then a number of people preferred to rely on their old sources. The four families at Tyler's Row, for example, maintained that their communal well water was 'that pure they'd never really take to that piped rubbish'. It was reputed to be one of the deepest wells in the neighbourhood and certainly a mugful drawn from its icy depths in mid-summer tasted ambrosial. A former resident, I was told, put a young frog into the well each summer and this practice ensured the water's purity. In later days, however, the ceremony was abandoned, whether by reason of a more scientific approach to such matters, or sheer laziness, or simply shortage of frogs, no one can say.

With the passing of the years, more and more householders have taken advantage of the mains water and most houses in Fairacre now have a bathroom and a water closet. One or two farmers were reluctant to provide these amenities for their labourers, but over the years they have faced the expense, knowing that a sound cottage with water laid on is necessary to keep a good farm-worker and his family.

Certainly it has proved a blessing here to have water piped into the houses. When I first came to Fairacre, I was young and active, and filling the copper with water to be heated was no hardship. I used a tin bath in front of the kitchen stove, and very snug it was to soak in the soft brown rainwater in the glow of the firelight. For the old folk in Fairacre, taking a bath was a major operation, and it is hardly surprising that some of them took one very seldom indeed.

Now I, and my neighbours, turn on the bath taps and watch the water rising, with undimmed pleasure. As for the privies in the gardens, no one mourns their passing. To be obliged to venture forth, torch in hand, on a bitter winter's night was enough to bring forth curses – and a common cold for good measure. Certainly, in the month of January particularly, we have cause to bless our comparatively new indoor sanitation in Fairacre.

But despite these innovations, many an old zinc bath hangs on its nail on the side of the shed in the garden. Spattered with bird droppings, just out of reach of the ivy's fingers below it, it waits there, in rain and shine, 'just in case'.

January is the month in which life is at its lowest ebb. Years ago, one or two of the wealthier inhabitants in the village went off on a winter cruise at the beginning of the New Year. Exotic post-cards of Madeira, Morocco or Malta arrived in Fairacre to be put on the mantel shelves of the less fortunate. In cottage homes, propped between the tin tea-caddy and the clock, they brought a touch of foreign colour to a dark winter. Everything about the card was studied minutely – the queer stamp, the odd names above the square white shops, the great palm trees 'like the one we saw in the park at Torquay on the outing. Remember?' It was an object of wonder. The mere fact of it having travelled so far was a marvel. Visitors were shown it with pride, and it had the place of honour for weeks on the crowded shelf.

Now hardly anyone in Fairacre goes away in the winter. Trips abroad are taken in the summer, and there are very few among the younger generation who have not been on a packaged holi-day to Spain or France. The postcards from overseas are not looked upon as any more remarkable than those from Broad-stairs or Bude, and find their way to the garden bonfire with the empty cornflake packets and seed catalogues.

But although we in Fairacre remain housebound in this bleak month, we make our plans for holidays overseas in the sunshine. The young people, whose elders seldom went further afield than Devon, and whose grandparents had possibly never even seen the sea, now leaf through the gay brochures and book up for a fortnight's coach tour in Europe or ten days' baking on the Costa Brava. They have money for such things these days, and only the more curmudgeonly Fairacre folk grudge them their fun.

Mrs Pringle, my cantankerous school cleaner, is certainly one of the curmudgeons and thinks it shameful that young people should waste their money overseas.

'When I was a girl,' she tells me, 'we was lucky to get an outing to Springbourne Park for the day. What's more, we was dressed decent. Black stockings and our best starched frocks and a good hat to keep off the sun. None of your bikinis and courting pneumonia, I'm glad to say. The old vicar would have had something to say from the pulpit, if we'd flaunted ourselves like that!'

Mrs Pringle does not agree with a great many innovations, but she is in the minority. Television, for instance, and the mobile library van, which calls once a fortnight in the village, are looked upon as time-wasters by this redoubtable lady. Most of us disagree.

For life in midwinter, in a village, is largely semi-hibernation and we are glad to have something to occupy us in our own homes. At teatime the curtains are drawn and there are five or six hours of darkness before we make our way to early beds.

I dislike the winter, and here it is exceptionally severe, but there is something very snug about an evening spent by a leaping, crackling blaze of logs with the curtains pulled against the bitter winds, and the cat companionably curled on the hearth-rug. In my case, there are usually exercise books to be marked, or lessons to prepare, before I can amuse myself with a clear conscience. But once these necessary chores are done, I do as so many of my neighbours do, and relax with knitting, or reading, or the television.

The men who work on the land get in soon after five, and it is usual for them to have a substantial tea then. The midday meal is at twelve, and a long afternoon on a tractor, driving it slowly up and down the great fields on the flanks of the Downs, exposed to the cruel winds or driving rain, means that a man is ready for a meal when he reaches home.

It has many advantages, this high tea. The children are just back from school, and as hungry as their fathers, no matter how generous school dinner helpings have been. The dishes can be washed and put away, and the evening is blessedly free from the further preparation of meals. A milky drink and a biscuit, at bedtime, suit most of us very well.

Others take their dinner between seven and eight in the evening, and enjoy inviting their friends to join them. And how particularly dear friends are in wintertime!

For, let's face it, we crave company and chatter in the chill of January more perhaps than in any other month. The excitement of Christmas is behind us. By Twelfth Night, the fifth day of January, the garlands are down, the candles vanished, and the Christmas cards collected together for use in the infants' room later.

At the time, it is almost a relief. The Christmas tree is dusty, and fast shedding its dry needles. The holly sprigs are withered, the ivy trails have lost their gloss. As for the Christmas cards, we are all heartily sick of picking them up from the floor every time the draught catches them. Two or three weeks before, each one was welcomed with cries of delight.

'Better than ever this year!' we say to each other.

'And even more of them! I've got two dozen on the mantel-piece and more on the hall table.'

They are a source of pride and joy. But by Twelfth Night, they have lost their early charm and are nothing but 'dratted nuisances every time the door opens'. It is good to be able to dust the shelves again and to see the rooms in their usual plain garb.

Sometime during the second week in January, the village school opens again. Mrs Pringle has done her scrubbing of floorboards and has polished the two great tortoise stoves which are the very nerve centre of our two classrooms in the winter.

It is the most trying term of the three in the school year. The days are dark, the weather wretched and germs abound. I always try to persuade parents to start the new entrants after Easter, knowing full well that, in the winter term, these tender young ones, suddenly transplanted from warm homes, with only a few in family, to our draughty school with a crowd of children coughing and sneezing, will so easily fall prey to influenza and the like.

Grown-ups too have their share of coughs and colds and plenty of home-made remedies are bandied about. Some are eminently sensible and involve such well-tried ingredients as lemons, honey and butter. Other winter ills, such as rheumatism, from which a number of the older people suffer, evoke rather more subtle recipes.

'You wants to tie a thread of scarlet silk round the waist, next to the skin,' was once quoted in this area; and another popular preventative is a raw potato carried in the pocket.

While we are all in these January doldrums, visiting and being visited has to be curtailed. Friends and relatives who live at a distance are not at all keen to undertake a long winter's journey. Most of them know from experience that if a blizzard strikes Fairacre they might well be cut off from civilisation by substantial snow drifts in these parts. Wisely, they prefer to pay us visits in the summer when the Downs are at their most delectable.

This makes the company of local friends and neighbours doubly precious in the winter. There is nothing more cheering than a rather special meal followed by the wagging of tongues round the fireside while the wind howls across the Downs and batters at our tight-shut windows.

Food plays an important part in keeping out the cold and helping to dispel the January blues. The standard of cooking has improved enormously over the years. Many factors have contributed to this happy state.

After the war, when rationing was slowly relaxed and finally vanished altogether, housewives were eager to try their hands at recipes which had had to be neglected during the time of austerity. Strange and exciting foodstuffs made their way into even the modest grocer's at Fairacre. Sweetcorn, yoghurt, peppers, chicory, and a host of exotic spices as yet untried by local women were broached tentatively and found acceptable to themselves and, more important still, to their menfolk.

A spate of first-class cookery books and recipes in the women's magazines added fuel to the fire. Trips abroad gave a further fillip to trying foreign dishes. Rice, in particular, hitherto used exclusively for 'a nice rice pudding', maturing slowly at the bottom of the oven whenever it was being used, was now found to be a valuable adjunct to dozens of tasty dishes. The advent of frozen foods brought new possibilities to the menu, and saved time if not money, in many homes.

Some of the Fairacre ladies who had cars took advantage of the cookery classes held in the evenings at Caxley Technical College. The Women's Institutes usually had several cookery demonstrations included in their yearly programmes. All these things helped the welcome renaissance of good cooking during the years following the war, and today's dinner parties are usually followed by an exchange of recipes.

Of course, the highlight of January's cooking is making the marmalade. Earlier generations might spend a number of days on this operation, preparing several dozen pounds of the preserve to last the family throughout the year. Few make such quantities today. Families are smaller, toast and marmalade, delicious though it is, has to be eaten sparingly by those who easily put on weight, and it is more fun to ring the changes by buying a pot from the shop now and again.

Perhaps no other home-made commodity gives rise to such a variety of recipes and advice. Some cooks swear by long soaking before cooking the fruit. Others partly cook it in the slow oven of their solid-fuel stoves. Some like a recipe with a lot of water, some prefer a little. Debates go on about granulated versus preserving sugar. Some admit cheerfully to using ready-sliced oranges in tins, and very good the result is.

Having very little spare time to stand over my cooker, I prefer to boil my oranges first, and then slice the cooked fruit finely before adding the sugar. The marmalade is quickly made, and I find it keeps well. Quite by accident one year, I bought Italian bitter oranges as I had missed the Seville ones, and in my opinion the flavour was better.

But whatever our methods and our ingredients, the aromatic scent which pervades our houses, redolent of faraway sunshine, is a unique and welcome part of our January life, and the results of our sticky labours give us pleasure for months to come.

Outside, on the farms, the work goes on. Most of the fields lie bare and brown. They were ploughed as soon as the corn was harvested last autumn. Every year, it seems, the time between harvest and ploughing gets shorter and shorter. The bright fields of stubble are quickly turned into chocolate-brown furrows, ready for the winter varieties of corn which need a long time to grow. There are no gleanings now after harvest. The combine-harvester and this early ploughing are one of the causes of the decline in the partridge population, it is said, and has caused many other birds to change their habitat and their habits.

Some root crops add a splash of green to the landscape. In the field behind my house some fine swedes are growing, but soon after Christmas, when the ground grew harder with frost each day, flocks of pigeons descended upon them and have steadily ripped away the foliage, until now all that remains are the tough ribs of each leaf. The farmer, Mr Roberts, plans to fold his in-lamb ewes on this field later. How much greenstuff, one wonders, will they find? Luckily, the roots are unmolested and should provide an agreeable change of diet.

The work with the animals goes on without ceasing. Mr Roberts is fattening some handsome Hereford cattle which are penned in the yard nearby. Every morning, his men take the tractor and trailer along with food, and with straw for bedding. His milking herd are the Friesians who clustered hopefully round the water trough on New Year's Day and watched their keepers' efforts to thaw the ice. There is no respite, whatever the weather, for those with animals to tend.

While growth is at a standstill, the men cut back the hedges. It is seldom that one sees the beautifully layered hedges which were such a work of art before the war. Now, more often than not, a vicious-looking circular blade whizzes along the hedge tops, and the job is done in a tenth of the time. The brittle trimmings are raked into heaps, and before long, bright flames quiver in the winter air with a joyous crackling.

Sometimes in Fairacre, we hear the ululation of the huntsman's horn, and see hounds and horses streaming across the fields on their way to a distant covert. If we hear them in school time, I let the children run into the playground to see this stirring sight. One of my predecessors used to shut the school and let the children follow on foot.

'You can't get lost,' he used to assure them. 'Look out for St Patrick's spire and make your way home by that!'

But I am not at all sure that I want the children to roam the fields in winter, and the roads of Fairacre carry a good deal more traffic than they did fifty years ago when following on foot was so popular. A quick glimpse of the hunt's glory over the playground wall is all that is allowed now.

Every now and again we hear gun-shots. An odd report or two is dismissed as 'someone takin' a pot-shot at a pigeon,' but when the local landowners have a shoot, our lessons are somewhat disturbed. The children are pleasantly excited. Some of the fathers will be acting as beaters, no doubt, and with any luck there will be a pheasant or two, or a fine hare, for a future meal. Mr Roberts usually leaves me a brace of pheasants once during the shooting season, and very much appreciated they are, both by me and my lucky guests. At one time, there was often a partridge shoot, but since the hard winter

of 1962–63 the partridge population in these parts has dwindled almost to extinction.

In the garden, the wild birds come flocking to the bird table and the bird bath. Sparrows, naturally, predominate, but I am lucky in having many blackbirds, thrushes and blue tits among my visitors. Sometimes a greater spotted woodpecker is bold enough to come to the lump of bacon fat hanging on the lilac bush, but he is erratic in his visitations.

Yesterday morning, cold, grey and drear, was brightened by three colourful birds drinking together at the bird bath. A blue tit, a robin and a male chaffinch, splendid in pink and blue, cheered the gloom of a winter's morning and gave a heartening glimpse of the spring to come.

Keeping warm is probably the main aim in January, and here in Fairacre we tackle the problem in a variety of ways.

In my own small school-house, four electric radiators have recently been installed and, placed at strategic points in the house, they provide me with much comfort. I light the open fire soon after four o'clock, using plenty of kindling wood, with which kind Mr Willet keeps me well stocked, a firelighter and small coal, for one thing which I abominate is lighting a fire for the second time when all the vital ingredients have burnt but the coal has not.

More and more houses in Fairacre are using electricity instead of solid fuel. There is no gas in the area, which is a pity. One can see the advantages of switching on heat just when it is needed. Heating by electricity is clean, for one thing. Curtains, loose covers, bedspreads and all soft furnishings remain pristine far longer than those belonging to open-fire lovers like me. There is no need to remember firelighters, matches, kindling wood. There are no sorties to be made to the coal cellar or log pile in the teeth of a roaring nor'easter – and no return trips hauling weighty scuttles. The chimney sweep, and all his hazards, are things of the past. Why don't we all change to electricity?

The basic reason, I believe, is our instinctive love of an open fire, something which crackles and blazes and alters its shape and tempo as we tend it. It is companionable as well as comforting. 'As long as I can still lug the coal in,' we tell each other, 'I'm keeping my fire going. Time enough for other methods when I'm too decrepit to cope.'

And then there is the satisfactory feeling that a well-filled coal cellar makes one happily independent of power failures. It is paid for, too. No future bill, remorselessly pointing out the number of units used, will plop on to the doormat and cast its gloom. And what could be more delightful than wooding? To bear home even the smallest dead branch from a country meander gives a sense of thrift and well-being. Sometimes I watch my neighbours, after a proper wooding expedition, pushing home a noble load on top of an old pram. Children straggle behind almost hidden by armfuls of branches, or tugging at a large bough trailing in the dust behind them. Even the youngest toddler carries a few sticks. They may look tired, but they also look triumphant. This will keep the fire going, their eyes seem to flash! We all have a strong streak of primeval man in us and fire-worshipping is a long time a-dying in Fairacre.

A number of the older people still rely almost completely on solid fuel or on paraffin oil, both for heating and cooking, but gradually the old kitchens are being replaced, and the steel fire-irons, zealously cleaned with emery paper, are finding their way to the village jumble sales as the new cookers are installed.

Those who can afford it have had oil-fired central heating put into their houses or electric night-storage heaters, and at any village gathering on these cold January days there is enthusiastic discussion of the rival merits of heating appliances. Many house-holders have lagged their lofts and their water pipes, and some have attempted double glazing. If you live on the Downs, you learn quickly how best to fight the winds which sweep them.

In school, Mrs Pringle's first loves, the slow-burning tortoise stoves, are our main source of heat. It is amazing how well these ancient monsters do their job. It is true that they smoke evilly at times, and that they can be temperamental if handled by anyone other than Mrs Pringle. Most of the heat rises to the steeply pitched roof high above us but, nevertheless, a cosy warmth

emanates from their jet rotundity and the long hot pipe which takes the fumes through an aperture high in the wall.

It is draughts which cause us most discomfort in our class-rooms, for the school was built in 1880 and, over the years, the door lintels have been worn by generations of nailed country boots, and the framework of our ecclesiastical windows has slipped a little awry. Above my desk is a skylight which has called forth the curses of all those teachers compelled to sit beneath it, for the wind whistles through its cracks, rain penetrates and snow collects upon it. It has defied the efforts of Fairacre and Caxley carpenters and glaziers for generations, and continues to exert its baleful influence to the present day.

But Fairacre children are hardy, and are seldom away from school for long. They are much more sensibly dressed than they used to be. There are plenty of good hand-knitted jerseys in use – knitted usually by grandmothers or distant aunts, for so many of the mothers are out at work these days and the evenings are spent mainly in cooking or preparing for the next day. Warm dungarees of corduroy or woollen material, or thick skirts and warm tights keep the children's thighs and legs warm. I can remember the days when children were sent to school, in bitter weather, in short ankle socks and shoes. A long expanse of mottled blue leg contrasted strangely with the muffled upper reaches of the body, sometimes clad in as many as six layers of wool.

Today, the chain stores offer robust and attractive clothes for children, and Marks and Spencer's shop in Caxley High Street provides many of the comfortable winter garments which brighten Fairacre School. Even the babies, still egg-shaped, sport smart little A-line numbers with diminutive frills at the skirt edge, and prink about the infant room displaying their practical finery.

They are better shod, too, than when I first started teaching here. Then it was difficult to get the children to take off their wellington boots in the classroom. Very few had anything else to change into. Now, indoor shoes are left at school, and there are very few who do not change automatically when they arrive.

They are gloved as stoutly as they are booted, which means fewer chilblains – that bane of my childhood winters – and the standard of dress on the whole is very high.

It has grown steadily colder during this last week of January and keeping warm has assumed a more vital significance. Frost at night has been prodigious, and one of my pre-school tasks is to take a kettle of boiling water to the bird bath to thaw the solid plate of ice, two inches thick, which so disconcerts the band of hopeful birds when they arrive to refresh themselves.

All heating appliances in Fairacre, both ancient and modern, are working overtime and Mr Willet, who is sexton at St Patrick's, forecasts an enormous bill for the church's electricity. New wall

heating was installed there recently, replacing a voracious coke-eating boiler in the basement below the vestry. From its vast body, a network of pipes wreathed about the church under the floor. Metal grilles, which clanged disconcertingly under the feet of shame-faced late-comers, allowed the heat to rise into the vast building, in a meagre sort of way. When, at last, the stove collapsed with respiratory troubles, it was decided to do away with such an antiquated mode of heating. Mr Willet, who had a certain love-hate relationship with this demanding old invalid, mourns its passing and is dubious about its modern successor. No doubt he will be proved right – he usually is – and the bills will be astronomical. At least it will bring him the satisfaction of being able to say, 'I told you so!'

Quite by chance, I read today the entry for 29 January 1799 written in his diary by James Woodforde, Parson at Weston Longeville, Norfolk, at that time.

'Tuesday . . . Very intensely cold, and a very hard Frost last Night and this Morning. It froze sharply within doors last Night and also this Morning. Nevertheless tho' the Weather has been and is still severely cold we have not had our beds warmed at all during the whole Winter as yet, neither do we intend to.'

I like those last five defiant words. James Woodforde was then within a few years of his death, not very strong, and usually rather nervous of his own health. But he is not going to give way to the weather, formidable though the Norfolk winter might be.

What would he think of us, I wondered, as I made my way to bed clutching a hot water bottle? Electric blankets and hot bottles were warming plenty of beds in the village tonight, I surmised, as my Fairacre neighbours prepared for sleep beneath their thatch or tiles. And we, poor weaklings, had been using these comforts for weeks now!

I fear that the good parson would not have approved of such

molly-coddling. 'Neither do we intend to' – this proud challenge to winter echoed in my ears as I climbed between my newly warmed sheets.

Truly, our forefathers were made of stern stuff.

February

Shed no tear – O, shed no tear!
The flower will bloom another year.
Weep no more – O, weep no more!
Young buds sleep in the root's white core.

JOHN KEATS

Strangers, visiting Fairacre for the first time, wax enthusiastic about its beauty. It is true that the main part of the village, called by the residents 'the street', is very much as it has been for well over a century. The lane leading from it to the church and the school is equally unspoilt, and a magnificent sycamore tree, halfway along, is a froth of golden leaf in early spring, the haunt of innumerable pigeons in the summer and a splash of tawny glory in the autumn. It adds greatly to the charm of the view towards St Patrick's and is much appreciated by the parishioners as well as their visitors.

We usually take our visitors 'the round walk' when we show them the village. On our way, we pass a picturesque quartet of thatched cottages called Tyler's Row, a score or so of others also thatched or attractively tiled, and a number of gentlemanly residences set back from the road behind trim lawns and hedges. There are very few gardens which are not well tended. Fairacre folk are great gardeners and the soil is rich after many years of digging and manuring.

A footpath which skirts the churchyard and the vicarage garden gives our visitors a glimpse of St Patrick's west end with its square tower topped by a stubby spire, and a fine vista of the vicar's great Georgian house, with its sloping lawns and two beautiful cedar trees.

Until recently, there was a village pond, complete with white railings and a dozen or more loudly quacking mallards, but two or three years ago it was drained and the railings removed. I was sorry to see it go. Too many ponds have vanished over the years. They were a source of pleasure to adults as well as to the children and the ducks.

Nowadays, we simply point out the site to our guests and lead them back to tea with a last view of the magnificent Downs behind the village.

'How lucky you are to live here!' they sigh enviously, as I fill their tea cups. 'It's all so completely unspoilt.'

But it isn't, and I tell them so. They have only seen the old village, the nucleus which has been virtually unchanged for one or two centuries. Certainly the roads have been metalled, kerbs laid and a simply ghastly cat's-cradle of wires criss-crosses the sky above Fairacre. Television aerials adorn our roofs and tele-graph and electricity poles proliferate. But somehow most people can take these things in their stride when the general aspect is so mellow and pleasing.

But, in common with almost all English villages, Fairacre has what is euphemistically known as its 'new development' and, on the whole, it is deplorable. Between the two wars, in the early thirties, a dozen or so new houses were built on the outskirts of the village, on the road leading to Beech Green and Caxley. Some were sizeable places, set back from the road in an acre or more of meadow land, some were bungalows on smaller patches. The old thorn hedge remained and served them all as their frontal boundary, and two or three oak trees were left to give a certain grace to the new site. All in all, the raw mess left by the builders was partially screened and, within a few years, the shrubs planted by the proud owners of the properties added their foliage and flowers to the scene.

Despite the folly of ribbon development, of which this was the beginning in Fairacre, the new houses soon took their place fairly acceptably on the southern outskirts of the village. But, a little later, a council estate was erected at the northern end and remains to this day a blot on the landscape, despite the fine gardens which now surround the houses.

They were built of a particularly hard red brick, which never weathers, but retains its glaring fish-paste colour throughout the years. The upper half of each house is embellished with concrete pretending, unsuccessfully, to be weather-boarding. The council paints the woodwork, guttering and drain pipes in a depressing shade of green which affords a fearsome contrast to the garish brickwork, and as the colour of the paint has never changed over the years, it can only be assumed that gallons and gallons of the wretched stuff were once purchased – probably cheaply, which is not surprising – and we must resign ourselves to this decor for many years to come.

Evelyn Waugh writes movingly of 'this huge deprivation of the quiet pleasures of the eye' as our English villages become enlarged. Sometimes, he continues, this makes 'for impotent resentment, sometimes for mere sentimental apathy, sometimes poisoning love of country and of neighbours'. Certainly, for every pleasing house which has gone up in our lifetime and is at harmony with its surroundings, there are twenty which are an affront to the eye.

Apart from the general ugliness of our village council houses, those in Fairacre have some appalling planning blunders. They are built in pairs, and the doors are at the side so that each tenant looks away from his immediate neighbour. So far, so good. Unfortunately, each tenant looks directly across a low wire fence into the side door of the next pair of houses, a few yards distant, so that there is little privacy. The conversations with the baker, the milkman and, worst of all, the rent collector, are clearly heard. So are the noises from inside the house, the everlasting radio music, the children's squabbles and the dogs' barking.

The one lavatory also leads off this porch – a source of embarrassment to some who dislike entering under the eye of their neighbour, and dislike even more being forced to emerge, to an accompaniment of crashing waters, to answer the tradesman who is standing one foot away.

Planners point out that there is a *front* door to each house which could be used. The answer is that it never is. Most tenants were brought up to 'go to the back door' and to keep the front one locked. The habit continues.

But perhaps the saddest part of our village's 'new development', echoed all over rural England, is the rash of bungalows built along two outlying lanes soon after the war, and yet another example of ribbon development, wasteful of land and completely uninspired. They are, for the most part, square box-like structures, all set back from the road at the same distance and all uncompromisingly facing in the same direction towards the lane, although in both areas this means that they are looking to the north-east.

These bungalows, though small and simple, were far from cheap. Their owners, from the first, took enormous pride in their property and the raw gardens were soon planted with wispy hedges of lonicera or privet, and frail flowering trees, lashed to posts three times their girth, battled for existence against the onslaught of the downland winds. New lawns sprouted where once the sheep grazed, and gravel paths were laid where cowslips used to nod.

Each gate differs from its neighbour. Here there is a black one of wrought-iron. Next door there is a wooden one shaped like a miniature five-barred gate. At the end of the row, there is a distressing number which emulates the rising sun, with rays which fan out from one corner and must be deucedly tricky to paint. The names which are upon them tend to be folksy: 'Green Fingers', 'Pixie Cot' or 'The Nook', and are usually found on oval slices of wood hanging on a little bracket nearby.

On the whole, there is a laudable attempt to be different. The paintwork shows this independence more obviously than any other feature, and the owners spend much time and money in attending to doors, windows and guttering. Of latter years, there has been a swing to mauve – not a colour which lends itself happily to exterior decoration, to my mind – and this clashes cheerfully with the more conservative white, black and green of the neighbouring paintwork.

The whole effect is, unfortunately, suburban, and completely foreign to the rest of the village. The lane was once tree-lined, a virtual avenue of noble elms whose branches met overhead and cast a welcome shade in summer and a protection from the worst of the weather in winter.

All were felled to make way for builders' lorries carrying material for the new bungalows. When I see the poor little alien Japanese cherries struggling to gain a foothold in the gardens, I remember those handsome giants who made that part of our village so gracious in their aged dignity, and mourn their passing. What kind of exchange is this?

The tragedy of it all is the sincere longing people have to live in a village and to take part in village life. They recognise its rightness. They can belong. They will know their neighbours. They will have peace. They will live in an old and small society where each man matters and where the surroundings have remained unchanged for generations.

But there are very few who can slip into one of the old houses, in its mature garden, and be readily absorbed by the community. I was lucky. The resident in the school house, man or woman, old or young, is accepted as part of the village, just as the vicar is, or the postmaster. Such people simply fall into the right position in the village. The fact that they are newcomers is of secondary importance.

It is the strangers who have fallen in love with village life who have the hardest row to hoe. They find that they are on the outskirts of the village both literally and figuratively. In a genuine desire to belong, they cheerfully take on local responsibilities which most of the true villagers shun like the plague. They become secretaries and treasurers of a dozen societies. They bring enthusiasm and new ideas. But are they wholeheartedly welcomed? The answer is in the negative although, of course, it is very agreeable to us villagers to have someone to do the work and then to be able to find fault with it. How much better, the curmudgeons say (usually within earshot of the hard-working one), things were managed in the old days when the gentry ran village affairs!

We older inhabitants are not all as unkind. We do our best to welcome the strangers, but perhaps we should do more. There was a lot to be said for the old-fashioned courtesy of calling upon new arrivals. Now no one calls. I suppose our friendliest gesture these days is to open a conversation when we meet the newcomers in the Post Office, or after church. Some of them, I know, are lonelier than they ever imagined they would be. Fearful of becoming too friendly with their immediate neighbours over the wire fence, they put up little barriers of reserve in the early months, and they find that the older residents are so engrossed in their own ploys that very little communication can be found there.

It is not wholly the fault of the older families. In recent years, there has been such an influx of newcomers that it is virtually impossible to keep pace with them. Two or three new families were soon absorbed into the old community. Thirty or more are an embarrassment.

'Went into the baker's today,' Mrs Pringle said to me one

morning, 'and there was ten people in the shop. D'you know, Miss Read, I couldn't put a name to any of 'em!'

And I can assure you that if Mrs Pringle is not able to recognise them, then we less sharp-eyed folk certainly will not.

Of course, no one imagines that the newcomers are desperately unhappy.

They are doing what they wanted to do. They are living in a village, shopping in its shops, attending its church and walking its ways. They are up to their eyes in gardening and settling in. Their children attend the village school, and are often among the brightest there. They enjoy the ineffable pleasures of fresh air and space and the enchanting company of small wild animals and birds.

Nevertheless, they also inhabit, through no real fault of their own, a miniature suburbia, and when one considers that this pattern is repeated a thousandfold all over the countryside, one can but echo Evelyn Waugh's heartfelt cry: 'This is part of the grim cyclorama of spoliation.'

It was, no doubt, the avenue of fine elms, and other local things of beauty, which attracted the bungalow dwellers to the village. When I remember the trees, the stitchwort starring the banks and the honeysuckle rioting over the old gnarled hedge in that lane, I remember, too, those true and chilling words:

'Each man kills the thing he loves.'

It has come at last. The snow, which has been prophesied by the weather-wise for the last week, began to fall yesterday afternoon, shrouding the Downs in undulating veils of snow flakes, and causing the schoolchildren untold exhilaration.

They were sent home early from school, but even so the sound of their footsteps was already muffled in its thickness, and their

footprints were covered again almost before they turned the bend in the lane.

It must have continued for most of the night, for this morning, under a heavy grey sky which presages further falls, the snow lay so deeply in our playground that it came almost to the top of my wellingtons when I went across to unlock the heavy old door.

Over the hedge, in the lane, there were deep drifts where the wind had caught the swirling flakes, and I thought, as I so often do in snowy weather, of poor Elizabeth Woodcock who encountered a February snow storm, so long ago, and was literally buried by it.

The adventure began on a snowy Saturday morning in February 1799. Elizabeth Woodcock, a farmer's wife of Impington, near Cambridge, set off to market on the back of her horse Tinker, with a little poultry, eggs and butter in a great basket before her.

She left behind her five small children and her hard-working husband, and although snow already powdered the ground and was still falling, she confidently expected to be home again before dark.

Having sold her produce she bought a few necessary things such as candles, some stewing meat for the family pot, and a pair of nut-crackers to replace the broken pair at home. Whilst making this last purchase, the shopkeeper presented her with a free almanac giving news of events for the year 1799 in Cambridge. It was to be of unexpected comfort to Elizabeth in the days to come.

She did not set off again until seven or eight o'clock. Some unkind people, who heard later of her ordeal, gave it as their opinion that she had spent some time in the Cambridge ale houses, and began her homeward journey slightly befuddled. No one really knows the rights of the case, but if Elizabeth did take a drop to keep out the fenland's biting cold, it is forgivable, and if that drop was rather too much, it is understandable when one considers that she had spent the major part of a cruelly cold day sitting on a stool in the windswept square of Cambridge market place, trying to sell her few poor articles to a public much depleted by the weather.

There is no doubt, however, about the next part of the story. About a mile from her home, as the horse was crossing Impington Common in a blinding snow storm, it took fright and bolted, precipitating poor Mrs Woodcock and her basket into the snow. She stumbled after Tinker, calling in vain, becoming more frightened and exhausted as time went on. She lost a shoe and, at last, sank hopelessly down beneath a snow-laden thorn bush to rest.

She must have fallen into a kind of coma, for when she awoke it was morning and she found herself completely covered by deep snow. Her breath had melted the snow close to her so that she was imprisoned in a tiny white cave.

She heard church bells ring out from the neighbouring villages of Impington, Histon and Chesterton and so knew that it was Sunday.

Meanwhile, the horse had returned home and the frantic husband organised a search, but in vain. Unbelievable as it seems, Elizabeth Woodcock remained trapped beneath the snow for eight days. It was on the next Sunday that a slight thaw set in, and Elizabeth managed to tie her red handkerchief to a twig and thrust it through a hole in the melting snow. Luckily, it was seen by a sharp-eyed Mr Munsey who quickly effected a rescue, with the help of Elizabeth's husband and neighbours, and the poor woman was soon put to bed amidst the rejoicing of her family.

She had passed the time, she told the many people who came to call on her, by listening for the bell of Chesterton church which rang at eight at night and four in the morning, and so she kept account of the passing days. The almanac was her reading matter, and a little snuff, which she happened to have in her pocket, gave her further comfort. The basket was too far away for her to reach, but was found later, and is now to be seen, with the nut-crackers, in one of the Cambridge museums.

Elizabeth never completely recovered from her ordeal, and died some months later. It must have been a sad time for the family, poor as they were, to lose not only a wife and mother but one of the bread-winners as well. It is to be hoped that local people took the delicate hint dropped by the *Cambridge Chronicle* in its contemporary account of the adventure.

'Mrs Woodcock', it reads, 'is the wife of a small farmer at Impington, four miles from Cambridge, in such circumstances as to render the contributions of the benevolent acceptable.'

Poor Elizabeth! It seems doubly sad to think that she succumbed at the early age of forty-three after enduring so bravely that eight-day burial alive. From time to time, her incredible story is retold, and there must be many people who are reminded of it – and the similar story of 'gurt Jan Ridd's' buried sheep in *Lorna Doone* – when the snow drifts rise, in awesome majesty, to hedge-height and above.

Dramatic weather revives old memories and country people have always loved to hark back to early recollections of similar circumstances.

Not long after I came to Fairacre, I talked with an old lady, now dead, who remembered the fearsome snow storms of 1881. She and a younger brother were sent off to school, well wrapped against the falling snow. The school was two miles distant on a bleak upland, the road exposed and steadily rising.

About ten minutes after the children had gone, the young mother, it appears, had sudden misgivings about their safety. The sky grew ominously blacker, the snow fell faster. In a panic, she threw on her coat and set off at a run to overtake the children. They were already halfway on their journey and had reached some crossroads where, buffeted by the fury of the mounting blizzard, they had sunk on the bank to rest.

The old lady said she never forgot the sight of her mother, hair streaming behind her, mouth wide open shouting their names, quite unheard by them in the wild noise about them. Frantically, she grabbed them and the three battled their way home again. She must have rescued them just in the nick of time, for they would never have reached the school against such odds, and could not have survived long in such cruel conditions. A carter and his boy were lost on the same day, not many miles away, and their bodies were not recovered for several days.

These links with the past are fascinating, and to talk to very old people, brought up in a way of life which had remained unchanged for centuries, makes history come to life. The celebrations of Queen Victoria's Diamond Jubilee are well remembered by a number of our older inhabitants, but when one of them recalled that her grandmother had been much praised as a child for reading aloud the account of William IV's death, it makes one realise how comparatively few human links are needed to span a great space of time.

Sir Maurice Bowra makes this point in his delightful book *Memories*. He tells us that he met Frederick Harrison of Wadham when the latter was ninety-two. He had come up to Oxford in 1848, and remembered the accession of Queen Victoria when he was seven years old. But he also provided a link with a still remoter past by a neat chain of circumstances. He had as an undergraduate met Routh, President of Magdalen, who died in his hundredth year soon afterwards. Routh in his boyhood had met an old lady, who had in her girlhood seen Charles II exercising his spaniels in Magdalen Grove.

But it is not only the lives of the illustrious which are so illuminated by the memories of the old. Here, and elsewhere in our English villages, we can hear first-hand accounts of rural work and play far removed from our own conditions – mainly by reason of the combustion engine – but little more than half a century removed in time.

Perhaps the most fascinating accounts come from the ploughmen and carters, the coachmen and grooms, now old men, whose horses were so great a part of their working lives.

They talk of an age when the horse was king, and they were his willing slaves. The horse's comfort and well-being came far before their own. He must be rubbed down, fed, watered and bedded, long before the man was free to pull off his own soaked clothing, eat and rest. As they tell you of creatures long dead, the eyes of these old men light up with affection, or with enjoyment at the 'devilry' of some lost companion. One has only to pace the empty stable blocks of old houses to see the splendour in which the horses lived, and to realise the hours of devoted work which went into their tending.

'Machinery ain't the same!' said one ancient farm-worker. 'A good team of horses was company when we was ploughing.' It is a remark which highlights a truth often forgotten. The old-time farm labourer or domestic servant was usually one of many. There was company in the house and on the farm. It made for comradeship and a sense of belonging. Quarrels there certainly were; jealousy and internal strife now and again, but never loneliness.

Today, a good farmer may manage several hundred acres with as few as three men. Machines have brought about this revolution but 'they ain't the same'. One man may spend several days ploughing a remote field by tractor and not see another soul while he works. But he may, of course, have his transistor set in the cab with him 'for company'!

As the snow slowly vanishes, the bare ribbed earth appears again in Mr Roberts' large field. Nearer at hand, on the patch of swedes whose greenery was so seriously depleted by the hungry pigeons, the in-lamb ewes are being folded.

My breakfast is taken to the accompaniment of the sound of a mallet knocking in stakes to support the hurdles. Every morning, the shepherd moves his flock to a new rectangle. While the ground is so hard, this is a long and hard job for the stakes need plenty of stout blows to ram them home securely. After that, the hurdles are moved, one by one, for they are surprisingly heavy, and after an hour or so's work the day's fresh allotment is enclosed. But still there is more to do before fetching the sheep from their overnight stand in the field next door. The shepherd loosens the great globes of swedes from the soil so that the flock can nibble more easily. The steady chock-chock of his hoe continues for half an hour, broken now and again by the sudden ring of metal meeting age-old flints.

This done, he moves slowly and deliberately to fetch his charges. Hurrying and stumbling, as fast as their pregnant bulk will allow, they stream towards the new patch, a woolly river of grey undulating backs. They hold their heads high as they bustle along, and with their splendidly haughty Roman noses they remind me of portraits of William Wordsworth.

The swedes will be finished in about a week's time which is roughly a week before the lambs are due to be born. It has all been beautifully worked out. As soon as this nourishing crop has been absorbed by the expectant mothers, they will move on to the sheltered sloping field, near the shepherd's house, for lambing.

And still the tractor rumbles by every morning, past the house, as it carries fodder to the store cattle in the yard not far away. The wild birds are as attentive at the bird table. The trees still make a winter pattern of black lace against a grey sky.

But, now and again, amidst this winter scene one catches a faint glimpse of the advent of spring. The stubby brown catkins have lengthened into powdery tassels. A faint rosiness begins to cloud the elm trees, as the buds swell. In the cottage gardens, snowdrops quiver beside the green-ruffed golden aconites, and the spears of crocuses thrust bravely upward. The autumn-sown broad beans are making sturdy growth, and from last year's stack of bean poles a blackbird tries his first notes.

There is a faint tremor of hope in the air, as though the bonds of winter are slowly slackening, and the earth relaxes. It affects humans as well as animals and plants. Housewives, in particular, respond to this first whisper of spring in time-honoured manner.

Up above the shabby thatch of Tyler's Row, the sweep's brush jiggles against the sky. Neighbours eye it approvingly.

'Time *we* ordered Mr Rogers for the chimney sweeping,' they tell each other.

'I had my winter curtains down last week,' says another.

'What! Before you've done with fires?' asks a neighbour, scandalised.

'They'm black,' states the first flatly. There is a finality about the statement that brooks no further discussion. And although her hearers may deplore her folly, they recognise only too surely the signs of spring fever which has already begun to grip them all.

Now is the time when cupboards are turned out, when drawers are supplied with fresh lining paper, and landing windows 'out of sight and out of mind', as people say, are suddenly attacked and burnished to crystal clarity.

At the first hint of a warm windy day, the village clothes lines dance with woollen jumpers and cardigans, children's leggings, thick bedspreads and all the other trappings of winter which have been 'waiting for the right day'. Dressmakers begin to think about looking out patterns for a new Easter frock. Gardeners pore over seed catalogues and wonder if the lawn mower will last another season. The house-proud make plans for re-decorating. Shall it be white paint again, or something quite different? And isn't it time that those dreary loose covers were scrapped and fresh ones made?

And where, we ask each other, ignoring the vestiges of snow under the hedges, are we going for our summer holiday this year?

'Bit soon, I'd say,' Mrs Pringle booms dourly, 'to start thinking of *summer*!'

But even she, still heavily swathed in winter clothes from stout boned corsets to ancient fur tippet, knows that spring fever has arrived, and knows, too, that no words of hers can dampen our rising spirits.

At this time of year, the congregations at St Patrick's are smaller than ever. This is understandable, as it is now that epidemics are most rife, and when the old, who constitute the major part of the regular churchgoers, are afraid to venture forth when paths are slippery or the weather unkind.

St Patrick's is typical of many rural English churches. Before the war, the average attendance at morning service was about thirty or forty people. At the beginning of the century, the vicar could expect to see an even greater number, ranged respectfully before him when he stood aloft in the pulpit. Nowadays, there might be a dozen faithful souls in the pews, with an almost equal number in the choir stalls, for Mr Annett, our choirmaster, helps to bring the musically minded regularly to church services.

What is the reason for this drastic falling off in church-going? There could not be a more saintly pastor of his flock than Mr Gerald Partridge. His concern for us all is deep and genuine. His sermons are laudably brief and succinct, and if he leans rather too heavily towards metaphysical hymns of obscure meaning and tends to quote the more mystical poets, at least such tastes are harmless and offend no one.

Before decrying the apparent godlessness of the younger generation, it is as well to remember that the pews, which were crowded in days gone by, contained probably half who were there under duress of some sort or another.

The Victorian father brooked no disobedience from his large brood. In rain or shine, the family set out to church and took their places decorously in the pews. There might be up to a dozen members in any one family present.

In the rear pews would be those servants who could be spared from household duties. Here, too, would be the farm labourers and their families, their gaze fixed on the backs of their employers' heads halfway down the church. It was plain common sense to conform in those days when times were hard, and an employer's eye was sharp.

'Didn't see you in church, Tom. What was wrong?' This was the sort of remark, made on a Monday morning, which might be the beginning of the end of a job for a man daring enough to assert a little independence.

But among those meek forms there must have been a number of inward rebels. With the slackening of parental authority, and the shortage of reliable workers, church-going has dwindled to the faithful few who go because the church and its teaching means much to them. Perhaps this gives some small comfort to present-day parsons. It certainly seems rather unfair to me that those who do attend are so often obliged to listen to the diatribes, delivered from the pulpit, on the subject of the back-sliders in the parish!

In Fairacre, fortunately, the Reverend Gerald Partridge is too mild and mannerly a parson to browbeat his small flock although he must often think of his predecessors' happier lot when the church was packed and the vicarage had its full complement of servants.

When that beautiful Georgian house was built in the eighteenth century, there would probably have been three or four servants indoors and two or three men employed in the garden and stables. The pattern would be much the same in the other sizeable houses in the village where the 'gentry' lived. In the truly great houses, such as nearby Springbourne Hall, the number of people employed would be nearer forty or fifty. Today it is owned by the National Trust, and cared for by three people.

Nowadays the vicar has two 'girls', both in their sixties, who live in neighbouring cottages in the village street, and who work for two hours, five mornings a week, keeping the lovely old house presentable. Mr Willet, the church sexton and general village handy-man, helps him in the garden. The Partridges consider themselves very lucky to have such help, for many owners of large houses have none at all. It is small wonder that such places are divided into flats, but this does not always solve the problem completely. Invariably, the garden suffers. If it is divided, the attention given to the various plots ranges from haphazard bedding-out to sheer neglect. If, in theory, the garden is maintained as a unit by all the tenants, it soon becomes a loveless waste, and those who remember it in earlier times mourn its decline.

The passing of domestic servants is noticed more keenly in the country than the town. Here, where generations of wealthy families were waited upon by generations of local families, the bond between those serving and those served was very strong and, in ideal conditions, was something rare and fine. An old man, once a family coachman, told me about a dinner party of long ago to which he had driven his mistress. She was a great beauty and he was proud to be her servant.

'The footman came out to me where I was waiting,' he told me. 'He said to me. "There's no one can hold a candle to your lady tonight!"'

The pride with which he recounted the tale told its own story.

'I'd like to go back and start all over again,' he ended. For him, at least, to serve such a one was a joy and an honour.

But, more important still, these faithful servants freed their masters to serve in other ways. The landowners and the professional men had time to give to many forms of public work. They served on councils, on committees, and on the Bench. Their wives could care for those in need locally, could visit sick people, could help to run clinics for babies, Cubs and Brownies, Women's Institutes and Mothers' Unions. They also had the leisure to devote to their individual talents, and many a charming book, or watercolour, owes its existence to the maid who coped with the housework, and the cook who relieved her mistress of the endless chore of preparing meals.

In our villages today, we hear so often about the benefactors who once lived in our midst and who gave both material and spritual help to those in need.

'No one bothers now,' is the complaint. 'No one has any time.'

To a certain extent it is true. Despite the labour-saving gadgets in the houses and on the farms, time seems shorter than ever. We all have more to do.

My own predecessors in the school house lived modestly, as I do myself, but a woman came in daily to help the school-master's wife even in such a small establishment. Today, I rise at seven o'clock, cook my breakfast and tidy my own house before going across to school. In the evenings, there are such jobs as washing and ironing, cooking and turning out to do.

Occasionally, Mrs Pringle, sighing heavily, comes to give me a hand. Otherwise, I manage alone and am glad to be able to do so. Most women in the village today have a family to look after as well as a job of some sort. It is hardly surprising that it is difficult to get anyone to take on the public work which was so cheerfully shouldered, in days gone by, by those who had their helpers beyond the green baize door to free them for such work.

All the more praise then to those who *do* find time. They are cherished members of a village community these days. A large proportion of them are the newcomers, determined to play their part in village affairs. They emerge from their gaily painted bungalows into the chill February night, and greet fellow committee members stepping out from thatched cottages which have housed the same families for a century, or from the few fine Georgian and Queen Anne houses which so delight strangers to Fairacre.

Later, crammed uncomfortably into desks in the schoolroom or fidgeting in the draughty Village Hall, the meeting begins. And there, in the shadow of St Patrick's which forms the focal point of the parish, no matter what form our particular religion takes, the work goes on, with gentry, cottagers and newcomers busy with the weighty affairs of their village.

March

Welcome maids of honour,
You do bring
In the Spring;
And wait upon her.

ROBERT HERRICK

Picking wild flowers is frowned upon these days, more's the pity. Of course, it is right that rare plants should be protected for the pleasure of all, but I feel sorry for children who have their natural joy in flower-picking shadowed by feelings of guilt.

The joy children get from the flowers of early spring is as much through the sense of touch as through sight and scent. When young, to run one's finger and thumb gently down the fine stalk of a blue violet, growing among dry wispy grass beneath a hedgerow, to the hidden knotted root, was a delight in itself.

The feel of the different stalks added to one's pleasure. Pink-stemmed primroses were faintly hairy to the touch, and the inner thread was an added surprise. Bluebells snapped with a satisfying popping sound, releasing their glutinous juice from cool satin stalks. Wood anemones were unusually tough and wiry for young fingers to pluck. But of all the wild flowers, the violet is the most precious to find in March, perhaps because it is so small and so well hidden among its heart-shaped leaves. I know that when the children bring me their first few blue and white treasures, they are as thrilled as I am. They are put in a Victorian doll's mug on my desk and, as the warmth from the stove releases their evocative scent, we breathe in the essence of spring.

As I pass cottage windows in Fairacre, I notice several similar posies on the sills inside, most of them perched in egg cups – a very suitable cradle for flowers which tell of the birth of spring.

Our first few violets were brought to school by one of the children on the very first morning in March. Far from coming in like a lion, the advent of this month was quiet, almost autumnal. The air was still, and a light mist hung over the Downs and bedewed the hedgerows. By chance, I came across Dorothy Wordsworth's entry in her diary for March 1st 1798. She was writing in Somerset and said: 'The shapes of the mist, slowly moving along, exquisitely beautiful; passing over the sheep they almost seemed to have more of life than those quiet creatures. The unseen birds singing in the mist.'

It was just such a day with us.

The sheep have now gone to the meadow near the shepherd's house, in readiness for lambing, and the field behind the school-house has just been ploughed.

Now the disc harrows are jingling over the clods, breaking the heavy soil into a finer tilth. This is not one of Mr Roberts' good fields. Here a cap of stubborn clay overlays the downland chalk, and it is difficult land to work. But once the harrowing has been done, the drilling will begin, albeit later than the rest of the farmland hereabouts. Seed and fertiliser will go in at the same time, but what the crop will be this year, I do not know. Selfishly, I hope that it will be corn of some kind, for it is lovely at all stages of its growth, and the whispering of the ears as they ripen makes a soporific background to my bedtime.

Planting is going on, too, in the village gardens, though there is plenty of argument about putting seeds into ground that is 'still winter-cold', as Mr Willet puts it.

Personally I find it too chilly to tempt me to work out-of-doors in the slowly lengthening evenings, although it grows increasingly heartening to see the first flowers coming out. The starlings and sparrows, ever-active, are equally delighted to see my polyanthus buds and the yellow crocuses breaking, and spend their time pecking at these luscious morsels and leaving them scattered and wilting over the lawn, thus adding insult to injury.

A few brave butterflies have appeared in the early spring sunlight. One beauty fluttered against the window pane of the schoolroom, opening and shutting its splendid wings as though testing their mobility after a winter's hibernation. The children, who were supposed to be im-bibing some facts about the Roman occupation of Britain, had their eyes glued upon the pretty thing, and I have no doubt that this rival to my efforts won easily.

The tortoise, too, has begun to walk about briskly in the midday warmth. This is earlier than usual. Gilbert White's emerged on March 14. He wrote in 1793 on that date: 'Timothy the tortoise comes forth, and weighs 6 lbs 5 ½ oz.' I must weigh mine someday, but I doubt if she would tip the scales at a third of Gilbert White's specimen.

The mortality rate of tortoises during hibernation is appallingly high in this country, and perhaps I may be forgiven if I set out my own method of tackling this problem, which has been successful in keeping one tortoise for seven or eight years, and another, the present one, for twelve, for the possible interest of any tortoise-owner who might read this book. [*See also* page 243.]

As soon as the weather begins to turn cold, the tortoise is

brought in to spend the worst of the winter on the hearth by the stove which burns night and day. Most of the time, she remains static with her head tucked into her shell, and rammed comfortably against the brickwork near the stove. She usually stirs a little in the morning and is then offered bread and milk, or lettuce, or dandelions, or any available fruit. A flat china lid (from a 'Gentleman's Relish' jar) is filled with water and from this she drinks occasionally.

If there happens to be a mild spell and the temperature of the room becomes too high for her, she stumps to a cooler spot, or if the sun is out I put her in her movable run in a sheltered spot, for an hour or two, with a straw-filled box on its side into which she can burrow.

I know that the experts advise putting the tortoise into just such a box, in a cool place, for the whole of the winter. Unfortunately, in practice, the box is usually put in some out-of-the-way spot, like a garage or garden shed, and is left there from, say, October to March. What happens, and this I know from experience, is that the poor creature rouses during a mild spell, looks for water and food, in that order, and, feeble from weeks without food, soon succumbs when none is available. It is sad to see the children, at this time of year, coming to tell me the painful news of yet another pathetic tortoise who had been doomed to hunger and an imprisonment in some frosty shed, and has been discovered in an advanced and horrifying state of decomposition.

I try to teach the children the basic facts of looking after all animals, but tortoises in particular, so cruelly out of their element in this country, need extra understanding. It is not generally known, for instance, that water should always be available, and placed in a low container which it can reach easily. A large light run, made of chicken wire, which can be shifted about the garden, and a sturdy wooden box for shelter, is all that is needed in the summer so long as the reptile has access to grass, clover, dandelions and the usual lawn mixture of the less impeccable garden. But tortoises also enjoy bare earth and stones now and again, and seem to like eating very small stones and bird droppings. Possibly they need the grit and lime, as birds do, for the formation of the shells of their eggs.

My tortoises have often been to school and are great favourites with the children. They like to draw them, to study their beady eyes, the leathery pulsing neck and to see the difference between their scaly curved front legs and the little straight back ones, wrinkled like loose stockings.

A friend of mine, who worked in a hospital, once watched idly as my present tortoise stumped away across the grass. 'Lots of our out-patients,' she observed, 'have legs like that!'

'Wind's getting up,' observed Mr Willet after school yesterday. He nodded towards my washing line.

'You wants to get your smalls in afore they ends up in Mr Roberts's.'

It was a good thing that I took his advice, for a gale has been blowing for the last thirty hours, and real March weather seems to have arrived. Everywhere is wet underfoot, for we have had our share of rain, but sometimes in a dry March when these gales occur, great clouds of chalky dust float across the ploughed downland and remind me of the two old Norfolk farmers who met, for the first time, in a powerful breeze.

'Where do your land lie?' asked one.

'When the wind's in the north,' said the other, 'it do mostly lie in Suffolk.'

Here, in Fairacre, we know how much devastation high winds can cause. St Patrick's church spire has only recently been repaired after storm damage, costing over two thousand pounds. We all cock a weather eye on the new steeple when the wind howls, and hope never to witness such destruction again.

Perhaps our school is one of the most sorely harassed buildings in the village in rough weather. Almost ninety years old and in continuous use, for all that long time, by boisterous children, it is hardly surprising that doors and windows are out of true, and that the stone step has a dip worn into it by generations of stout boots. In windy weather, the draughts are unbelievably penetrating, and every time the door opens papers blow madly about the room causing disruption to lessons. In any case, wild weather makes children as skittish as it does cats, and when the wind buffets the windows outside there is inevitably twice as much noise and fuss as usual inside the classroom.

Otherwise, it is amazing how well this old building has survived. It is typical of the hundreds of rural schools which still stand, and supply remote neighbourhoods with our children's early lessons. Almost all, these days, house children from five to eleven, the older pupils going to a larger school for the remainder of their education. Many of these small village schools have been closed in the last twenty years or so, and I fear that Fairacre's days may too be numbered. It is a sad thought.

It is interesting and salutary to remember that a large percentage of elderly people in this country had all their schooling at just such schools as Fairacre's. Those early memories contribute in a large part to the nostalgia which people feel for village life, particularly those whose lot it now is to live in a large town. They remember their classmates with uncommon clarity for there were not a great many of them to remember, and usually they remained the same from the time they entered school together until they left. They shared the same teacher for years on end, were subject to the same vagaries of that teacher's temper, and the working conditions around them.

And not only in school were they thrown into close companionship. The walk to and from school, often a mile or two, cemented many a friendship, though sometimes caused a long-term feud. There was plenty of bullying on the long walk home, when high spirits broke out into horseplay which would have been checked if the teacher's eye had been upon the children. I have often observed, when listening to old people's tales of their schooldays, that the happenings outside the school played a much larger part than those which took place in the classroom.

The village school at the turn of the century reflected very closely the village itself. There were several large families, so intermingled by marriage that uncles, aunts, nieces and nephews all jostled each other on the long wooden forms, and there might be only a dozen surnames in the register whilst forty children sat in class. These ties of kinship contributed to the feeling of unity in the school. In a minor way, they had their influence on discipline, too, for mighty little happened that was not recounted first-hand to parents. If 'our Nell' poked out a tongue at the teacher and was 'Caned for Impudence', as the entry in the school log-book faithfully recorded, then you may be sure that brothers and sisters would pass on the delectable news as soon as they reached home. Alternatively, the threat of 'telling-on' could be held over the young malefactor, and a nice line in juvenile blackmail initiated.

The subjects taught were few, and the set times for teaching them were adhered to zealously. The three Rs were the main ones, with Scripture and Needlework playing important roles. The aim of the infants' class teacher, who took the pupils up to the age of seven, was to teach each child to read, to give it a grounding in addition, subtraction, multiplication and division, and to implant the multiplication tables firmly, as well as to introduce each child to the mysteries of farthings, pennies, shillings and pounds. On the whole, most of the children achieved these aims.

Writing, in a clear copperplate style, took much time and energy, but the success of this early teaching may still be seen in the beautiful penmanship of a fast-dying generation. A steel nib was used and dipped into inkwells which were the depository of many strange objects – scraps of paper, seeds, dust, morsels of chalk and so on – flicked in there by idle fingers. To be appointed ink monitor meant extracting the inkwells once a week, putting them in a tray made for the task, bearing them to the lobby and refilling them from a special ink-stained can with a long spout. Mixing the ink itself was usually done by the teacher, by diluting blue-black powder to the right thickness. Some weeks the ink would be unnaturally watery; sometimes it would be thick and strong. Exercise books varied from week to week, displaying essays now pale, now near-black, according to the ink mixture. To be ink monitor was an ambition fostered by many a child, if only for the joy of being out of the room in the blessed privacy of the lobby whilst the other children chanted their tables or the Ten Commandments.

For a great deal was learnt by rote then – a form of imbibing knowledge now much frowned upon, although it still has its advantages. Children of five or six learn very easily by this method, enjoy doing so and retain that knowledge, often for a lifetime. It seems a pity not to utilise this. Poetry, in particular, learnt at this stage of development stays in the memory for years. No doubt the method will return before long. In education, as in fashion, if one waits long enough, the same thing reappears and is hailed as the very latest advancement.

By present-day standards, the lessons which our grandparents and great-grandparents endured were tedious in the extreme. Today, each child finds out for himself. He is trained to work at his own pace. He is given attractive apparatus and constant encouragement. The variety of interest offered to the child is enormous. Whether, at the end of his schooling, he goes out into the world better equipped for coping with it than his forebears, is a matter of debate. He will undoubtedly be livelier, more questioning, more conversant with the arts, maybe, and certainly less in awe of what his grandparents would have called 'his elders and betters'. But will he have their patience, their tenacity and, above all, their clear recognition of what is wrong or what is right?

There was a lot to be said for the religious teaching which took up such a sizeable amount of time in so many of the rural church schools in earlier times. A child likes to know where he stands. Moreover, he needs to be reminded of the right way to conduct himself, over and over again, if he is not to slide into slackness. In today's permissive atmosphere, where stealing, lying and swearing are everyday happenings, and where cruelty to one another, and to the animals whose lives are in our hands, is accepted as a necessary part of modern life, it is hardly surprising that children succumb to temptations. In fact, it is remarkable if they recognise temptation as their elders did.

The children who first sat in the classroom at Fairacre knew all about the Devil and his works. He was rather too dominant a figure in the place, we may feel today, but we have certainly gone to the other extreme. The sober fact of the existence of evil is completely ignored, and the present-day child is ignorant, to a large extent, of its influence. What weighs with him now is what he wants. If it is not readily forthcoming, he contemplates ways of getting it which his great-grandparents would have rejected instantly as unthinkable.

They were thoroughly grounded in the Ten Commandments and the Catechism. It was constantly drubbed into them that they had their allotted place in society – a lowly one in which respect and obedience to those in authority were paramount. Of course, the motives behind such teaching were more selfish than altruistic. Without a subservient poor, how could the middle and upper classes expect to get cheap labour? No one in his senses would wish, even if it were possible, to return to such methods.

But nevertheless something valuable was imparted. A strong sense of moral values became part of their fibre. They knew the rules, and they knew that if they followed them little harm could come to them. Furthermore, they knew only too well that retribution overtook those who broke the rules. Punishment was too harsh, maybe, and out of all proportion to the offence, but it taught the lesson it was meant to teach – that giving way to evil is not acceptable to the community. Today's children, without this sheet anchor and adrift in troubled seas, are much to be pitied for they are more sinned against than sinning.

Well-meaning parents and teachers, the easy prey of child psychologists whose science is yet in its infancy, are full of self-doubt. Will their actions affect the child emotionally? Should they thwart it in any way? Isn't self-expression the main thing? Better not say 'No'.

For the lazy parent and teacher, of course, this laissez-faire attitude is a godsend. Letting a child learn only when he is ready, or allowing him to change his activity as soon as he tires of it, provide a wonderful excuse for doing nothing. Perseverance, once so prized, is a faded virtue. A long job conscientiously done is given less praise than a painting slapped down in five minutes. It is small wonder that young children find themselves in trouble eventually, and sadder still to see parents arriving too late at the conclusion that, despite all the theories on child-upbringing which they have imbibed, something has been missing all the time. Ambitious, as they usually are, for their children's well-being and social advancement, they have forgotten to show them the plain difference between right and wrong.

The children who once learnt their lessons at the village school, and who look now from faded photographs in their sailor suits and black boots, would have envied today's children their freedom, their material prosperity and, above all, the gaiety and colour of today's teaching methods. The old painful drudgery of such things as an hour spent copying pot-hooks and hangers, when a blot was a crime and cramped young fingers could be rapped if they slowed down, or the slow growth of an eye-straining sampler executed in fine cotton with a small needle, has vanished, and no one regrets it. What has vanished, too, perhaps, is the pride in completing a piece of painstaking work, of accomplishing something which demanded sustained persever-ance. The Victorian child of the village might not have enjoyed his lessons particularly, but he learnt how to work, and this knowledge that 'it's dogged as does it' stood him in good stead when he left school – the earlier the better was his outlook – and found a place in the world.

Flora Thompson, in her fascinating book *Lark Rise to Candle-ford*, gives a vivid account of rural schooling in the 1880s. The school which she attended was at Cottisford in north Oxford-shire, the village known as Fordlow in her trilogy.

She brings out clearly how great was the pressure on the boys and girls to get out into the world to earn their keep. In such a farming area, the labourer's wage was pathetically low and usually his family was large. Once a child had attained a certain proficiency in reading, writing and arithmetic, and had struggled up to and through the rigours of Standard Four at the school, he might leave school, often as young as twelve. The shilling or two he could earn as bird-scarer, say, all helped to swell the meagre family income. A girl, if she were lucky, might be taken on as a maid at a good house nearby, and learn her job ready for later promotion in a larger establishment, perhaps in London; and though her wages would be low, she would be kept and housed, and so would relieve the congestion in her own home.

It is not surprising, when one reads these annals of the country poor, to find that the ambition of most of their parents was to see their children as wage earners as soon as it could be managed. The children do not appear to have minded overmuch. School must have been irksome to many an active child in those days, when sitting still and keeping silent were the rules to be obeyed before learning itself began. To be freed at last from a desk and the confines of a small classroom must have seemed like heaven to a tough boy of twelve, ready for outdoor life, no matter how rough, and working with men older than himself who would teach him his skills and probably a great many other things, both desirable and not. Young though he was by present-day standards of school-leaving, he was probably ready for work.

June

It is full summer now, the heart of June,
Not yet the sun-burnt reapers are a-stir
Upon the upland meadow where too soon
Rich autumn time, the season's usurer,
Will lend his hoarded gold to all the trees,
And see his treasure scattered by the wild
*   and spendthrift breeze.*

OSCAR WILDE

Although I love May better than any other month, with its fresh greenery and growing warmth, yet there is no doubt about June taking pride of place, for most people, as the loveliest month of the year.

Perhaps this is why so many outdoor functions are planned for June during the dark winter and why, when the month comes, it is horribly clear that there are not nearly enough Saturday afternoons in June to accommodate the junketings planned.

'Fancy Beech Green British Legion holding their bazaar on the same afternoon as Fairacre Fête!' is the sort of aggrieved remark one overhears.

In Caxley, and other similar market towns, internecine warfare is apt to break out as Townswomen's Guilds, Electricity Boards, Rotary Clubs and a dozen churches of one denomination or another find themselves clashing with each other's sports, Mammoth Fairs, Garden Parties and a bevy of other convivialities.

Primarily, these days, they are money-raisers, which may account for the proliferation of the events. In the old days, these entertainments were usually connected with a more important motive. The big Michaelmas Fair at Caxley, for instance, was usually the hiring fair when workers such as carters and shepherds – often carrying a symbol of their calling, a whip, say, or a wisp of wool or a crook – stood in the market square awaiting a new master.

Many of the old fairs, of course, originated as festivals of the saints and took place on the appropriate day. When the calendar was changed in the eighteenth century, many of the fairs forsook the saints' days and settled instead for a regular date, such as the second Thursday of September. In the Middle Ages, the importance of fairs as places of trade was considerable, and men came from all over the country and from the Continent to attend such famous markets as Stourbridge Fair, St Giles' at Oxford (particularly for books) and Barnet Fair (where horses and ponies were the speciality).

It is interesting to see how many of these fairs have continued into our own times. They still function as meeting places for traders in a minor way, but their main function nowadays is a social one. Crowds are still drawn, as by a magnet, to the garish stalls, the blaring music, the unsophisticated entertainments and the general jollity. And if the motorists find their way barred by 'No Entry' notices on these occasions, it is a small price to pay for the pleasure the local fair gives to many, and the annual respect paid to time-honoured custom.

In Fairacre, as in most villages, we have an annual fair, but it is a very modest occasion and comes, not on any settled day, but whenever the fair-owner comes into the district on his way to the great ancient fair at the county town. A local farmer lets out a field for this one-night stand and we are well content with a roundabout, swing-boats, coconut shies and the more traditional booths.

But this event occurs sometime in September when our social calendar is less crowded. It is in June that the real fever takes us, and we are all busy erecting marquees, coddling our cabbages, grooming our geraniums, making fancy dresses, begging for produce for our stalls, and always – with fervent hope – praying for fine weather.

It always seems pathetically foolhardy to me that so much work and preparation go into an event which is to be staged *outside*. With such unpredictable weather, why not have it in a hall and bill the occasion as 'or in the vicarage garden, weather permitting'? I suppose that one of the main attractions is the outdoor setting, and certainly some of the wonderful gardens which are opened by their generous owners attract as many people as the event itself. Certainly, all the efforts seem to be blessed with a sound financial reward and if the heavens open, as they so often do, sending us scurrying for shelter with plates of cakes and bowls full of raffle tickets, it is really only to be expected and, as we tell each other with true British phlegm: 'The gardens can do with it!'

I like to hear the older generation talk about their village junketings. In those days, it seems, the competitions were geared very closely to the work going on. There were prizes for the best turned-out wagon and horses, the most obedient sheepdog and, for the women, the finest piece of crochet work or the best jar of jam. Such things are still with us, to a certain extent, and competition is still as keen at local horticultural shows and fêtes, but the rewards are interesting to compare. Quite often these days, there is a money prize – five shillings, say, for a first place, half-a-crown for second, and a shilling for the third. It is a simple solution to the problem of what to provide in the way of prizes. Often prizes are donated, and a committee finds itself with some embarrassingly useless articles – possibly unwanted Christmas presents – which they must dispose of in as delicate a way as possible for fear of giving offence. Many a hurried trip has to be made to the local grocer for boxes of chocolates or bottles of wine to replace the hot-water bottle jackets or fearsome vases first donated.

Prizes were eminently practical at the beginning of the century and I have heard an old lady relating with honest pride the story of how she was given five yards of good stout calico for winning the girls' skipping race.

'It made lovely pillowcases,' she told me earnestly. 'They lasted for years.'

Sometimes the prize was a pair of boots or sack of potatoes – and very welcome such things were in those days.

In our village, it is pleasing to see that similarly acceptable prizes are given by local tradesmen. A voucher for the free repair of two pairs of shoes by the shoemaker, and another for a hundred-weight of coal from the coal merchant are received with as much joy today – by grown-ups, at least – as ever they were. Naturally, children prefer to be presented with sweets or toys, the gaudier the better, and any properly run village bean-feast has plenty of these for their delight.

As for balloons, those enchanting frivolities, no summer function worthy of the name can do without them. Seasoned organisers order them by the hundred, knowing that for every one balloon flaunting its beauty in the air, there are a dozen, in fragments, being trodden into the grass, watered, without doubt, by their late owners' tears.

Today, our village fêtes and fairs seem very sedate compared with the rumbustious activities of our forebears. True, at a neighbouring village which clusters along the rushy banks of a little river, which later joins the Cax, they have a spectacular tug-o'-war across the water. Everyone gets deliciously drenched, spectators included, and it is the real highlight of the proceedings. But such boisterous fun is a rarity today.

Climbing a greasy pole, in order to win the leg of mutton balanced atop, was a common entertainment. Pie-eating, bobbing for apples and eating sticky buns suspended from a string with no help from one's hands were all sure winners at drawing crowds. There is still in existence a poster announcing the festivities at Cambridge, which accompanied the Coronation of Queen Victoria in 1838. Some of the attractions billed give an idea of the riotous nature of the frolics on Midsummer Common on that memorable June day. Biscuit-bolting, a ram race, a grinning

match ('Which is the ugliest phiz!!') and dipping for eels, are just a few of the excitements. The rewards offered to the winners include: a Victorian waistcoat, a new white beaver tile (i.e. hat), a new pair of boots and something coyly designated as 'a pair of velveteen inexpressibles'. What fun they must have had!

Such home-made pleasure was an important part of village life before the First World War. In this area, tableaux were much enjoyed, particularly by the ladies who took great pains to get every detail of their historical costumes correct. Many hours were spent on music. The glee club was as important as the church choir, and the standard of singing at village concerts was high. The ladies in the big houses organised play-readings and musical evenings and fostered many a talent which might have been overlooked in a larger community. It is still noticeable, on the rare occasions when the village joins in song, as, for instance, in 'Jerusalem' at Women's Institute meetings or 'God Save the Queen' when public affairs end, that the older generation produce the best notes and have far more musical understanding than their grandchildren.

It is, I suppose, yet another sign of the decline in self-expression. The oft-repeated complaint that we are becoming a nation of spectators has some truth in it. In company with the rest of the inhabitants of these isles, we sit and watch television. Even in the loveliest month of the year, villagers drive their cars, or catch the bus to Caxley to watch wrestling matches or films or to sit, heads down-bent for hours, in a bingo session. The older ones may watch cricket, but it is not easy these days to get enough interested young men to make up a good eleven. Still more difficult is it to get willing workers to maintain a pitch, and many a village hall committee ponders over the problem of maintaining, in the face of apathy, something which an earlier generation struggled hard to bring into existence.

Today's diversions have their points. Television, in particular, has proved a boon to many a house-bound person, but they have quenched much that was vital in the life of small communities, the gaiety and ingenuity which local entertainments brought forth, and the fostering of individual talents for the common benefit.

There is one place in the village where life is as rich and varied as ever it was. The Beetle and Wedge is the only public house in Fairacre and is representative of a hundred other such cheerful centres.

It abides primarily as a meeting place, but also as a haven from the weather, from the cares of a working day, from the scolding of women's tongues and the clamour of insistent children. Here news is exchanged, advice given and – sometimes – taken, village affairs put to right and, now and again, the nation's affairs as well. Here there is a welcome. This is where the pulse of the village body beats, and whether one spends every evening here or simply calls in occasionally on business other than drinking, one is conscious of the feeling of relaxation and warmth which inspires the well-run country pub.

In these days, when organised activity in the village hall meets with little response, and when the church gets scant attention from the majority of the community, it is interesting to notice that the public house thrives. The fact that it sells liquor is a minor one. It is the social side which attracts the customers. Here the village dweller feels that he belongs. The pub is one of the true focal points of his little world, and even those who never enter its hospitable doors recognise it as a key point in their territory.

This awareness of territory is particularly strong in a village community. Until quite recently, people from as little as five miles away were looked upon as foreigners, and treated with some reserve. Some innate wariness, a throw-back, no doubt, to times when a neighbouring tribe might invade one's own domain with malicious intent, still lurks within us. The urge to defend one's territory is stronger than the modern world recognises, and recently a book, entitled *The Territorial Imperative* by Robert Ardrey, an American writer, elaborates this point. He maintains that there is conclusive proof that this animal compulsion to own and to defend territory, the basis of self-preservation, patriotism and general security, is greater, probably, than the reproductive urge although, alas, not half so profusely documented.

Certainly, in a village, the place itself means much. In that garden, Uncle George, long-dead, grew the largest gooseberries in the county. In that house, Mother's family lived for generations. In the churchyard lie parents, brothers and schoolmates. The kinship and the locality are closely connected, and the community is small enough to appreciate its unity. In the ordinary course of events, this unity may not be readily apparent to the onlooker. Family feuds have ever been the bloodiest. But let some outside danger menace a village, and its inhabitants become a band of brothers overnight. Let a motorway be proposed, which will cut across a local farm or destroy a fine grove of trees, and we villagers are up in arms, spoiling for a fight with any ministry of this and that, in order to safeguard 'our patch'.

It is in the local pub that the news of such things is first heard. This is the place to go, not only for private solace and refreshment, but in times of national crisis, to celebrate a victory, to plan the next stratagem in a campaign, or simply to hear what the next enemy move is to be. The local pub is one of the important nerve centres of the village body, receiving and transmitting messages which vitally affect the whole system.

This applies equally, of course, to the town 'pub at the corner' which serves a small area and whose clients are closely knit, less by ties of relationship as in a village, but just as strongly by the bonds of a shared district. It is small wonder that men and women, uprooted from their village, or an old street in some small densely populated area of an ancient city, fail to settle happily in the new towns.

Planners omit to take into account the loyalty which people have to their own district, and the real suffering which occurs at the uprooting of any living thing whether it be a man, an animal or a plant. Factories in reeking areas, truly 'dark Satanic mills', have been rehoused, at enormous expense, amidst fields under an open sky. Houses, upon which the ingenuity of architects and builders have been expended, go up to accommodate those who have hitherto lived in slum conditions, either in the town or the country, and what happens? Very often the factory's output drops. People are not happy. They miss 'the old place', the pub on the corner, the neighbours, the sights, the sounds and smells of home – those very things, in fact, which to the planners were so abhorrent and from which, they congratulated themselves, they were rescuing the workers and their families.

It is tough being a planner today, for everything grows bigger and bigger, and higher and higher, and more and more people are crammed into larger and larger units. It is flying in the face of Providence, as a few – a very few – wise men are beginning to realise.

There is a limit to the size of the district and the number of his fellow-beings to which the average man can adjust himself happily. Good luck then to such enlightened people as those who recognise this basic fact, and are trying to create small and pleasant communities, and are aware of the age-old compulsion in men and women 'to belong' to a territory.

As Kipling summed it up:

Mrs Griffin Sends Her Love

God gives all men all earth to love,
But, since man's heart is small,
Ordains for each one spot shall prove
Belovèd over all.

We are blessed this year with a fine June, a rare occurrence it seems when one reads former diarists and letter writers. Horace Walpole maintained that, 'The contents of an English June are hay and ice, orange-flowers and rheumatism.' And added, 'I am now cowering over the fire.'

Gilbert White, writing on the longest day in 1792, commented, 'A cold harsh solstice!'

But when June is warm and sunny then the English country-side displays a thousand beauties. The frail dog-rose begins to star the hedges, poppies fleck the growing cornfields, tall butter-cups and the coral spires of dock freckle the meadows. Down by the river, the yellow irises are in flower in the water meadows and the pungent scent of mint, growing at the river's edge, is the very essence of summer.

Out in the sunny fields, the hay is being cut, the tedders and the balers thumping their way rhythmically round and round. The farmers work feverishly, their weather eyes cocked at the sky so blandly blue above them. But who knows how long this will last? Farmers are suspicious fellows, and press on urgently with their hay-making while the sun shines.

This is the first of the year's great crops. Within living memory here, on the downland farms, nearly all farm-workers owned and could use a scythe. This fine art is dying out, and the rhythmical flash of the blade and the swish of the cut swathe are rarely encountered today. Then most of the hay was turned by hand, either tossed with prongs or raked. The hay cocks were left standing until they were dry, and then loaded into wagons. The

great creaking vehicle, dropping fragrant hay as it brushed the hedges, would lumber to the place where the hay rick was to be built. Later, the thatcher would be called in to thatch the new ricks with wheat or rye straw to make them weatherproof enough to withstand the winter onslaught.

Today, the whole job is quickly done, the neat bales stacked in the barns, and those glorious picnics in the hay field, remembered as the highlight of summer childhoods, are rare indeed. The practice of making silage by cutting the young grass has also limited the production of hay in June in the traditional manner, and no one would deny that the stench of a silage pit is a very poor substitute for the evocative fragrance of fresh hay on a warm summer's night.

In the gardens, the roses begin to make a brave show, and irises, lupins and peonies tower above the smaller flowers in the borders. Clematis plants, of every colour from pure white to dark purple, present their flat faces to the sun, and look particularly fine against the dappled brickwork of rose-red and grey in which this area is so rich.

The cottage gardens display great patches of yellow and red musk, which is a prolific grower and makes a gay splash in the beds. There are still old people here who can remember the scent of musk but, alas, it has gone, and no one can say why. Pansies, London Pride, columbines and pinks add to the profusion of blossom.

It is interesting to see how many plants are duplicated in neighbouring gardens. When autumn comes, and we are busy splitting up large clumps, what is nicer than to be able to present a root to an admiring neighbour, and to receive one of his treasures in return? The 'good doers' are always recommended to one's friends, and in these days plants which demand the minimum of attention, but provide the maximum of pleasure, are always welcome.

The long spell of sunny days has made the bird bath doubly attractive, and thrushes, blackbirds, starlings, finches and a host of sparrows, both house and hedge varieties, enjoy the water for bathing and drinking.

Two tit boxes in the school-house garden are occupied. One by sparrows, unfortunately, but the other by those for whom it was intended. The parent birds have been busy for the past week or so, flying back and forth to feed the clamorous young who keep up a faint high-pitched murmuration from the minute they hear the rustle of nearby leaves, as their parents alight, until they have flown off again to forage for more.

I allowed myself one glimpse of the babies while the parent birds were absent. When the front of the box was removed I could see eight babies, very quiet, their bright round eyes looking at the world so soon to be theirs. They were exquisitely coloured in new feathers of soft blue and yellow, uncannily like the irises flowering in the border nearby. I replaced the lid carefully, and only just in time, for the mother bird arrived in a frenzy of scolding, and I retired hastily.

The feeding continued for another few days, but now they have flown, and the nest awaits new occupants next year. Once I was lucky enough to see the emergence of some tit babies from their box. There were seven all told. The first six, encouraged by little cries from the parents, came out of the tiny hole, one by one, and settled on the branches of the ancient plum tree which shadows the box. They clung there, like some exotic flowers, gazing around them wonderingly.

But the seventh bird was not so bold. He remained in the nest, with his head protruding from the hole, and squeaked loudly. The mother bird flew down and back repeatedly, as though showing him how easy it was, but he did not dare to come out for over an hour. At last he struggled out, landing on a nearby twig, and the family was united again. Within another hour, they had all vanished. I like to think that this year's family are descendants of those which I watched, with such pleasure and instruction, a few years ago.

Another joy this year has been the return of wrens to the garden. After the cruel winter of 1962–63, the wrens vanished and did not come back until last year. This spring, a pair has nested in the old thorn hedge and their metallic song, so surprisingly loud for so tiny a bird, has echoed through the garden, and even made itself heard above the noise of children shouting in the playground hard by.

The bird bath in the garden is filled daily, but by nightfall there remains only a pathetic muddy drop of water. Two bowls are put out in the school playground but, rather naturally, are used by the birds only when the children are inside or have gone home. Needless to say, the children have quite as much fun with the water as the birds do.

This downland area is by nature a dry one. One or two ancient dew-ponds survive and are used by the sheep. The birds flock there in dry weather and also visit the water troughs which have superseded the dew-ponds since the coming of piped water.

The passing of our village ponds, in company with hundreds of others up and down the country, is a source of real regret. There were three at one time in this village, and only one remains.

The surviving pond is in Mr Roberts' farmyard. The older generation remembers the great carthorses that were watered at this pond, but now the largest animal that drinks here is Mr Roberts' sheepdog, Bess. A low wall divides the pond from the road, and over this wall one can watch the life of this delectable piece of water. A flotilla of Khaki Campbells is the main attraction, and when the ducklings hatch in the spring, these animated balls of yellow down delay the children so long with their endearing antics that there are plenty of late arrivals at school.

The two public ponds were formed by the drainage of surface water from the road. One was near the Beetle and Wedge, and local gossip had it that, over the years, two or maybe three home-going revellers from the pub met their ends in its watery depths.

Before the advent of mains water, nearby cottagers fetched a bucket of water from this pond for household jobs. It was clean enough for washing flagged floors, or for providing drinking water for fowls and pigs, and saved many a trip to the hand pump some distance up the road.

We were sorry when it was drained. It is now used as an untidy car park by the descendants of those who dipped their pails in the murky water, and only the sparse clumps of stiff reeds give any hint of the pond vegetation which used to add its green beauty to the scene.

The other pond was some half-mile away along the Beech Green road. It was always a dark pool, shadowy and secret, overhung by trees whose branches swept the silky veil of scum and small leaves upon the surface. It was supposed to be dangerously deep but this rumour had grown up, I suspect, to deter children from playing there. No one, I think, really regretted the passing of 'the black 'un', as I once heard a child call this lonely pool, for there was something sinister in its silence. Nevertheless, it was a feature of our village which added its interest to our surroundings, and the present dusty pancake, embellished with rusty tins and gaudy plastic objects no longer needed, is a poor substitute for the dark mirror which reflected darker trees in all seasons.

I think that we should fight more lustily for the retention of our country ponds. Apart from their looks which add enchantment to a rural scene, they provide water and cover for all types of animal and bird life. Where, for instance, are the frogs these days? When I first came to the village, only a few years ago, it was a common occurrence to meet dozens of young frogs after a shower of rain, most of them originating, no doubt, in the two village ponds. Far too often, for my peace of mind, one encountered poor flattened reptiles on the road, but in the last year I have been hard put to find even one frog to show to the children in a nature lesson, and the tank of frog-spawn in the classroom, which we watched so eagerly for the first tadpole, is no more.

All of us, grown-ups and children alike, are the poorer for the passing of our ponds.

If the ponds have gone, at least the rivers are not far away, and it is in June that the fishermen have their heyday in these parts. The

Cax and the Waybrook both provide good trout-fishing and when the mayfly (which the *Concise Oxford Dictionary* describes prettily as 'an ephemeral insect') comes into its brief season, then fishermen, and their friends, can expect trout on the menu.

With luck, too, strawberries will be ready in the gardens. It is almost impossible to grow them here unless one has a fruit pen to protect them from the ravages of the birds. They attack the fruit long before it is ripe, and I have watched a young thrush gulping down hard white strawberries with much enjoyment. Are birds tamer then they were, or is there less untainted food for them to eat? Certainly, they seem to be fearless these days, approaching far closer to habitation than before, and taking less notice of people near them.

To my mind, the strawberry season is all too short. It is a fruit which, above all others, is exquisite when served with the minimum of fuss. The perfect way to enjoy strawberries is to pick them on a sunny day, and to eat them within an hour or two with fine sugar and cream. It always seems a pity to me to mix strawberries with other fruit, or to kill their delicate flavour with wine or liqueur, but no doubt with some of the tired berries one sees in the shops it is forgivable to do this.

As a child, living among strawberry fields in Kent, it was a joy to be let loose among the crop – *after*, let me add hastily, the farmer had collected all he wanted. We could pick as many as we liked for, I believe, sixpence a pound, and they made excellent jam, if they ever survived a mile-long journey in the care of ravenous eight-year-olds. The smell of sun-warmed strawberries and the golden straw on which they rested in those far-off days is with me yet.

This is not a great strawberry-growing area here among the Downs, although further south there are farmers who specialise in this chancy crop. A few are grown in gardens, but raspberries, loganberries and black and red currants are the usual soft fruit crops to be found in our gardens. For some unknown reason, gooseberries seem to have fallen out of favour. Perhaps the cruel thorns have something to do with this, but I miss the different types, ranging from green through deep red, to the enormous yellow hairless variety which used to be known as dessert gooseberries, and broke so delicately in the mouth, releasing a flavour as heady as champagne. A bush of these treasures grew, among lesser gooseberries, in the tangled garden of an old lady I knew as a child. I used to call there to collect a younger child on the way to school. No doubt I was particularly assiduous about this little duty during the gooseberry season. Certainly, I was given the run of the gooseberry patch, and it was towards the dessert variety that I turned first. I still hope that gardens will revive their interest in this neglected fruit.

The gourmet has his hours of bliss in June, particularly if he is a gardener as well. The very earliest new potatoes begin to appear, and what is more pleasurable than digging for this buried treasure and watching the fork turn up globes of gold? Broad beans, pale green among their velvet-lined pods, fitting as snugly as sovereigns in an old sovereign case, are at their best, and I know few dishes better than a good gammon rasher with new potatoes flavoured with fresh mint, and broad beans served with parsley sauce. If there are home-grown strawberries to follow, then here, surely, is the perfect June meal.

Asparagus and cherries, tomatoes and cucumbers from the greenhouse, with salmon, trout and mackerel at their cheapest and best, all help to make June the cook's heyday. No wonder that those with deep freezers are working overtime, surrounded by mounds of peas to be shelled and masses of young vegetables and fruit to be attended to.

Sometimes I wonder, when I see the amount of work being done by these good housewives during the bright summer days, if I am not better off eating my way carelessly from day to day, eating as many broad beans or strawberries as I can afford, and a helping from some mundane tin when winter comes. But when the long cold months approach, those busy housewives, and their fortunate guests, can recapture the bounty of summer as they unthaw their precious polythene packets.

In this hot weather, nothing is enjoyed more by the children than their weekly trip to the swimming baths at Caxley. The older children pile into the bus in the lane, soon after school dinner has been demolished, and they return to school just after the afternoon break.

Very few leave this school, nowadays at eleven, without being able to swim a little. I doubt if half their parents could match this record, and their grandparents, more often than not, were unable to swim if they were born and brought up in Fairacre. The Waybrook offers one or two pools suitable for splashing about in as it meanders towards the Cax, but it is not an inviting brook, overhung as it is by willows, and flowing sluggishly through meadowland frequented by cows, who muddy the water for most of its length. These pools, and the old village ponds, were the only places where a child could bathe, and were more suited to an unsatisfactory paddle rather than any active swimming. The older generation, who rarely saw the sea, therefore grew up with a healthy respect for water and a genuine admiration for the brave fellows who served in the Royal Navy and the Merchant Navy.

'If the Almighty had meant us to swim,' I have heard one ancient worthy say, 'He would have given us webbed feet. Going into water's against Nature!'

But going into water is just what the children love, and 'swimming afternoon' is the highlight of the week. When they return, with their damp hair plastered to their skulls, they look unnaturally fresh and clean. Quite often, too, I notice that there are damp patches on their frocks and shirts, for not only do they dry themselves somewhat sketchily, but all too frequently a garment is dropped into a puddle on the wet concrete of the changing-room floor.

When the sun blazes, we usually take the last lesson of the afternoon outside on these occasions, and dry off in the warm sunshine.

Usually, I read them a story, but as they sit or lie on the grass with the murmur of bees about them and Mr Roberts' hay-baler thumping somewhere in the distance, I realise that the blissful aftermath of physical exercise has dulled their wits, and that they are content to drowse in this rare June heat, absorbing all the joys of a summer day.

And, for that matter, so am I.

COUNTRY MATTERS

The First Fortnight: January 1963

The period of snow in early 1963 certainly was memorable, and Dora started to keep a diary while she and Doug were more or less housebound. I came across it after she died, and think it is worth including as a record of that time, and observation of the local wildlife.

Tuesday January 1st

The snow which first fell on Boxing Day still lies very thickly. Drifts between here and Wickham are up to six and seven feet, and although tractors and Land Rovers can get to Wickfield by going part of the way along the edge of a field, nothing can get beyond the Wickfield turning towards Wickham. The Wickfield people are collecting crates of milk from the Waseys' house next door, and taking them home on the tractor. Newspapers and letters were left at Shefford Woodlands Post Office today.

Yesterday, Jill was lucky to get to Oxford in a Land Rover. The road from Hungerford to Wantage was badly hit with deep drifts, and two buses and a snow plough blocked the hill into Wantage, we heard.

The garden is about eight inches deep in snow, with drifts up to a foot or more where a bitter north-east wind has swirled it through the gate and gaps in the front hedge. Dozens of birds have come for food. As well as house and hedge sparrows there have been blue tits, great tits, a coal tit, several robins, starlings, blackbirds and thrushes. The new wire feeding basket hanging on the copper beech has been in constant use. The starlings sit in it and gorge, but this does not stop the tits, for whom it was primarily intended, from hanging underneath and pecking like mad.

Seven partridges huddle in the field behind the house, a sorry sight. They scratch in the snow, but I fear that they find very little. No sign of our cock pheasant today.

Wednesday January 2nd

Still a fierce north-easter. The band of beech trees across the road has sheltered us a little. We are told by local people that we should have had much more drifting on this road, Ermin Street, if the wind had been in the north-west.

Dug paths today and cleared snow away from the house. Birds still busy eating scraps, coconut hanging on the lilac tree and lumps of fat festooning the japonica. They seem to leave the oats in the chicken corn thrown out to them, but eat all the other grain readily.

Thursday January 3rd

Saw a cock and hen pheasant today sitting on our garden hedge, but too timid to come for the corn near the house and impossible for us to throw it any nearer. Can only hope they come when we are not about. Still very cold, but the wind is less. The north side of the house is glazed with ice, and a freezing rain, which fell this morning, has covered the windows on that side with thick ice, heavily pitted, so that it looks like old-fashioned frosted glass. The trees are encased in ice, each twig heavily coated so that the whole effect is of a glassy tree. The hedge of beech and privet is the same and crackles when it is touched.

Tinker, the cat, is very bewildered by the snow on the rare occasions he ventures forth. He hardly leaves his basket by the fire.

The road between here and Wickham is still blocked but the Wickfield people go by on the tractor two or three times a day. The baker from Great Shefford, the milkman from Newbury and the butcher from Hungerford all came today – a stout effort, but the laurels really go to the newspaper boy last Sunday who cycled from Froxfield to Hungerford to collect his papers and then did his rounds on the bicycle.

Friday January 4th

Much better today, milder altogether. A watery sun came out for an hour or two and a slow thaw has begun. The ice on the branches has been loosened and comes rattling down with a tremendous crashing sound, particularly from the oak at the corner of Strouds Field, as it rushes through the glazed ivy leaves round its trunk.

The freezing rain has left a thick crust over the snow and this is covered with pieces of grey ice under the trees where they have thawed. Some of the pieces are as big as test-tubes, some like fine long crystal beads, the sort we used to call bugles.

The ice on the overhead electric cables and telephone wires is also crashing down on the ice below – a most exhilarating sound, freedom from bondage! Full of zeal, we dug out the snow from the garage to the road. We chopped it along in lines with our shovels, then at right angles, and lifted each great block of ice and threw it against the hedge. It is easy to see how igloos are built when snow is so substantial. One has a feeling of great satisfaction in lifting something so big and yet so light. Nevertheless, it made my arms ache.

We got the car out and drove to Hungerford, three miles away, and felt very adventurous, our first outing for over a week. The Wantage–Hungerford road has been well cleared, but the snow has drifted in the hedges to a depth of eight or ten feet in places.

People in Hungerford were busy buying loaves and greenstuff and all sorts of necessities. There were far more tractors and Land Rovers than cars in the parking spaces today. It is amazing to see the array of colours which people have put on. Quite rightly, all the warmest clothes have been donned, and purples and yellow, pinks and greens, with no end of scarlet, are seen cheerfully mingled to keep out the weather.

We posted our letters, bought some sweets, some scones for our tea and collected the meat to save the butcher a journey tomorrow. Rather perturbed because he could not find anything specifically for the cat's food, he charged sixpence on the bill already made out, and cut him a wonderful wedge of shin of beef which I am sure is worth three times that. Tinker, I trust, will be duly grateful.

Saturday January 5th

The sun has gone again, and it has been raw, slightly foggy and very still. We walked as far as the Pheasant Inn to see drifting there. John Pallet was on his roof clearing snow from a gully. We called in and asked the family to tea. Our telephone has been out of order for two days and on our way back we unwound a hanging wire and put it safely out of the road on to the snow drift. Several wires are down broken by the weight of ice. As we came in the front door our telephone was ringing! It was Jill. All's well at Oxford. We must have mended our own telephone.

I took some photographs of the snow yesterday while the sun was out, including one of the icicles hanging from the Waseys' thatch. Some are a foot long, and they look like a thick row of splendid crystal carrots. There was an equally fine row along Miss Stevens' house today.

Tonight it began to thaw again, and we went to bed with the welcome sound of ice crashing down every now and again.

Sunday January 6th

Another raw day. We walked towards Newbury today. The snow plough has opened this route after about ten days. The snow is deeper here between the Wickfield turning and Oakhanger than anywhere else nearby. We met Vera Wasey with the two Labradors, Bracken walking sedately in the road, but Nick, the young dog, leaping up to the snow peaks and tearing up and down the slopes in great excitement.

Monday January 7th

Were to have spent the evening at Chieveley but frost was so severe, and hard-packed snow so icy after dark, that we decided to postpone our visit. Also the snow plough has choked their entrance with snow and there is nowhere to park.

Bitingly cold all day with strong north-easterly wind. Did not venture further than the garden. At dusk, as I was drawing the curtains, I saw a hare running across the field. He sat up and listened, then tore across the field to Templars. He looked enormous against the white field.

I took down the holly wreath from the front door. It was a mass of fine red berries on Christmas Eve. Now not one berry remains – the birds have seen to that.

Tuesday January 8th

Had my first trip to Newbury since Christmas. The trees still laden with snow in the Sutton woods and several grey squirrels hopping about. There is considerably less snow near Newbury and the streets have been well cleared, but the yards and passages are still slippery with hard-packed ice.

The men were busy at Shefford mending the telephone wires, no easy job as it is difficult to get near the posts because of drifts.

A beautiful clear night, the moon almost full and casting sharp shadows on the snow. The cat quite pleased to go out and loth to come in at bedtime.

Wednesday January 9th
The first really bright sunshine since Boxing Day. Quite exhilarating with sun glittering on ice-crusted snow, but a wind so keen that my eyes watered as I came back facing it from the Post Office.

There are a great many dead partridges and pheasants about, and the hares are getting painfully thin. Any greenstuff not covered by snow has been eaten by the starving birds and animals. Vera Wasey saw the pigeons digging a hole in the snow by her spring broccoli and eating well below the surface. There are dreadful tales tonight on the News of sheep and cattle frozen to death further west.

Thursday January 10th
Went to London today catching the 8.45 train which arrived almost on time at Paddington. The white wastes of snow each side of the railway line between Newbury and Reading looked very lovely, and the Thames and the Kennet very black and sinister winding between them. London looked drab with hummocks of snow here and there, but black, with bits of paper, dust and shavings frozen into them. An icy wind at every corner.

Friday January 11th
More birds than ever in the garden today, including six partridges. Can they be the ones we see so often in Strouds Field? I dug a patch of snow away in the shrubbery and threw corn, chopped apples, scraps of suet, sago and soaked bread for them. They whirred away across the road at my approach, but all the other fowls of the air swooped joyfully upon this largesse. Later

on, the partridges returned and seemed to find enough to please them. They came very close to the house in their search for food.

We drove to Chieveley through cliffs of dug-out snow. North Heath is still very thick. Chieveley's main street has quite a high bank of snow edging it. A clear night but wickedly cold. It was extra good to see friends again. We are all getting low and liverish being obliged to keep to the house. Everything is an effort to do – getting up, going into the garden, facing the cold at every turn. This sort of weather makes one realise the spirit that made Arctic explorers the heroes they were.

Saturday January 12th

For the first time that I can remember we kept the electric fire on all night in our bedroom, and still felt chilly when we woke this morning. We heard later that there were 20 degrees of frost here, but 29 degrees at Lockinge.

A slight fog had formed hoar frost on the trees and bushes. Very pretty but deathly cold.

It continued bitterly cold all day and we stayed indoors. The outside lavatory has a burst pipe despite an oil stove in it night and day. We heard on the Six o'clock News that temperatures have been 12 degrees below freezing point. (It came as no surprise to me!) The Thames is frozen at Windsor and a cutter is going up and down keeping a clear path for boats. At Slough, people skated on the canal there.

Sunday January 13th

We took Jill back to Oxford this afternoon. People were sledging down the slopes at Boxford. The Newbury–Oxford road was clear of ice, and we saw one or two people in Oxford carrying skis and skates.

We came back on the Wantage–Hungerford road. Still very icy

on the top of the Downs, this side of Wantage. The snow blows across the road and silts it up. Nevertheless, had a good run home, and nothing we saw on our travels during these fifty miles exceeded the wintriness of our own stretch of road from here to Wickham.

The six partridges came again to the garden, and we also have four pigeons, two yellowhammers, three robins, and scores of tits, sparrows, blackbirds, thrushes, starlings etc, as regular customers. I must buy more corn.

Monday January 14th

Sunshine, and a blessed rise in temperature to a degree or two above freezing. A slow thaw set the snow sliding from the roofs in Newbury where we spent most of the day. It was wonderful to see puddles again, and to see people walking casually, with arms relaxed instead of hunched against the cold.

Electricity was cut off in London, we hear, and in other places, too, owing to a 'work-to-rule' campaign. Our own supply was diminished for a time, but not actually cut off.

We lit the fire at teatime and saw the smoke blowing across the garden. The wind has gone round to the north-west at last, and we feel unspeakable relief. Can this mean that, after three wicked weeks, we are through the worst?

Note As we now know, we were very far from being through the worst. Electricity was cut further, gas supplies dwindled and the temperature dropped further than ever. On the night of January 21st at Shefford Woodlands, where the writer lives, there were 35 degrees of frost. The icy spell did not end until early March.

Mrs Griffin Sends Her Love

Our nearest shop is in a village almost two miles away. Town friends, who plod up and down their High Streets daily with weighty baskets dragging their arms from their sockets, are very sorry for me marooned out here in the midst of fields. But my sympathy is for them, for all my goods are brought to the door, even through the shocking winter of 1962–63, with time for a heartening gossip thrown in.

The baker calls on Tuesday, Thursday and Saturday bringing lovely crusty loaves from his own bakery three miles away. His rounds of scones, Thursday's speciality, arrive warm from the oven. The butcher calls on the same days, and the weekly groceries arrive on Wednesday morning without fail.

I need never set foot in a shop. There's freedom for you! On Tuesday morning, I sit by the telephone and give my meat and grocery orders for the week. And if, as always happens, something has been forgotten, I know that another travelling grocer is calling that afternoon with a van packed with everything from sausages to sherbert dabs, and I am saved again.

But perhaps the most sociable day is Friday. The greengrocer calls in the afternoon in comfortable time for the weekend catering. He brings wonderfully fresh vegetables, salad and fruit, as well as new-laid eggs from hens who still have their freedom. If I am out, a basket in the porch overflows on my return. 'Don't leave any money!' he says cheerfully, as do all the other tradesmen. 'Pay me next time!'

It is on Fridays, too, that the fishmonger calls in his neat van carrying plaice and cod, herrings and kippers, and one large turbot 'for the gentry'. The boxes are lavishly sprinkled with ice and sometimes covered with sprays of fresh greenery for extra protection. The cat accompanies me to the van, and we are given news of friends he has called upon along the way. Surely, town shoppers, battling with baskets, indifferent assistants and the clock, can never feel the lift of spirits that I have when the fishmonger, uncovering his boxes, says: 'Before I forget it . . . Mrs Griffin sends her love. Any fish'm?'

Georgie Giraffe Comes in Sixth

The cars begin to trickle through the village while we are having our elevenses. By lunch time, Land Rovers, shooting brakes, cars and motor cycles are streaming through, nose to tail, packed with children, aunts, uncles, rugs and large supplies of food and drink. The first race at the Easter Monday point-to-point begins at 1.45 and one needs a substantial lunch to withstand our downland weather.

We cycle the mile to the course on our venerable bicycles, hugging the hawthorn hedge and hallooing at overtaking friends who honk remorselessly at our wobbling back wheels. The cars bump into Farmer Henry's meadow and draw up in neat lines near the rope that marks the course. We prop our bicycles by an elder tree, confident that their age will protect them from even the most hard-pressed bicycle thief, and buy our race cards from a cheerful man with bow legs and a blue nose.

The first race is soon to begin and the horses are being led round the paddock. Some tittup demurely, some prance alarmingly near children, who hang over the ropes with their mouths open in adoration. Others are plainly bored, and lean heavily on their sweating grooms.

'Let's back Georgie Giraffe,' begs my young companion, a

staunch *Rainbow* reader. I identify him as a particularly lolling chestnut, with a wicked eye, who is giving his groom the deuce of a time. But I am persuaded, and we make our way to the Tote, a marquee as imposing as the one next to it marked 'Refreshments', and receive for our florin a pink ticket.

Now the horses, riders up, are trotting from the paddock to the start. We make for a small hill, topped by five pine trees, from which we can get a view of most of the course. Sunshine roofs are being pushed back and people are scrambling up on top of their cars.

We are all bundled up in our warmest clothes here, for the wind cuts wickedly. I am reminded of the advice given on 'Woman's Page' this week about the necessity of dressing attractively and suitably for these occasions. I doubt if she would approve of the countless travelling rugs worn squaw-wise which are to be seen. Most of us look like those wooden Russian dolls, shapeless, imperturbable and cheerful. This is no time to be over-finicky about our appearance. The woman I envy most wears a fur coat over a camel hair one, a plaid rug pinned round her middle, the sort of boots I imagine they attempt Everest in and a fur balaclava which leaves the minimum of face exposed.

The starter, on a gigantic horse, raises his pistol.

'What a lovely white horse,' I remark to my companion.

'*Grey!*' she screams back, shocked. I apologise.

The horses make a sketchy attempt at a line. There is some preliminary shouting, the pistol cracks and they pound away to the first jump. There are about a dozen entries and they keep together in a bunch for the first half-mile. Race cards flutter, field glasses are snatched from hand to hand, an ambulance edges nearer a jump and my young companion bounces ceaselessly up and down, piping 'Georgie Giraffe' in a reedy refrain.

Now they are coming into the second and final round. An enormous bay shakes the earth as it gallops by. Yards behind come four more. Georgie Giraffe follows them at an easy pace. He obviously 'won't be druv' and wears the expression of one who is only doing this because, at the moment, he likes it.

'He isn't even trying!' wails his backer.

The bay maintains his lead. His rider is Mr Henry, whose fields these are, and he is a popular winner. Georgie Giraffe, as fresh as when he started, comes in sixth.

'Well,' sighs my young companion, 'that's that ! D'you know, there's a man over there selling the loveliest, *cleanest* candy floss you've ever seen!'

I take the hint, and hand over sixpence for this consolation.

Between races, in this green plot, we meet more of our friends and neighbours than we have seen through all the long winter months. We make up for lost time and exchange news of births, marriages, changes of address, our pet influenza cures and the progress of our gardens.

By five-thirty, it is all over, and we walk across the bruised grass to collect our bicycles from the elder tree's custody. As we wobble homewards, returning the waves of the children who flatten their noses against the back windows of the passing cars, we feel well content. A fine afternoon behind us and mounds of toast and pints of tea ahead!

Dora regularly drew on her experience of village life for her fiction writing. The next three pieces, each presented as fiction, were published in The Lady *under their 'Country Matters' section, and are three good examples. She used a variety of names for her characters – always avoiding the names of people she knew – often using one more than once to give a sense of continuity.*

Buying Logs

'Tip some more coke in,' suggested old Bates as we huddled round the stove in the village hall. Waiting for our chairman is always a lengthy business at Parish Council meetings.

'I left a good fire at home,' said the doctor sadly. 'Some apple wood. Makes a good fire. We burn no coal to speak of . . . just our own wood.'

'You're very lucky to be able to burn your own wood,' said Mrs Trent forcefully. 'Very lucky indeed! Why, I paid that old rogue Rogers five pounds for a load last month!'

There was a good deal of throat-clearing and foot-scuffling for old Rogers is brother-in-law to our Mr Bates, and you can't be too careful in the village.

'Five pounds!' repeated Mrs Trent, raising her voice above the protective sound barrier, 'and a more measly lot of damp box wood I've yet to see!'

The vicar deftly turned the subject into more peaceable channels. 'I believe we get ours by the bushel. A very pleasant young man from Danbourne calls once a week with bushel sacks and keeps us well supplied through the winter.'

'More expensive that way,' said the doctor.

'I've met that young fellow,' said Mrs Trent ominously.

' 'E don't give fair weight,' said old Bates.

A thick column of smoke suddenly belched from the stove, and we all coughed together.

Mr Pettitt recovered first and spoke through the fumes. 'How many bushels to a load?' he asked.

Mr Pettitt has only lived in our village for two years, and is reported to be writing a book about us. Not that we hold it against him. As old Bates very fairly says, 'We all gotter live, ain't we?'

The vicar looked at him with the same expression that he wears during Sunday School, a blend of irritation and patience.

'It depends, naturally, on the size of your load.'

'Quite, quite! Let us say then, how many bushels would you get into a two-ton lorry?'

'About forty or fifty, maybe,' said old Bates.

'Put it another way,' burst in Mrs Trent. 'How many logs would you get in a bushel sack?'

'It depends entirely on the size of the logs,' said the vicar blandly. 'But I should say about twenty-five on average.'

'And how much do you pay for those twenty-five, sir?' asked Mr Pettitt, hot on the trail.

'Half a crown.'

'I never give 'im more'n two bob,' said old Bates.

Mr Pettitt waved him aside. 'So you pay him a little more than a penny each. Now, Mrs Trent, how many bushels did you get in the load that cost you five pounds?'

Mrs Trent looked blank. Mr Pettitt breathed heavily and leant forward, wagging his finger.

'You see what we are trying to do? We're trying to find if it's cheaper to buy logs by the load or the bushel.'

Mrs Trent continued to look blank.

'What sort of lorry was it?' persisted Mr Pettitt.

'A big red one,' said Mrs Trent truculently.

Mr Pettitt slumped back in his chair and seemed to have some difficulty with his breathing. At this moment, our chairman stamped in cheerfully.

'Perhaps *you* could tell us the best way to get logs,' said the vicar.

'Logs?' roared the chairman. 'Why, I tell the men to fetch down a couple of tidy-looking trees somewhere on the farm, and they see us through the winter.' He settled himself happily at the head of the table. 'Now, first thing on the agenda . . .'

'We've 'ad that all right,' said old Bates.

The Peasants' Revolt

During the summer months, we villagers wear a preoccupied air as we pad about in our sandals, and our eyes are glazed or glaring, according to temperament. For this is the season when mothers, sisters, dear old school friends and adorable but exhausting grandchildren arrive in their shoals to stay with us.

'Not that I don't love seeing them,' Mrs Trent assures me, dashing back a white lock with a distracted hand, 'but Anne has four now, you know, and all under six . . . and the food and bedding . . . which reminds me! Can you possibly spare the playpen again?'

At the bus stop stands Miss Hughes. She is wearing her best spotted silk and the chunk of amber on a chain. Clearly her batch is just arriving. She hails me to her side.

'I wonder if I might borrow your camp bed? My sister, Miriam, may bring the biology mistress with her, in which case . . .'

I explain that the camp bed is being slept on by the baker's brother-in-law from Coventry, who has promised to erect it, on his departure, for the butcher's son's friend who will be down from Oxford for the fruit-picking. In the event of his non-arrival, it is already bespoken by Mrs Pettitt who is expecting her son and his family for their three months' leave from Africa. 'Otherwise . . .' I begin, but the bus arrives.

Miriam and a severe-looking companion alight, and I continue my way to the Post Office.

Here, my neighbour Miss Gray is making agitated enquiries about telegrams to South Kensington. Her cheeks are flushed and she seems distraught.

'Churlish, it may seem,' she said as we set off together, 'but what can one do? At times I dread the summer. My sister Phyllis and her two girls arrive today, and my aunt wrote to say she would arrive this afternoon and spend three weeks with me as she couldn't afford a real holiday this year. What do you think of that?'

I make diplomatic noises.

'And poor Mrs Baker,' she goes on, 'tells me that her daughter in Birmingham has decided to come for most of the school holidays, as she finds the children too much for her on her own.'

'And Miss Miller,' I reply, 'says that her sister has written to say that as she is saving up to go for a cruise early next year, she'll "make do" at Miss Miller's for a fortnight next month, and look upon it as this year's holiday.'

'Incredible!' says Miss Gray, stopping suddenly in the middle of the village street, and nearly capsizing a dreamy man on a bicycle. 'All through the winter months we moulder here, without sight of hair nor hide of a friend or relation. Do *we* ever get invited to stay with *them*?'

I assume that this question is rhetorical, and make a non-committal noise.

'Are we, in fact, ever thought of at all until the sun comes out and all these people think how pretty the country must be looking, and how much good it would do them to smell fresh air instead of exhaust fumes . . . and how nice it would be to have someone else to cook and shop and make beds for them . . .'

I murmur that this is perhaps taking rather too gloomy a view, when young Mrs Thomas approaches us. Her aspect is careworn.

'My husband's brother and his family are arriving next week,' she says, after we have greeted each other. 'I wonder if either of you could lend me a camp bed, a push-chair, a baby's cot, or even . . .'

She breaks off to stare at Miss Gray who is looking as though she has been left a large fortune.

'My dear,' says Miss Gray in a determined voice, 'you can have my whole house then. I've just decided to invite myself back to Phyllis's for the rest of the summer. Why didn't I think of it before?'

Felling the Tree

So they were cutting down his tree!

When John first heard the news he felt as though someone's fist had hit his chest and winded him.

'Yes, that's what the noise is,' Mrs Parker had said to a customer, as she rumbled potatoes into the weighing pan. 'Miss Miller told me herself: "They're taking down my dirty old yew tree tomorrow," she said to me.'

Dirty old yew tree, indeed, thought John furiously, and he flung himself out of the shop without buying his sweets. Quite clearly, above the thumping of his heart and the thud of his shoes, he could hear the rhythmic squealing of a saw.

Slowly, steadily, without mercy, they were killing his friend.

By the time he arrived at the gate, there were several people watching the two men at their sawing. The postman leant on the handlebars of his bicycle, a child with a puppy on a lead hopped up and down by the palings, and Mrs Trent with a shopping basket stood nearby. Old Mr Potter who lived next door emerged from his house, head shaking, red eyes watering, his walking stick in his trembling hand, just as John had always known him.

Miss Miller herself was there. She wore a bright red frock and a bright wide smile as she surveyed the scene of destruction. John could not bear to look at her. It was bad enough that she lived in the house where he had been born and brought up. The thought of her sleeping in his mother's bedroom, eating in their kitchen, walking up their stairs, was almost more than he could endure, but this . . . this cutting down of his tree . . . was worse than everything put together.

He had played under the yew tree as soon as he could stagger about the garden. He could feel now the dry prickly dustiness of the dead leaves as he pawed them into heaps, squatting down beneath its wide low branches. On the day he was four, he found he could climb halfway up and could see into his mother's bedroom. There was her white counterpane, and there, buzzing on the other side of the glass, was a fly desperate to escape. He had scrambled down through the green scented branches, his legs shaking, his hands scratched, but his heart bursting with pride. He could climb the yew tree!

The squeaking of the saw stopped suddenly, and the two men straightened themselves. One pressed his hands to his aching back and looked up at the feathery topmost branches dark against the blue sky. The other fumbled in his pocket for a cigarette, kicking moodily at the trunk of the tree with a steel-tipped boot. Fragments of brown bark flew off to reveal the pink fleshiness below.

'Had enough already?' quipped the postman.

'It must be hard work,' said Mrs Trent to old Mr Potter, 'though I must say I just hate to see a tree being cut down.'

'You're quite right,' quavered old Mr Potter, putting a knobbly hand on the garden palings for support. 'I don't like to see a tree cut down either. Especially a yew tree. Very unlucky it is to cut down a yew tree.'

'I never knew that,' said Mrs Trent.

'It's perfectly true,' said the old man. His head shook more than ever, and the water from his eyes ran down his withered old cheeks, but something about his voice made them all turn to listen. 'It's the guardian of the house, you see,' he said. 'It looks after it, as you might say. My old mother told me that people planted yew trees to keep the Devil away from their homes. Stands to reason, if you cut down a yew tree the house will suffer.'

'Well, I don't know about that . . .' began Mrs Trent doubtfully, but Miss Miller broke in.

'Old wives' tales, Mr Potter,' she called heartily. 'You don't have to put up with the mess I get from this dirty old tree. Nor the noise it makes on the roof on windy nights. And you don't have to clear out the gutters when they're choked up with leaves.'

John's eyes turned to the tree. The cruel saw was embedded in its stout old trunk. Three or four branches had been lopped off on the road side, and the raw wounds gaped like open pink mouths. This had been done, John knew, so that it would fall away from the road and into the open part of the garden.

One of the men was busy with a rope as black and greasy as a Chinaman's pigtail. One end was already tied round the trunk, high up, within a few yards of the topmost boughs. It was hitched, John noticed with a feeling of sickness, just below his favourite seat, a forking horizontal branch which was shiny with the rubbing of his trouser seat over the years. From that perch, John had watched his mother pegging clothes on the line. She was curiously foreshortened, and her white parting was very noticeable in her black thick hair. He had looked down on neighbours passing in the road, viewing the tops of their hats and the contents of their baskets. The secret glee he felt in his hiding place always excited him. One day he had called to his dog, rolling on the grass below, and laughed and laughed to see the bewilderment as it dashed about seeking for its master.

It was a different world up there near the sky, level with the sparrows on the roof. The branches gave off a resinous perfume as he sat there, his back pressed comfortably against the friendly trunk, listening to the whispering of a million green leaves. Sometimes he picked at the flaking brown bark, and down would flutter the dark brown outer skin, then the paler brown, until the pink sappy flesh showed through.

The man left the rope and returned to the saw. He was carrying two wedge-shaped pieces of wood which reminded John of cheese.

'You're nowhere near wanting those yet,' grumbled old Mr Potter. 'No need for wedges if the tree's trimmed properly.'

Miss Miller's laugh rang out, hard and shrill. 'Perhaps these men know their own business best,' she said snappily. 'Pity other people don't look after their own!'

The postman took the hint, put a heavy black boot on his pedal, and pushed off. The child with the puppy moved a foot or two further back, and Mrs Trent with her basket tossed her head and walked away. But old Mr Potter did not take the hint. Nor did John. He had no intention of deserting his old friend in its last hour. His heart was heavy, his eyes smarted, he could not speak for the ache in his throat, but his place was here and nothing should budge him.

The two men bent again to the saw, and the dreadful squealing began again. To John, it seemed as though the tree shrieked for help in its agony.

There was a sudden creaking and the saw stopped. Carefully the men withdrew it from the deep cut. Sawdust fluttered from its shining blade as they propped it against the palings. One of the men picked up the wedges and lodged them squarely in the crack. The other man returned to the rope. The first man raised a sledge hammer and swung it steadily, first at one wedge and then at the other, forcing them gradually into the gap. Back and forth swung his arm. Chock-chock went the first wedge. Chuck-chuck went the second one as they drove deeper and deeper into the widening split. The whole tree quivered like poor Mr Potter who trembled in sympathy behind the palings.

Miss Miller had bustled away to get a garden broom and now stood waiting to sweep away the yew tree's dead leaves and twigs for the last time. Her face was triumphant, her smile brighter than ever.

There was a terrible cracking sound from the wounded tree and the man with the slege hammer straightened himself.

'That'll do it!' he called to his mate. The other man was holding the rope taut, and looking intently at the topmost boughs which waved their dark plumes against the sky for the last time. Then he planted one foot behind him and began to pull steadily on the rope.

'It's coming!' screamed the child joyfully.

'Mind my garden bed!' shrilled Miss Miller.

John closed his eyes and clung even more tightly to the palings. He could hear the panting of the heaving man and the intolerable groaning of the yew tree. The dreadful struggle seemed to go on for years.

'Stubborn old brute!' shouted Miss Miller.

'Brave, brave old tree!' shouted John's heart.

A crack like a pistol shot rang out and John opened his eyes. His yew tree was heeling over like the mast of a sailing ship, amidst a roaring and snapping of branches. Leaves whirled through the air, dust flew and the wedges, released from their bondage, bounced on to the trodden ground, the earth shook with the thunder of the impact as the giant crashed, shuddered, and lay still.

It was uncannily quiet, and from the smooth pink circle of the newly sawn stump there arose a sharp resinous fragrance which seemed to John to be the very spirit of the tree. Suddenly he realised all that had gone in those last dreadful minutes. It was the end of his tree. It was the end of his own childhood. All was past and gone.

'Next year,' he heard Miss Miller saying exultantly to poor old Mr Potter, 'I shall plant forget-me-nots there.'

And anger returned to comfort him.

THE JOY OF WORDS

Easy Knowledge

Have you ever thought how much you have learnt without trying? It was brought home to me the other day when walruses cropped up in the conversation. I found myself speaking to my rather disbelieving hearers with surprising authority. They live only in Arctic waters, I told them, and they like shellfish to eat, prising them off the rocks with those useful tusks. They are also very united as a herd, and if one of the flock gets hurt then the others rally round in the nicest possible way.

How do I know? Well, I once had occasion to look in the encyclopedia for information about Sir Robert Walpole – the Walpole who mopped up the mess when the South Sea Bubble burst, you remember – and the walrus happened to be on the same page. My knowledge of Sir Robert has faded, but the walrus evidently remains.

The same sort of thing happened last week when I needed some information about the Roman poet Virgil. I can't tell you much about him, but under Viruses I found that the best seed potatoes come from Scotland because it is too cold there for the greenflies to survive.

Some of the best snippets of knowledge are picked up whilst doing the crossword. I don't mean the knowledge gained from writing in the correct answers. That is much too straightforward to stick. But think of all those bits of information and advice in the adjoining columns! How to cure your baldness, for instance, or that nasal congestion which you have so foolishly been confusing with an ordinary cold in the head! And I wouldn't mind betting that you know all about a new stamp recently issued in Norway to commemorate the bicentenary of a musical society in

Bergen, that is if you read the same Sunday paper as I do, and attempt its crossword.

Telephoning brings masses of indirect information, particularly from a public call-box where posters on nearby walls can be seen through the glass. Do yon know, for instance, the risks you are running by not having your telephone properly cleaned and fumigated? I do, but I shan't distress you with the details.

As for those chance pearls cast by friends – well, I've picked up enough for a three-rope necklace. The funny thing is that they are usually tossed off at the beginning of some lengthy explanation on another subject.

'There are nineteen different kinds of gum tree in Australia,' begins one, 'and the amazing thing is that one of them . . .' But you are not listening. You are too busy picking up that first fat pearl. Nineteen different gum trees! Think of that!

Did you know that there are nine sorts of tit in this country? A friend dropped that casually before embarking on detailed advice on how to protect my seeds from all the other birds in the garden. I've forgotten how you do it, but I'm glad to know about the tits.

And talking of gardens reminds me that I must get on with my autumn gardening list and find out more about penstemon for the border. Better look up William Penn of Pennsylvania, I suppose, if I really want to remember.

The Lighter Side of Authorship

Thackeray's tart rejoinder to one of his devoted readers is relished by writers. The good lady complimented the author on producing 'such easy reading'. Thackeray's somewhat harsh reply to this civility was: 'That easy reading, ma'am, means damned hard writing.'

For all who take up the pen – even if only to write an overdue letter of thanks for a Christmas present – the labour of writing is oppressive. It was Robert Browning who said, with his customary forthrightness, 'I never sit down to my desk without revulsion, and I never rise from it but with relief.' To know that the giants of the literary world suffered such feelings is some comfort to the small fry who share their pains with no hope of attaining their pedestals.

But, luckily, there is a pleasanter side to writing. For one thing it is work which can be done at home. This gives a writer every possible excuse to put off the dread hour when he must seat himself, in cold blood, and face a blank sheet of paper. There are always telephone calls to be made, household affairs to be seen to, callers to be rapturously welcomed (don't they postpone the evil moment?) and a host of activities which the writer can persuade himself need his urgent attention before committing himself to the hateful task of writing. He is spared uncomfortable daily journeys to and from his work. He can work at any hour he chooses. He is – almost – his own master.

I say 'almost' because, naturally he has editors and publishers with whom he must deal, and although they may be his taskmasters they also provide a good deal of the brighter side of his literary career – his money, for instance, free copies of books, and, if he is very lucky, delicious luncheons at expensive restaurants.

Publishers, and I speak personally here, treat one with so much indulgent concern that it is as well to be on one's guard against becoming hopelessly spoilt and unbearable. Can it be that authors are looked upon as temperamental, naughty children who must be humoured in case they have a fit of the tantrums and refuse to finish the work in hand? Whatever the motive the result for the writer is extraordinarily comforting and definitely on the credit side of the career.

Another agreeable facet of authorship is the correspondence with readers. Some of my most interesting letters have come from American readers who are flummoxed by the odd English word. 'What on earth', asked one, 'are *plimsolls*? I guess they must be what we call *sneakers*.' 'These *vegetable marrows* you write about . . . and make jam with . . . are they like our *pumpkins*? And can you send me a recipe?' But my favourite query came only the other day. 'What exactly is a *grig*? And is it always merry?' This sort of thing makes one look carefully at one's use of words.

Sometimes the letters are more shattering. Had I noticed, asked one hawk-eyed reader, that one of my characters had a birthday in April and again in October? No, I had not noticed, I was ashamed to admit, in spite of reading the wretched book at least six times before publication. Nor, incidentally, had several other conscientious proof readers.

But, on the whole, the letters are kindly. It never ceases to touch and amaze me that readers will take the trouble to write and say that they have enjoyed a book.

Sometimes, of course, one meets a reader face to face. Better still, he sometimes carries a book of your own which he has actually *bought*, and, as any author will tell you, the book buyer is doubly dearer than the book borrower. Of course, writers know quite well that libraries have to buy books before they can be lent, but there is something particularly endearing about someone who has fished in his pocket and plonked down eighteen good shillings for his own copy, and now asks you to deface the title page with his proffered ball point pen.

Writers are often called upon to answer questions about their work, and two which are frequently asked are: 'Do you wait for inspiration?' and 'Do you put real people into your books?'

A *Punch* writer once said that all the inspiration he needed was last quarter's coal bill propped up in front of him. That set him going beautifully.

'Putting real people into books' is not a very common habit of authors. The law of libel still holds terrors, and in any case the characters which a writer makes up are far more credible than those he meets in real life. Just occasionally, of course, one comes across somebody so exquisitely eccentric that temptation is strong, but the wise author resists it. No one would believe in him anyway, and the critics would point him out as 'a grossly overdrawn character straining the reader's powers of credulity'.

I suppose that reading critics' comments could be put on the lighter side by many authors. Not all, of course; Hugh Walpole and Virginia Woolf, for instance, were unduly sensitive. For many writers the critics' remarks hold no sting, for the work under scrutiny is now behind them and beyond their interest. Aldous Huxley is among this number, and most writers would agree with his statement: 'The critics don't interest me because they are concerned with what's past and done, while I am concerned with what comes next.'

'Concerned with what comes next'. There, in five simple words, is the brightest gleam on the lighter side of writing. The writer lives in hope. What he has accomplished he does not dwell upon. The book stands upon the shelf like any other book. He might look upon it with a little proprietary affection. He might take it in his hand, now and again, and read a little, but ten chances to one he will come across some phrase which makes him groan in spirit and he returns it hastily to the shelf.

The book upon which he is engaged will be too urgent, too demanding and too close to give him any comfort. It is his wrestling partner, his tormentor, his inseparable companion until it is done. The book which comes after that . . . Ah, that will be the one! Now and again, as he comes up for air from his present writing, he gets a glimpse of that distant masterpiece. It shines like the morning star. It flickers like some celestial will o' the wisp beyond the swamps in which he now flounders, and beckons him on to Parnassus itself.

Of course, there are sober moments of cold truth when he knows that this lode star will become as dim and insignificant as the rest, but these moments are rare and easily forgotten. As soon as the present pedestrian plodding is done, he will take wings, he will fly, higher than ever before.

'What comes next', his blithe spirit tells him, will take him to the stars.

The Author and the Artist

Some twice-blest authors can illustrate their own writings, which seems mighty unfair to those of us who find writing on its own quite testing enough. But how lucky they are to be able to put down exactly the image in their mind's eye without having to describe it to another!

Edward Lear, Beatrix Potter, Hugh Lofting and dozens more were writers who were able to illustrate their work exquisitely. Others, primarily known as artists, have the added gift of writing remarkably felicitous prose as Mr Edward Ardizzone and Mr Ernest Shepard have proved. Some authors pick their own artists, but for most of them the artist is chosen by the art editor of the publishing house which is producing the book.

It is usual, of course, as a matter of courtesy, for the writer to be shown the rough illustrations at an early stage. There are

factors, such as cost, type of reproduction and so on, which vitally concern the art editor, but which the author does not consider when he first looks upon the visual image of his familiar characters. His prime interest is in the truth of the scene. Does it really portray his own ideas? Is the result pleasing? Does the type of picture catch sympathetically enough the spirit of his book?

Some authors are more painfully touchy on these points than others. Speaking personally, I have been uncommonly lucky with a perceptive art editor and several equally understanding artists. Mr John Goodall, in particular, who has illustrated all the Fairacre books, has a flair for detail which is a constant delight. The old armchair, casually mentioned, is there with every Victorian button in evidence. The Edwardian hat is right, to the last curled feather. In fact, this observant artist sometimes shows me things more clearly than my mind's eye has done. This happy relationship is of great importance for it doubles the impact of the book upon the reader.

In children's books, of course, the importance of the illustrator is even greater, and the author of a children's book would be the first to agree that artists in this field should be well paid.

Illustrations mean so much to the young child as anyone who can recall his own delights or revulsions will testify. The dreadful cocoa-coloured plates in our home copy of *Lorna Doone* kept me from reading it for years, whilst the beautiful, if grisly, steel engravings in *Robinson Crusoe* held our interest in that long story. For some of us, Arthur Rackham was the other half of Hans Andersen, just as Tenniel was as necessary to *Alice's Adventures in Wonderland* as Lewis Carroll himself.

This is why the authors of children's books tend to be so critical of their illustrators – and rightly so. I suspect that art editors find this particular brand of author the most trying of all. Authors cannot bear to see their fascinating young heroes and heroines depicted as brutal delinquents, with undershot jaws and thick fringes hiding their eyes. What the artist may call 'strong and realistic' the author may call 'downright ugly' and it is the long-suffering art editor who must mediate.

Colour, too, can be a sore point. Patient art editors can explain till they are blue in the face that coloured plates will be hopelessly expensive, but authors never really believe them. And if the artist does present one or two, how often they appear to the writer as far too gloomy, or much too garish or pathetically pastel and wishy-washy! As for the book jacket, that really is a problem.

The author expects it to be so eye-catching that it gleams from the bookseller's window like a goldfish among the lesser minnows. On the other hand, he wants it to look as dignified and beautiful as the text inside. It is probably the book jacket which causes more heart-burning than the rest of the illustrations put together.

Harmony between author and artist is really necessary to a successful book. There must be respect for the other partner's work and recognition of the difficulties in the other's medium of expression. That authors and artists, who can so easily be antagonistic, are usually prepared to sink their differences for the common goal of the book's success, is plainly evident from the fine books now being produced for the delectation of the reader.

Brief for John Goodall

When Robert Lusty asked Dora if she had any ideas for an artist for Village School, *she said she had seen some pictures in the Midland Bank, signed only JSG, and that she thought something of that sort would be ideal. Robert Lusty laughed, and said that was just who they had in mind.*

John and Dora worked extremely well together. They were both conscientious and punctual, and submitted their work on time. Dora had an enormous respect for John, and frequently said that the illustrations made the books; she thought of it as a partnership.

She said of him: 'He has portrayed the English countryside and the people who live there with an incomparable combination of skill, affection and humour which has always delighted me and, I know, countless readers.'

It is not always remembered that John Goodall was an author in his own right. He produced beautiful

books of pictures which told their own stories, many with
Victorian and Edwardian settings.

Dora sent the following brief for The Year at Thrush
Green *to Michael Joseph Ltd, to be forwarded to John. This*
was the last book John was to illustrate, as he died after a
serious illness in 1996. He followed the brief for January,
but made his own decisions on the other months and the
cover, possibly because by that time he was very unwell and
wanted to do scenes with which he was familiar.

The Year at Thrush Green (for 1995)

I should like to arrange the book in twelve chapters, one for
each month. Probably 5,000–6,000 words in each chapter.
Village Diary fell into this pattern comfortably; and if you plan
to ask John for, say, twelve pictures, the format came out very
successfully in that early book.

About the illustrations – this might give John some ideas for
the first three months. 1) a snowy setting for **January**, 2) the
discovery of an abandoned, but well-kept young dog in its basket
in the church porch. This is found by Piggott, and later taken to
Dotty. (This could be the **February** picture.) 3) in **March**, a tall
blond American is noticed wandering about. Great speculation
in Thrush Green! It turns out that he is grandson (great-grand-
son? I'll have to check) of Mrs Curdle, and is over here to find her
grave. To pay tribute to his forebear he gives a conservatory-
annexe to the old people's home on Thrush Green. He meets Ben
and Molly Curdle, and possibly revives the May Day fair, in a
small way.

Subsidiary happenings include Nellie Piggott taking over the
Fuchsia Bush, Winne Bailey's lunch party with SOFT FOOD for the
aged friends, a visit from Miss Watson and Miss Fogerty and
more about the solicitor, Justin Venables. I think I'll bring the

Youngs in more prominently this time. He can supervise the new addition in his architectural role.

Much the mixture as before, I fear, but it will be good to be in Thrush Green and not that pesky out-of-date Fairacre School. Any ideas welcomed.

What about an autumn jacket? He'd be marvellous with autumn leaves, and little boys playing conkers, and Mr Piggott sweeping up the leaves. And with *windy* scenes. I always thought *Winter in T.G.* was one of his best.

A MEDLEY OF OTHER WRITING

Lost to Science

The science exercise book, mentioned in this article, came to light after my mother had died, and is much as she described. It certainly wasn't her strongest subject.

Years later, when living at Chieveley, Dora noticed an elderly woman cycling past, and was considerably taken aback to recognise her science teacher from schooldays. Thinking she must be mistaken, she made some enquiries, and found it was indeed Miss Titchmarsh who was then working as the cook at a local preparatory school. It would be interesting to know whether Dora showed her the exercise book.

Miss Titchmarsh – known at that school as Titch – became a very good friend and, through her, we came to know the rest of the staff, and were regularly invited to visit the school. We used the swimming pool and joined in many of the school's festivities, not least the wonderful Guy Fawkes celebrations.

This piece and the following two were probably written for the Times Educational Supplement, *and are therefore slightly more serious in theme.*

For many years, I kept my *Elementary Science* notebook as a corrective against overweening pride.

It was a shiny red book with a neat white label on the front bearing my name, in the vile script of a careless eleven-year-old, and the added information that I belonged to Upper Three A. Inside were alternate plain and lined pages which I filled laboriously week by week, through three terms, with accounts on the lined pages of experiments undertaken in the laboratory, and diagrams purporting to make the whole thing crystal clear on the facing plain pages.

When the book reappeared some years after I had left school, I was so appalled at the untidiness of the writing and the lop-sided appearance of beakers and gas jars, not to mention the slovenly way the *menisci* (or possibly *menisca*) stuck out through the glass on each side of the receptacles, that I thought it prudent to keep this reminder by me in case I should be tempted in later years to wonder why my children were so exceptionally backward and careless.

The book served its turn but vanished about five years ago. Indeed, I had forgotten all about it until I saw a young man studying *The Electronics Weekly* in the railway carriage last week and wondered if I too should have turned the pages back and forth so vigorously and with such profit and pleasure if I had had more encouragement as a child.

From my far corner, I could only see the advertisements and it grieved me to discover that I did not understand even those. They all seemed to depict metal boxes. Some had wires hanging from them, some had a knob or two, and some had grids on them. Each time that the page was turned I looked hopefully for some familiar science-shaped object – a retort, say, or one of those great glass jars with wicker round them, that Messrs Heal turn into attractive lamps these days, but which I remember used to lurk in a smelly corner of our school laboratory near a glass lean-to whose function I never knew.

'Mind the Kipps' Apparatus, dear,' the voice of authority called when we approached this mysterious miniature green-house, and we always retreated hastily. It is now quite plain to me that my sort of elementary science led on to branches other than electronics, and I am sorry. I should like to have enjoyed those boxes as keenly as the young man did.

But not all is lost. I could still run you up some beautiful chunks of crystal from saturated solutions, white, blue, orange or black, although I am a little shaky about which solution produces which colour now that I have lost my notebook. But I am quite clear about setting up the apparatus with a glass rod across a beaker. I can see it now with 'careless' written beside it in red ink.

Or should you prefer something less frivolous I could prove to you that a heated copper ball is bigger than an unheated one (as if you didn't know!). As I recall, it was dangling from a substantial black hook ('Use a sharper pencil') above a hole in a sheet of metal. It dropped through as clean as a whistle before we applied heat from an adjacent Bunsen burner ('Smudgy'), when it swelled, turned awkward and refused to do its tricks.

Of course, some diagrams remain clear to the inward eye but what they were meant to prove has faded over the years. What was the point, for instance, of those two U-tubes, one upright and one on its side? The one on its side, I remember, had its *menisci* standing on end as I had turned the book round to draw it, and there were some rather savage red lines round my efforts which spoilt the effect. Could it have illustrated the well-known fact that water finds its own level – although, as someone sagaciously pointed out, 'It seems to prefer something a little lower down'?

Then that drawing of two pipettes – well, five or six, actually, if you count the faint ingrained shadows of those that had been rubbed out – what on earth was that about? Or the flask with arrows inside it, showing the direction taken by a dissolving purple crystal, which I can clearly recall dropping in. What was that proving? There are sad gaps in my elementary science, as you can see.

But, on the whole, how pleasant it was to mess about with pots and liquids instead of pen and paper! What a joy to collect gas in gas jars! Don't ask me how we made it – the recipe evades me now, although something about chips of marble floats in the sluggish backwaters of my brain. But the delightful way one put the gas jars in the trough of water *upside down* and watched the bubbles glugging up, and the brisk clapping on of glass lids – Vaselined, if I remember rightly, to keep the stuff from escaping – all added up to a slightly demented and wholly enjoyable cooking session.

Weighing things was less fun. Those fiddling little bits of platinum in their prissy little velvet beds were bound to end up on the floor under a bench somewhere and let one in for 2s 8d of one's scarce pocket money. Any scales which needed to be stored in a glass case were bound to cause trouble, and when a pair of tweezers was needed to negotiate the weights it was the last straw. A wettened forefinger did quite as well, and indeed was a great deal safer, but this was forbidden by pettifogging authority. We were all glad to shut up the glass cases and return to more robust joys such as pouring acid on sugar and watching it froth blackly, fizzing and cascading down the side of the beaker. I should have liked a colour slide of that experiment.

The last picture that I can remember in my science book showed a thermometer with some rather fetching cross-hatching at the bottom where the mercury lurked. To my mind, it was no more untidy than the other drawings; in fact, it had a monolithic grandeur, standing stark and black on the page with only the slightest woolliness round it where the rubber had been busily at work. But I suppose that something about it had snapped the last frail threads of my science teacher's patience, for it was crossed through and the ominous words 'See me' were written nearby.

Kindly Nature has erased all trace of that interview from my memory, but I can't help feeling that from then on my grip on scientific data began to loosen. But for that, who knows? I might have been a regular reader of *The Electronics Weekly* – a contributor even – and have been able to let you into the secret of those metal boxes. As it is, you will have to look elsewhere for scientific advice, and I am very sorry indeed to have let you down.

Deadly Sins

A child does not have to be long in this world before he discovers that some things are frowned upon and called wrong, and others are acceptable and called right. His Victorian counterparts were told a great deal about the two, as well as the deadly sins, the path to ruin and the awful necessity to withstand temptation.

Today's child, though not quite so harried, still recognises that there is an enemy to be fought. It has always been an uphill battle, and who can wonder if some succumb?

Lying, for instance, comes as naturally as breathing to a child, a hard fact that seems to be overlooked by conscientious parents, teachers, child psychologists, probation officers and a whole heap of other worthy people who should know better.

Greed is equally natural, but is not so frowned on as it was.

'I like to see a child with a healthy appetite,' says Mother, cutting a substantial slice of cream cake for her overweight son.

But the allied sins of covetousness and envy, which have always played so great a part in childhood, are still sharply and rightly corrected by those in authority.

'Why can't I have an airgun? Bill Brown's got one.'

'Why can't I have a pony? Jocelyn's got two.'

'More fool the parents,' is Father's short reply, while Mother, primed with the latest child-psychology article in her weekly magazine, struggles, pathetically, to explain.

Wanting other children's toys and envying other children's attributes cast a real gloom over our tender years. Looking back, it is interesting to see exactly the things which made one an easy prey to two of the Devil's temptations.

At the age of about three, I remember, I would have given my newly cut eye-teeth for a doll possessed by the child next door. It was a hefty specimen of calico stuffed with horse hair. Hair, face, arms and legs were printed on the material, but what particularly entranced me were a pair of green-striped stays that ran down to long-legged drawers. It was all so neat and practical. There was no shoving of doll's legs through knicker legs too small for them. No buttoning of under-bodices. No tapes to tie. Probably my fingers were too young to cope easily with these tiresome matters, and this gave Bertha's doll's underwear an added glamour. It was the only doll I really cared for.

My sister's splendid collection left me cold. They had romantic names like Guinevere and Imogen and wore wonderful creations. They even had evening gowns with trains and beads on the bodices. They were a dressy lot altogether. Mine were clad in the throw-outs from their wardrobes, old shawls and outworn baby garments of my own. They spent, I seem to remember, most of their time in the dolls' cradle where I felt that they were safe and warm and, above all, no bother to me. But if I had owned Bertha's doll, ah, what cherishing those divine stays would have had!

It must have been about the same time that envy of another child overcame me. When visiting my grandmother, I was put on her bed to take my afternoon rest. Needless to say, I got off it the minute the door closed. This door had panes of coloured glass in the top half. After viewing the landing through the small red pane (the Fiery Furnace), the yellow one (a Sunny Day) and the blue one (Under the Sea), licking the pleasantly cool china door knob, re-arranging those ornaments within my reach, unscrewing the door handles on the bedside table and pulling out any loose fringe from the rugs, I used to take my stand by the window.

The garden below me was unremarkable, but next door there lived a girl of about twice my age who did not have to suffer the indignity of an afternoon rest, but was sent to play in the garden.

I remember her as very pale, very pretty, with curly ash-blonde hair and – the cause of my envy – a completely white outfit, from white fur bonnet to white kidskin button boots. She was quite beautiful and, young though I was, I recognised beauty when I saw it. The fact that it was an odd get-up to play in did not strike me, and in any case, Eileen was no mud-pie maker. She spent her time walking round and round the narrow paths beneath the pergola, pushing a small wicker dolls' pram and keeping sedately to the very centre of the gravel so that the box edging did not soil her splendid boots. How I longed to look so pretty, so cool and so clean! I have never achieved it.

Later, boys' possessions were the things to covet. Why could not I have an iron hoop instead of the wooden one I owned? Why did girls have to be content with small tops which needed whipping while the boys had beautiful heavy peg tops wound up with string which they threw nonchalantly to the ground and then stood, hands in pockets (no pockets for us!), lost in admiration? And look at the sensible penknives boys had! Who wanted a mother-of-pearl midget with no pick for horses' hooves? Envy and covetousness are certainly at their deadliest at this stage of one's life.

In the teens, one's longing became more feminine. I yearned for a pair of patent leather ankle-strap shoes, for curly hair and a smaller waist. But, as the years pass, so do the agonies of wanting things. The fires burn lower, thank heaven. One is content with less. As the Provincial Lady pointed out, a comfortable bank balance and sound teeth really outweigh the passions, and so it is with envy and covetousness.

Apart from an exquisite French cupboard, which I still mourn, I have been free of the pangs of envy for years. Too large and too expensive for me, the cupboard went eventually, I was told, to Shell-Mex House in London and I have often wanted to drop in to assure myself that it is being cherished as dearly as it deserves.

Sometimes I feel downright sorry for the people who create advertisements aimed at whipping up envy in the middle-aged. Do they realise that they are flogging a dead horse? They should really turn their attention to the eight-year-olds so easily tempted, so covetous, so racked with the fever of possessing. Those are the ready customers.

Perseverance

Perseverance seems to be a rather old-fashioned virtue these days. No doubt some of you remember, as I do, the adage that was drummed into our infant ears:

> *If at first you don't succeed*
> *Try, try, try again.*

and how maddening it could be when one was aged four and bent double over a pair of button boots that just wouldn't do up.

Nowadays, we are told that children will come to things when they are ready for them, and that it is a pity to urge them to activities beyond their powers. This is probably basically sound, but it certainly ignores the fundamental laziness in us all, I feel. There is certainly not the same pressure on sticking at a task as there was when we were young, and not so many tales of perseverance to be found in today's children's books. Personally, I was heartily sick of Robert Bruce and his tiresome spider by the age of seven.

But perhaps unconsciously the moral stuck, for later one began to realise that there was a great satisfaction to be felt from overcoming a difficulty. For perseverance implies a challenge, a mustering of the spirit to meet that challenge, and tenacity of purpose to overcome it.

The case of Douglas Bader comes to mind when thinking of overcoming physical difficulties of an outstanding order. People like Captain Scott, Ernest Shackleton, Sir John Hunt and all his Everest team are justly famous because they were challenged by numberless forces and faced them with courage and persistence until they were overcome. This is perseverance on the heroic scale, but there is ample evidence of the less spectacular but no less worthy sort.

Anthony Trollope, the writer, for instance, continued to write industriously for many years with little recognition and hardly any monetary reward. But he persisted. He says in his auto-biography: 'During ten years I did not earn enough to buy me the pens, ink and paper which I was using.' This doggedness he carried into his daily life as a writer, rising at 5 every morning, working at his novels for three hours before breakfast, and then setting off to his daily work at the Post Office. He was not by nature an energetic man, he assures us. He was as much disposed to putting off the job in hand as we are ourselves. And this, I think, brings out clearly another aspect of perseverance.

It is the antidote and answer to that deadly sin which besets us – sloth. While we persist in our efforts, we live in hope, and our progress, however slight, rewards us with cheerfulness. Once our perseverance slackens and sloth creeps in, then we become dissatisfied and miserable.

Sir Harold Nicolson has a wise word to say about sloth. 'I regard sloth', he says, 'as the major cause of melancholy in that it provokes a sense of inadequacy, and therefore of self-reproach, and therefore of guilt, and finally of fear. Melancholy is caused less by the failure to achieve great ambitions or desires, than by the inability to perform small necessary acts.'

That 'inability to perform small necessary acts' is known to all of us. We sit in our armchairs and wish we had written that letter to Aunt Maud, or stuck at the ironing and finished it instead of rolling up the awkward things like the sofa-cover 'for another time'. If we do get to our feet, of course, and set about the work, strangely enough we feel even more energetic than when we started. This is due in part possibly to an unaccustomed feeling of virtue, but I suspect that a stimulated liver has a lot to do with this wonderful glow. Certainly perseverance brings its own rewards.

As well as being an antidote to sloth, it is the very essence of dogged endurance. How long can perseverance persist before finding success? Well, William Wilberforce started campaigning for the abolition of slavery, you may remember, in 1789. He continued to struggle for over forty years, and in fact died very shortly before the Bill was passed in 1833. Dozens of other examples of patient persistence will occur to you, and it is this 'It's dogged as does it' attitude which is perhaps the finest aspect of perseverance and the one which can be most readily applied to our lives.

Look back for a minute to your own childhood and think of

the many things you managed to learn just by persevering. Take knitting, for instance. How easy it looked as your mother worked away, and how impossible it was even to hold the needles correctly yourself. But by sticking to it – and perhaps by hearing that aggravating 'Try, try, try again' exhortation – it was mastered. My own outstanding effort was to teach myself to whistle at the age of seven. I don't think I have ever brought such concentrated powers of perseverance to bear on anything since then.

As a nation we are renowned for hanging on when the battle seems lost. 'The English never know when they are beaten', our enemies have said sourly, on many occasions. It is really a delightful compliment, and those of us who can remember 1940 can be thankful that the quality of perseverance came out strongly then.

So there it is, this somewhat overlooked virtue, perseverance. I commend it to your notice for it can enrich your life, in everyday small affairs just as steadfastly as it helped in the overcoming of Everest or a mighty enemy. It is the key to success, whether we are simply trying to stick to that three-week slimming diet, or whether we have some greater ambition, as William Wilberforce had, and need the spirit to sustain us for a battle of many years. Certainly, very little of true value has been accomplished without it.

The Fabulous Coat

The following article is the story of a wager that a coat could be made from shearing to wearing 'between sunrise and sunset on a summer's day'.

Two similar attempts were made later: on 21 September

*1991, an identical Newbury Coat was produced in exactly
the same manner, and beat the previous record by a whole
hour. This second coat can now be seen in the West Berkshire Museum in Newbury.*

*The second was in 2009, during the 600th anniversary of
the Throckmorton family at Coughton Court in Warwickshire. A 21st-century version was created and presented to
Mrs MacLaren-Throckmorton's grandson, Marcus Birch.*

One hundred and fifty years ago, the market town of Newbury in Berkshire was the scene of an outstanding specta-
cle. June 25 1811 was a red-letter day for its inhabitants. Bells
rang, all manner of junketings took place in the streets, and the
day ended with a mammoth feast.

The fun began as the result of a wager. Early in the same year,
John Coxeter, a leading clothing manufacturer in the town, was
boasting that he had recently had new machinery installed in his
Greenham Mills which would revolutionise the trade. So proud
was he of its efficiency that he guaranteed that he could take the
wool from the sheep's back in the morning, speed it through the
subsequent processing, and have it tailored and ready to wear by
the evening – the time being defined as 'between sunrise and
sunset on a summer's day'.

Sir John Throckmorton, who owned property in the Newbury
area as well as an estate in Warwickshire, came to hear of John
Coxeter's statement, and sought him out. He was so impressed
with the tale that he asked John Coxeter to make sure of his
facts, and added that if it could be done he would lay a wager of
a thousand guineas.

Coxeter went systematically round his mill and made careful
reckoning of the time taken for each process, and assured Sir
John that it was possible to do as he had said.

Accordingly, early in the morning of 25 June 1811 Sir John's shepherd, Francis Druett, led two of his master's Southdown sheep to the open space outside John Coxeter's mill hard by the canal. Here, as the clock struck five, he began to shear them. People had already begun to gather, for the challenge had been widely advertised and there was great excitement and speculation. Pedlars set up their stalls, a greasy pole was erected for the enjoyment of spectators and as a challenge to the young men of Newbury to try their luck at securing the leg of mutton balanced on the top, and Newbury prepared to enjoy a rollicking holiday. Meanwhile, John Coxeter and his helpers bent their energies to the day's work.

As soon as the first clippings were ready, they were scoured, carded and spun. Then the yarn was spooled and taken swiftly to the loom where John Coxeter began to weave the cloth. More processes followed for, as a contemporary account in the *Reading Mercury* says: 'The cloth had to be burred, milled, rowed, dyed, sheared and pressed. It was put into the hands of the Tailors by 4 o'clock that afternoon.'

Eleven hours had now gone by. Meanwhile, Sir John had been measured by the master tailor, Isaac White, and as soon as the cloth had been delivered to him, he had passed it to his son, James White, who cut out the coat rapidly and distributed the pieces to the waiting tailors who stood with their needles ready threaded in their hands.

Excitement mounted as the minutes and hours ticked by. The crowds grew thicker as the people hurried from all parts of the town and neighbouring villages to see how the project fared. At the end of two hours and twenty minutes, the tailors' work was done and the completed coat was handed to John Coxeter. He hurried into his house where Sir John waited.

A platform had been erected outside his drawing-room window and when Sir John emerged upon it wearing the coat, the clock showed a little after six o'clock. The crowd had now grown to 5000 and pressed forward eagerly. 'The air,' says the *Reading Mercury*, 'was rent in acclamations.' The whole undertaking had been completed in thirteen hours and twenty minutes, and Sir John's wager had been won. 'The Cloth,' continues the account, 'was a Hunting Kersey; the colour, the admired dark Wellington.' This was a deep purplish-brown shade. The coat was double-breasted, with turned-up cuffs and long tails.

Sir John wore it that evening when he and about forty other gentlemen were sumptuously entertained by John Coxeter at the Pelican Inn, Speenhamland. This same inn, it may be recalled, found fame in the rueful rhyme:

> *The famous inn at Speenhamland*
> *Which stands below the hill,*
> *Might well be called the Pelican*
> *From its enormous bill.*

The two sheep that had provided the wherewithal for such a memorable occasion had not yet finished their services, for they were slaughtered (rather unfairly one cannot help feeling) and roasted whole that same evening. One was enjoyed by the work people at Coxeter's factory, and the other was presented to the public who boarded the *Prince Regent*, a vessel drawn up on the canal nearby, for the feast. As a hundred and twenty gallons of strong beer were also presented to the throng, there is no doubt that the day ended in the greatest rejoicing.

The coat is still in the possession of the Throckmorton family and appears to be known as either the Newbury Coat or the Throckmorton Coat. It is displayed at Coughton Court, Alcester, where Sir Robert Throckmorton still lives. It was shown at the

Great Exhibition in Hyde Park in 1851 and has been exhibited many times since.

Newbury's magnificent record has often been challenged, and the latest attempt was made in June 1960 at Pitlochry by the firm of woollen manufacturers, A. & J. Macnaughton. A jacket was made for Mr Blair Macnaughton on this occasion in just over six hours but, of course, with the advantages of modern machinery. It was interesting to see that a member of the Throckmorton family was one of the referees on this occasion.

John Coxeter's effort was recognised by the Royal Agricultural Society who presented him with its Silver Medal for his part in the achievement. A local artist, Luke Clint, was commissioned to paint in oils a picture of the scene, showing the processes involved in the wool-to-wearer performance. The result is charming, and records not only the portraits of the leading characters but the background of boisterous excitement which made that June day, a hundred and fifty years ago, such a memorable one for Newbury.

'Embarrassed Reptile'

Vicky, our tortoise, is a young female reptile of character. Her gait is brisk, her eye clear, and she takes everything in her stride, including the rockery. Her taste in food is catholic, ranging from cucumber to babies' cereal. While other people's tortoises are decently asleep, Vicky hibernates, in a perfunctory manner, either under the sofa in the sitting-room or with her head rammed into a corner of the hearth.

She has become much attached to this particular hearth since making her home with us, and has always been able to find her way to it from any quarter of the room; but recently, I discovered that her knowledge of the geography of the house, and the garden, too, is considerably more advanced than we had supposed.

It happened like this. One afternoon of summer heat, Vicky was grazing at large on the lawn when, finding the sun a little too much for her, she decided to return to the shelter of her hearth and home. She advanced briskly down the slope of the lawn to the doorstep. This is a shallow one, made of brick paving, but even so it offers a formidable barrier to a tortoise.

After watching Vicky make several gallant attempts to scale it, I put down a tile against the step, and this, after some inspection, she used to get up on to the step. Once over the door sill – a tobogganing effort – on to the door mat, she stopped, looking around her. The dining-room door was open on her left. She entered this room and was lost to view.

Soon afterwards I was conscious of thumpings at the further door that led into the hall. Vicky was bumbling up and down, her nose to the crack, and her shell bumping, as she looked for an exit. I opened this door for her, and she crossed the hall, to continue her nosings and thumpings at the sitting-room door. Once inside, she made a beeline for the hearth, and settled herself in her accustomed corner.

I must confess that I thought she had accomplished this feat with more luck than judgment, and later I took her out into the garden. She at once set off again, repeated her journey, and regained her resting place.

One morning there was an amusing variation in her trek. 'Walking elate, and, as it were, on tiptoe,' as the Reverend Gilbert White said of his much-loved tortoise, she entered the back door, and instead of turning left at once, she advanced rather further into the kitchen than usual. Behind the open door stood a kitchen chair, and this time, as she turned left and advanced, she found herself between the chair legs and confronting a wall. Her neck stretched further and further out as she contemplated her predicament, then shuffling round, she retraced her steps, found the open door, and set off in quest of the hearth.

'Pitiable indeed seems the condition of this poor embarrassed reptile,' wrote the Reverend Gilbert White of his pet, 'to be imprisoned, as it were, within his own shell, must preclude, we should suppose, all activity and disposition for enterprise.' He goes on to say that only for a week or two in June are the exertions of 'this most abject reptile and torpid of beings' at all remarkable.

How unlike our dynamic Vicky this sounds!

There is certainly no doubt that, had she been fortunate enough to have stumped across the path of the Reverend Gilbert White in the halcyon days of 1789, such a forceful personality would have gained herself a place among the immortals in *The Natural History of Selborne*.

The Queen of Hearts

Dora could turn her hand to many types of article, including matters involving a good deal of research. This piece about Ashdown House, the atmospheric building in its lonely position on the Lambourn Downs, is typical of the more factual approach she adopted on occasion.

Ashdown House was given to the National Trust in 1956.

If you travel north-west from Lambourn, the Berkshire village renowned for its racehorses, you rise steadily towards the ancient green road, the Ridgeway, which runs along the crest of the Downs.

The countryside here is strange, remote and beautiful. There is a feeling of immense antiquity about it, hardly surprising when you realise that you are heading towards the Vale of the White Horse, and are among fields that knew King Alfred's battles, and earlier ones, too.

Before long, on the left-hand side, a remarkable house comes into view. It looks for all the world like an outsize dolls' house, cream in colour, set among its bower of trees.

No one is quite sure which architect designed Ashdown House, but it may have been William Winde, who built old Buckingham House in London. He had been brought up in Holland, and the Dutch influence is obvious at Ashdown House.

Between the road and the house lies a meadow scattered with large grey stones like so many sleeping sheep. Indeed, legend has it that the magician Merlin turned a flock of them to stone here, but the true name of these stones is sarsens, derived from the word Saracen or foreigner, for these stones are foreign to these parts, and were probably brought by the movement of earth during the Ice Age.

Ashdown House is built of white clunch or chalk with stone dressings, and stands four-square to the cardinal points of the compass. It has five floors in all, with fine large windows, but the most noticeable feature is the octagonal cupola, crowned with a golden ball.

Inside, a magnificent staircase of chestnut runs right up to this roof top, and is the main feature of the house. Fine portraits line the stairway, the hall and landings, showing members of the Craven family to whom the house belonged. But, surprisingly, there are also many portraits of Elizabeth, Queen of Bohemia – or the Winter Queen, as she is sometimes called – and her family, too.

And this brings us to the most poignant reason for the existence of this lovely and lonely house.

William, the first Earl of Craven, had it built soon after the Restoration of Charles II. All his life he served the Stuarts, but Elizabeth, the daughter of James I, inspired his greatest devotion.

She was a romantic figure. The Queen of Hearts was one of her nicknames. At sixteen, she married Frederick, Elector Palatine of the Rhine. In 1619 he became King of Bohemia, and thus found himself in opposition to the mighty Habsburgs. He and Elizabeth reigned for just over a year – the Winter King and Queen – before being driven into exile, settling finally in Holland. He died there in 1632, leaving Elizabeth very poor and with ten children. One of them was the gallant Prince Rupert who later supported his uncle, Charles I, in the Civil War.

Despite her poverty, Elizabeth's gaiety was undimmed, and her letters are full of high spirits. She had a small pension from Charles I, but most of her help came from such generous friends as the Earl of Craven. He kept her creditors at bay with his own money, did his best to deal with her household problems and those of her children. He was laughed at by some contemporaries who dubbed him 'the little mad mylord'. Years later, it was even suggested that he and the Queen were secretly married, which was totally untrue. His was a completely selfless devotion. In all his letters to Elizabeth, there is no word of love, simply of respect and loyalty. He was ten years younger than the exiled Queen, whose vivacity had captured so many men's hearts. Robert Burton, John Hampden and the great John Donne himself had all written poems in her honour. Lord Craven's steadfast support reflected their sentiments.

He bought one house because Elizabeth had lived there as a child. He built another on the model of her Bohemian castle, and Ashdown House, we can be sure, was consecrated to the Winter

Queen who did not live long enough to inhabit it. He spent his life, his energies and his fortune in her service, and it was to one of his homes that she came eventually when she returned at last to England after the Restoration. She stayed at his house in Drury Lane until an official residence could be found. But the move proved too much for her, and she died a week later.

What Lord Craven must have felt, we can only guess. He was to live another thirty-five years, and was over ninety when he died.

His beautiful romantic house stands as a memorial to his unswerving loyalty, and to the fascinating Queen he served so chivalrously all his days.

The Last of Glory

It fell today. A wild burst of wind, which made the windows rattle like gunfire and wrenched the last leaves from the creeper, tore it from the gutter and hurled it – a scrap of grey paper – into the bushes below.

Seven months ago, the decorations went up. Here, in our village, we were as busy and excited as the important people up in London who were fixing their arches in the Mall and strewing Regent Street with roses. We hung at perilous angles from our windows or stood below, eyes cocked critically at the lofty labourers. We ran into each other's cottages borrowing carpet tacks and ladders and incredible lengths of string. Cries of 'It's nowhere near central . . . Try it the other way up . . . Hitch it higher, it hardly shows!' echoed on all sides. We were loving it. Here was a big occasion and we rose to it.

Of course, there would be a tea for all the village, new seats for the recreation ground and a fine new tree to plant; but, somehow, this was different. This joyous garlanding and festooning of our cottages was a personal thing, our own individual offering to national rejoicing.

The house which was robbed today was one of the gayest in the village at Coronation time. Streamers of unbelievable beauty, red, white and blue, crossed and re-crossed its modest front, from gutter to door-scraper, from slate to cobblestone. Above the iron porch two huge Union Jacks hung which, for a full month, entangled the postman's cap and the milkman's white locks, but neither evoked a 'Drat!' nor any stronger expletive. Why, who would be so curmudgeonly as to resent a flick in the eye by the old flag?

We did ourselves proud with flags here. Not only Union Jacks but flags of all nations bedecked our cottages, the rising sun of Japan flapping amicably by the crescent moon and star of Turkey. One of the finest flags was a Duster of some sort, we told each other. Red, or was it white, we'd heard? No, not blue . . . we were pretty positive it wasn't blue, but there . . . if you live as we do in a snug inland county it is difficult to be quite certain of these nautical matters. That it was magnificent we all agreed, and it rode the breezes proudly for many weeks.

But at last the flags came down, and were folded and put back, either in quiet attics with trunks, old school photographs and bamboo occasional tables, or taken to outhouses and returned to their former companions, the tennis markers, bundles of bass and towers of flower pots. The criss-cross of paper was unravelled from the gay house, bedraggled it's true, but ready to make its last contribution to festivity as a bonfire in the back garden. Just one shred of scarlet escaped the funeral pyre. High up in the gutter, it flaunted its freedom, rebelliously tossing, fluttering its challenge to the winds that tugged at it in vain.

Through the long summer and the mellow autumn it clung

tenaciously, growing paler daily as the creeper below it glowed more rosily, until no one would have guessed, when November came, that the cobwebby wisp of grey had once been as bright as a poppy. But the creeper's beauty waned, the leaves whispered down to the ground, and the house stood naked, adorned only by that gallant tatter of paper.

Just now, at the end of the old year and the beginning of the new, we look forward to many things – to watching next season's cricket from the comfort of our Coronation seats, to drinking from our Coronation mugs and to seeing the first leaves put forth by our new tree. These tokens of the Coronation remain with us: they will be part of our future. But it is good, too, to look back behind us, to the glory of the past year whose beauty lay in the things that were fleeting and ephemeral, of which that last flutter of paper was a tangible sign.

All are gone – the beds of salvias, lobelias and alyssum, the streamers, the flags, the music, the full-throated cheers – gone to bare earth, the bonfire, the silent store room or the winds of heaven. Only backward-glancing Memory can catch and hold that bright glory now.

Talking in Trains

Friends of mine frequently tell me how much work they get through on train journeys. 'Last month,' they say, 'I read *Gone with the Wind* or *War and Peace*.' 'I plan the family meals for the week,' says another. 'I'm studying Russian,' says a third.

Good luck to them! They are more fortunate than I am in trains.

Cross my heart, I have yet to make a lengthy train journey without being drawn, most reluctantly, into conversation.

Perhaps I have a kind face. If so, it masks an extremely cross disposition on these occasions, I may say! Perhaps I look lonely. I just don't know. But whatever the cause, the result is the same. Before two stations have rattled by, I am holding a fistful of family photographs and hearing about little Nigel's abdominal operation . . . no, not *that* photo, that's Brian, she'll tell me a story about him in a minute that will make me cry with laughing. With frustration more likely, I think morosely, trying to shuffle rapidly through my handful.

Naturally, I always arm myself with a newspaper before setting out on my travels, but I have found, by bitter experience, that this is not enough. If I am alone in the carriage and another woman enters, I make a private bet with myself that she will have opened a conversation within five minutes, despite my absorption in the newspaper. Men are less bother on the whole, particularly young ones who usually have reading matter of their own. But older men who find that their eyes tire easily soon start looking about in a predatory manner. This where I cower behind the paper. In vain, of course.

'Do you mind the window down?' is the usual ice-breaker. And after this, it is only a matter of minutes before I have heard all about the old friend he has been visiting, their respective careers – particularly their service in the First World War which introduces a host of unknown characters with such names as Dusty Miller and Nobby Clark – which leads to much laughing on *his* part, then coughing which in turn leads to the catalogue of respiratory diseases he has been unfortunate enough to contract, and which I am now unfortunate enough to have to hear about.

Children's overtures I enjoy, although I am not so rash as to encourage them too far. No woman, however devoted to children, wants to have one standing on her new skirt from Reading to Paddington while he licks the windows or capsizes the ashtray into her shoes. But at least their comments are short and direct.

'Do you have your hair dyed? Mummy does.' Or 'I'm going to the dentist. Are you?' are the sort of things I can cope with, knowing full well that the child's attention will soon be withdrawn from me by an outraged mama. But with adults, alas, it is not so simple.

Sometimes I toy with the idea of hanging a placard round my neck saying MY DOCTOR FORBIDS ME TO SPEAK, or simply DO NOT DISTURB, but it might look a trifle eccentric. In any case, I can guess what would happen. Before those two stations had rattled by, there would come the familiar tapping on my knee.

'Excuse me,' someone would begin, 'I do hope you won't think me curious, but that little notice you're wearing . . .'

And there I shall be, cornered yet again.

Ringing Off Gracefully

At some time or other, we have all suffered from those tireless chatterers on the other end of the telephone line. Indeed, quite often they are our dearest friends. The difficulty is this . . . how on earth can one ring off gracefully without cutting them to the quick? That hoary old one: 'I mustn't keep you. You must be awfully busy', is useless. An eager voice says, 'Don't worry. All the family are out. I'm quite free.' And you are back where you started.

People with children are provided with wonderful excuses, of course. 'I must hang up. Baby's eating the coal', or 'turning on the gas tap', or 'pouring honey into my shoes'. A quick click, and it is all over. What's more, it may well be the truth!

Pets are equally useful. 'Heavens! I can see Pip digging up my new tulip bulbs! I must fly!' Or 'The dog's just brought in a poor little rabbit, mouse, bird, grass snake! I shall have to rescue it!' No one, surely, could be offended at such humanitarian reasons for being cut off.

If you live surrounded by farmland, as I do, all sorts of helpful situations can crop up.

'Believe it or not,' (a good opening this!) 'there's a cow in the rose-bed eating Madame Butterfly.' Or 'I must rush! I can see a sheep on its back. It looks pretty groggy already.'

Imaginary kettles and saucepans boiling over provide an understandable excuse. As for milkmen, grocers and the like, both real and fictitious, calling at the door, they are an absolute godsend.

But one of the neatest solutions to this problem was told me by a friend some time ago. Her telephone stands near the front door. When her patience has really worn threadbare, she opens the door, presses the bell firmly, gives a well-simulated squeal of surprise, and says: 'Someone at the door, dear. Must ring off!' Isn't it superbly simple?

And now that I come to think of it, that's *exactly* what happened when I rang her yesterday. Well!

From the Introduction to
Miss Read's Country Cooking
or to cut a cabbage-leaf

This book was first mentioned in a letter early in 1967 when Dora mooted several non-fiction ideas to Michael Joseph Ltd. It appears from the correspondence that it was put on the back-burner while she wrote two other books already under contract, but Peter Hebdon, the company's Managing

Director, wrote saying: 'I won't bother you about the cookery book suggestion, but give you fair warning that I shan't forget it!'

The recipes are fairly traditional, and the family enjoyed trying them out while the book was being written. There is Winter Rice Pudding, Pheasant with Apple, Kedgeree, Marmalade, three recipes for her much-favoured gooseberries, and Grasmere Gingerbread for which she became well known among her friends. She was a good baker, despite the following complaint in a letter to her sister:

'Have just made a sponge and some small cakes and the lot have turned out like leather and about half an inch high! Honestly – aren't sponges temperamental swine? Made with the same old recipe, usually sure-fire.'

'**D**o you think', asked my publisher, when I first suggested this book, 'that you are *greedy* enough to write a cookery book?'

It would have been more delicate, I felt, to use the phrase 'interested in food' rather than 'greedy'. It sounds so much more rarefied, and I am vain enough to hope that it would be nearer the truth.

For, I'm happy to admit, food fascinates me. 'We are what we eat,' say some, which is a pretty sobering thought. Do cannibals really imbibe, as they hope, the courage of their victories as they tackle a brave late-enemy's heart? Are vegetarians less bloodthirsty than carnivores? Does a heavy consumption of milk actually make one bovine in outlook? And what's all this one hears about honey being an aphrodisiac?

There is still a modicum of black magic mixed up with our ideas of nutrition and I, for one, enjoy the relics of ancient folk lore which still crop up in cookery books.

Certainly, there are many snippets of country wisdom that present-day cooks would do well to heed. Celery and brussels sprouts, for instance, *are* better after frost. Blackberries *are* always nicer in September than October, for in the latter month, as every country child knows, the Devil trails his coat over the fruit and spoils it.

It is this interest in food, which so many of us enjoy, which makes memorable dozens of literary meals. Do you remember Mr Woodhouse in *Emma*? One might almost think of him as the arch-priest of *non-eating*.

'A small basin of thin gruel', writes Jane Austen, 'was all that he could, with thorough self-approbation, recommend.' He did however propose to Mrs Bates at one supper party that she venture on an egg – a very small one. 'One of our small eggs will not hurt you.' Luckily, Emma was dispensing minced chicken and scalloped oysters throughout her father's anxious pleadings, so that the guests were adequately refreshed.

As for Parson Woodforde, who was rector of Weston Longeville from 1774 until his death in 1803, his diary fairly bursts with food. Listen to this dinner for fifteen people.

'We had for dinner a boiled Rump Beef 45 pd. weight, a Ham and half a dozen fowls, a roasted Saddle of Mutton, two very rich puddings, and a good Sallet with a fine cucumber . . .'

No wonder that the good parson often has recourse to 'a dose of Rhubarb before retiring'. And one of the most poignant entries in the diary, commenting on a sleepless night of indigestion, consists of these four succinct words: 'Mince Pye rose oft.'

But the interesting thing to note, after one has got over the sheer stupefying bulk of the meals, is the large proportion of meat eaten. How different is the picture drawn by Flora Thompson a hundred years or so later. It is true that the labourer's home was a modest one compared with the parson's, but the main meal simply consisted of a tiny cube of bacon from their own pig, and any vegetables available from the garden, including potatoes, and a roly-poly pudding tied in a cloth and made from flour from the gleanings at harvest-time.

All went into the pot together and were dished up when the man of the house came home from the fields and the children back from school. The bacon amounted 'to little more than a taste each'. They filled up empty corners at other times with bread and lard, or bread and home-made jam. Milk and eggs, which one might have thought plentiful, were extremely scarce. When one considers the length of a man's working day, and the tough conditions he endured – ploughing a vast field of north Oxfordshire on foot behind a team of horses would have made even Mr Woodhouse hungry – it is amazing how little they managed upon.

I suppose that the moral to be drawn from this is that 'the rough plenty of the poor', if plenty you call it, was wholesome food. The pig was well fed, sometimes better fed than the children. The vegetables and fruit were nourished by natural organic matter, and the nearest the cabbages got to being sprayed was a bowlful of washing-up water cast over them from the back door, interspersed with rain showers. When the housewife-cook wanted to prepare the meal, 'she went down the garden to cut a cabbage-leaf' and it was in the bubbling water within minutes, fresh, firm and fragrant. The tired produce that we are so often forced to buy would have been chucked into the pig's sty to make future bacon.

Lettuces, pearly spring onions, crisp radishes, all would be plucked from the soil, washed and eaten within the hour. And always, no matter how poor the garden, there would be a few herbs to add relish and piquancy to the monotony of the diet.

This cookery book has many short-comings. It does not

supply at the end, as so many more ambitious books do, those lovely recipes for furniture polish and cough-cure. Nor does it tell you how to engage a parlour-maid or how to order your dry-goods quarterly.

And just because it is called 'Country Cooking', please don't expect the book to be aggressively bucolic. You won't find any of the 'take-a-calf's-head-cleanse-nostrils-remove-tongue' type of recipe here, for the simple reason that I cannot face such horrors. Nor will you find any of those dainty recipes about crystallising rose petals – a two-day procedure as far as I can see – for I think that most of us prefer to buy half an ounce when needed, perhaps every tenth year or so, and reckon the money prudently spent.

Similarly, it is not all syllabub-and-cottage-pie. We live in times when the produce of the whole world is available to us, at a price, and our tastes are increasingly sophisticated. There are recipes here from all manner of countries and climes, but don't let us lose sight, amidst the welter of exotic out-of-season food that tempts us, the satisfaction of cooking meat, fruit and vegetables in season when they are at their freshest, cheapest, and most delectable.

THE BIRTH OF MISS READ

The Lucky Hole

*Dora taught as a supply teacher for just one term at Pease-
more School in Berkshire in the early 1950s, but it made a
great impression on her, and had a considerable influence on
her writing about the fictional Fairacre School. It was a
downland, one-teacher school, with a leaking skylight like
Fairacre's and a similar log-book dating back many years.
Dora said on more than one occasion that if she had not
married, she would have been very happy with the life of a
rural headmistress in such an attractive village.*

Interestingly, when the first illustrations for Village
School *came through from John Goodall, the setting of the
school with the arch over its entrance gate, and the church
just beyond, was almost identical to Peasemore's although I
understand he had never been there.*

*Dora cycled to the school from her home in Chieveley,
and on the way into Peasemore passed a very fine flint and
brick wall. A flint was missing at about child's eye level, and
local people would put a sweet or small treat into this hole
for the next passing child to find. This inspired her to write
the article called* The Lucky Hole, *which appeared in the*
Observer *in 1953.*

The children first showed me the lucky hole when we were
out for a nature walk. It was one of those pellucid afternoons of late autumn, when the bare fields stretching away
beneath an immense sky remind one of Dutch landscapes. Far
away, in the distance, stood a clump of yellow elm trees, for all
the world like stumps of cauliflower in piccalilli.

We had skirted a ploughed field and were returning up the hill to the village, bearing hips and haws, travellers' joy, bryony and a few nuts and blackberries stuffed precariously into disgraceful handkerchiefs. As we approached the church the children broke into a run, close by the flint wall. They stopped in a bunch, John with his fingers inserted in the socket of a large grey flint.

'Miss, this is the lucky hole!' they explained excitedly.

'Sometimes there's a sweet in it!'

'Or nuts!'

'Eric found a penny once!'

'Who puts the things in?' I asked.

'Anybody as likes,' they said casually. 'Our mums, or us does ourselves. Then the next one finds it, see?'

We trudged on up to school, the sun dazzling our eyes. It was almost like summer, we agreed.

But winter came overnight. As I cycled the three miles to school next morning there was a cold mist and the grass was grey with frost. The dahlias, so brave yesterday, stood wet and brown in the cottage gardens. The mist grew thicker as I pushed up the Downs, and by the time I reached the crossroads it was impossible to see more than a few yards ahead. Clammy and mysterious, the mist swirled across the lane.

'Here she is!' said a voice close by me, and two small figures appeared through the fog. Eric and John, who often met me near the school, had chosen this, of all mornings, to greet me two miles from their own village.

I looked at them with dismay. They had no overcoats, and wore thin grey flannel suits. Their legs and hands were mauve with the cold and their skimpy sandals sodden; but their eyelashes were glamorously festooned with mist and their gappy smiles were undimmed.

'We was a bit early,' they explained, 'so we just come along in case you was lost.'

Touched though I was by this solicitude, I was not going to be bamboozled by these blandishments.

'You know quite well,' I said, 'that you are not supposed to come beyond the church to meet me. I must go on because the others will be waiting, but you must follow as fast as you can.'

I remounted. 'Keep together!' I shouted back through the mist. 'And *run* . . . or you'll have shocking colds!'

'Goodbye, Miss, goodbye!' they called cheerfully. I could hear their feet pounding obediently in my wake, the sound growing fainter and fainter behind me.

It was getting much colder, and I was worried about them. It would take them over half an hour to get to school. I might, I thought remorsefully, have been a little kinder to the poor dears. They could have had my scarf, for one thing, and the dilapidated raincoat that was strapped to my bicycle. I imagined them falling exhausted by the lonely road; meeting mad bulls, escaped lunatics and, worst of all, their own irate mothers.

By this time I was swerving along the flint wall which held the lucky hole. I felt in my pocket for a small paper bag containing a few sticky mint humbugs. Peering closely at the wall, I came at last to the yawning lucky hole. As one who brings a votive offering to the gods, I poked the bag into the gap. Perhaps, I told myself, the luck would work for both the giver and the receiver. At any rate, it was the least I could do to salve my pricking conscience; their last half-mile should have the solace of a sweet and bulging cheek.

At school we said our prayers, sang our hymn and learnt an encouraging snatch of psalm, while outside the trees dripped. The ancient clock on the wall said half past nine, and with some vague, unhappy recollections of first aid for those suffering from exposure, I tipped the children's milk into a saucepan and set it on the stove to warm. The children exchanged delighted glances. Winter had really come!

Surely, I thought, they should be here by now? Could they have lost their way? Fallen down? Gone home? Broken a leg? I could see the headlines in our local paper . . . 'CALLOUS SCHOOLMISTRESS REPRIMANDED BY MAGISTRATE'. In another ten minutes, I told myself agitatedly, I must certainly ring for the police. I began to write up the seven-times table on the blackboard with quick, distracted strokes and, as I bent to write the last cramped line, I heard them. Never were children's footsteps more welcome!

'Miss,' they said as they burst in, bringing with them a trail of mist and an overpowering smell of mint humbugs, 'Miss, it was lovely out! And look what we found in that hole we showed you yesterday! Ain't that a real lucky hole, now, ain't it?'

At the Sign of the Mermaid

Letter from Robert Lusty, director of the publishers Michael Joseph Ltd, dated 9 November 1953. It was addressed to Miss D. J. Saint c/o the Observer.

Dear Miss Saint

I would like to congratulate you very warmly on your delightful article in yesterday's Observer. As I read it, it seemed to me that a most entertaining and valuable book might be written, describing experiences of this kind in the life of a village school mistress. Such a book could conjure up in a most interesting way village life today and give a most useful picture of education in rural areas.

If this suggestion appeals to you at all I hope we may have an opportunity of discussing it, and meanwhile I enclose a copy of our most recent list, so that you may have some idea of the books we publish.

Yours sincerely, Robert Lusty

Mrs Griffin Sends Her Love

Extract from a letter dated Saturday 14 November 1953 from DJS to her sister Lil.

Dear Lil

  This is just a quick scribble to say I'm coming up to town next Friday & wondered if we could meet. You aren't free to come back with me on the 6pm for the weekend, I suppose? That would be best of all & I hope you'll feel able to; but failing that perhaps we could have tea if you feel it's worth the fag of coming up to town after school.

  Michael Joseph wrote after the Observer thing & is throwing out feelers for a book. I shall know if he still feels like it – me too! – after we've met. The appointment is for 3 o'clock next Friday & their offices are Bloomsbury Street, so if we don't meet at Paddington, as I very much hope we might, to have tea, perhaps you know of some dive round there, but en route for Pad. for us to meet. I imagine the old Ariston would suit, but it would be nice to go somewhere different if you know one.

The following is combined from My First Book, *an article written in 1993 for* The Author, *the magazine of the Society of Authors, and the piece DJS wrote for* At the Sign of the Mermaid, *a collection of articles by staff and authors published to celebrate Michael Joseph Ltd's fiftieth anniversary in 1986.*

I was extremely nervous on the great day, but summoned up my courage to enter 26 Bloomsbury Street where I was met by a small bird-like secretary who took me upstairs to what must have been, in its early life, the master bedroom overlooking Bloomsbury Street.

It was a large square room with a blazing coal fire surrounded by a club fender. A red and blue Turkey carpet covered the floor, and Robert Lusty stood behind a massive desk. He was a tall, heavily built man with a rather sad face and greying hair. He must have been in his mid-forties then, but he seemed ten years older. He waved me to a low chair.

That chair! It was really a mini-sofa with a seat so deep that one could either sit primly on the edge, or right back with one's legs sticking out like a toddler on a bus. I sat on the edge, and Robert Lusty asked me which magazines had taken my work.

I told him *Punch*, the *Times Educational Supplement,* the *Observer, The Lady, The Countryman* and any other publication willing to take a chance.

'Quite *reputable* journals,' he muttered. 'Really quite reputable.'

We talked of this and that, and I liked him more every minute. At last I dared to ask him how many words were needed for a book.

'Oh, about 70,000,' he said casually.

I fell back, stunned, upon the mini-sofa. When I had struggled up again, I said, 'Then I can't do it. I've never written anything longer than a thousand.'

He waved a large dismissive hand. 'Oh, you won't find it difficult,' he assured me. 'Just make a start and you'll find it quite easy.'

He continued to try and reassure me, then stood up and accompanied me politely down the stairs. I was still in a state of shock, but was conscious of the secretary's bright eyes watching our progress from her office at the foot of the stairs. We made our farewells on the doorstep of Number 26, and I tottered to

Dryad's Handicraft shop nearby, and there sought normality among the wooden beads and hanks of raffia.

Extract from a letter dated Wednesday 25 November 1953 from DJS to her sister Lil.

Dear Lil

It was nice to see you on Friday although it was for such a short time.

I got home by 10 to 8 & since then have drafted out an outline for Mr Lusty & have just finished typing it. Later I must compose a letter & send it all off by this afternoon's post. It's probably clean off the beam so I don't propose to start anything till I hear more.

Extract from a letter dated just Thursday but presumed to be shortly after the previous letter from DJS to her sister Lil.

Dear Lil

Mr Lusty has given my synopsis his warm blessing & it now remains to write the ruddy book. I hope to get it started (just!) before Christmas & if I'm lucky get it done before the end of 1954.

A concluding extract from My First Book *for* The Author *magazine.*

A day or two later in November 1953 I began my first book.

In October 1954, I carried the typescript to our village post office. On the way, I met a friend who knew all about the contents of my parcel, and who asked if she could spit on it for luck.

So spat upon, in the most lady-like way, it went on its way to Robert Lusty.

On 5 November, the telephone rang and Mr Lusty told me that he liked it. So, he said, did two other readers, some people in the office, and the general feeling was that it would do well. It would be published in September the following year, he continued. He would send me a contract, my advance would be £75, and he hoped I was pleased.

I was, I croaked down the line. Very pleased indeed. *Village School was* going to be published!

Extract from a letter dated 10 November from DJS to her sister Lil.

I had a phone call from Mr Lusty to say he likes the book & would like to have it – so I'm going up to see him tomorrow at 3.30 to find out more about it. It probably wants a lot done to it. This news has shaken me severely – I should have been quite bobbish had it been turned down!

Extract from a letter dated Wednesday 17 November from DJS to her sister Lil.

I saw Mr Lusty last Thursday & must hasten to tell you that so far I have signed no remunerative contracts but we cleared the ground a bit, & I feel a lot happier about the whole affair. He is sending me his agreement to look at in a day or two; & he let me see his reader's report & the legal one. Since then I've done a few alterations & am going up to post it back to him when I post this. I'm so glad he's decided to get it illustrated, which I think will be a good thing. Doug & I are now spending all the money – mentally only, I fear.

Village School *was indeed published on 5 September 1955 and the advance of £75 was paid on publication. By the time the second book,* Village Diary, *appeared in 1957, the publishers must have been pleased with their new protégé, as the advance was £250.*

In January 1956, Dora received her first royalty cheque for Village School *and wrote enthusiastically to her sister: 'I have received a large & luscious cheque for £360 from Michael J's – £200 of which is earmarked for income tax, isn't it CRUEL? However, I have treated myself to a Hi Fi gramophone out of the bit that's left & it's come today.'*

The Birth of Miss Read

This was written for The Countryman *in 1978. Dora always enjoyed visiting the Sheep Street offices of the journal in Burford.*

Miss Read was born fully clothed in sensible garments and aged about forty. She was born, in fact, some twenty-five years ago when I was struggling to write my first book and needed a village schoolmistress as the narrator.

That book, *Village School,* was being written in the first person, and I remember trying to think of an ordinary kind of name by which this central character would be known. My mother's maiden name was Read. There seemed no reason to seek further.

When the time came for it to be published, Robert Lusty, one of the directors of the firm of Michael Joseph Ltd which was to publish this book (and all the next couple of dozen, I am thankful to say), suggested that it would be a good idea to let it appear under the pseudonym of 'Miss Read', thus creating a modest secret.

I was not known anyway. I had been writing for several years, mainly for *Punch* and the *Times Educational Supplement* and occasionally for *The Countryman* and other distinguished journals. In those distant days, soon after the war, *Punch* and the *TES* had nothing so frivolous as authors' names attached to their contributors' efforts. A little later, *Punch* cautiously allowed initials to appear, and heady stuff I found it.

It was only revealed to me recently that kind Robert Lusty had felt some qualms about my possible disappointment at not seeing my real name emblazoned on a hardback cover. In fact, I was grateful. It spared me a good deal of publicity, and I sheltered behind my pen-name for several years, with considerable relief.

But it is always difficult to write in the first person. The veracities of time and place worried me horribly. Strictly speaking, if Miss Read described a scene she should be present at it. But how could a respectable middle-aged spinster be present when drunken Arthur Coggs faced Mr Willet in his night-shirt at past midnight? It was unthinkable. Luckily, readers were good enough to ignore the difficulties which confronted me, and we made the leap into the unknown together.

But it was much less trying to write in the third person and, tiring of Fairacre, my imaginary village, after three books about it, I resolved to find another village. There was one ready to hand, a perfect setting not far from *The Countryman*'s offices.

During the war, I had lived with my husband and young daughter in the pleasant Oxfordshire town of Witney. Almost every afternoon I pushed the pram northward up the steep hill which led to Wood Green. Here the road divided, the minor left-hand one skirting the spacious green, past the church and the Three Pigeons pub and going on to New Yatt and North Leigh, while the main road went on to Woodstock.

A number of delectable houses stood round the green and, years later, I was to people them with imaginary characters and rename their village 'Thrush Green'. Mind you, I was pretty ruthless with that village, ignoring quite a few real residences, inserting some others and a village school, and even letting Harold Shoosmith take over the Witney Urban District Council offices for his own abode.

This period in Witney confirmed my love for the Cotswolds, and one of our excitements in those times of petrol rationing was a trip on the bus to Burford from Witney. There was usually time for a saunter along Sheep Street where it is 'always afternoon' for me, before the bus turned round at the bottom of the hill by the river Windrush and we ground up again between the lime trees and the Cotswold stone buildings to the windy heights above.

We pushed our daughter's pram to Minster Lovell, to Duck-lington, to the Leys. We brought back precious second-hand purchases on it from Mr Jones in Corn Street. In fact, the oak table, on which I have always written, came from that same delightful shop, although I hasten to add that the baby did not have to suffer that weight on her pram. All these experiences, and subsequent visits to the area, gave me a rich background for the Thrush Green novels which frankly I enjoy writing rather more than the Fairacre ones.

The first one, *Thrush Green*, appeared in 1959 under the same pen-name. It dealt with the events of one day, and was a literary

exercise which I set myself and enjoyed tackling. Later, I tackled another similar exercise. It has always seemed to me that one person must mean a great many different things to a number of people. One woman can be a wife, a mother, a painter, a dress-maker and so on, making contact in all these different spheres with different people and influencing them. Some books later, I wrote *Emily Davis* and let the characters whom she had met during her lifetime tell of the impact she had made upon them. Actually, it became ten or a dozen short stories, but linked by Emily herself. It was interesting to do.

A year after *Thrush Green* was published I was delighted to hear that *Village School* was to appear under Penguin's imprint. This meant a lot to me, as I had happy memories of buying several of the first ten Penguin books, which came out in 1936, if I remember aright. I certainly remember that they cost sixpence each, were well printed, nice to handle, and included such giants of literature as Somerset Maugham. I was proud to find myself, some twenty-odd years later, in such distinguished company.

By now, of course, Miss Read was my *alter ego,* and I answered as readily to my assumed spinster's name as my married one. As the years passed, the secrecy began to wear a little thin. In any case, my immediate circle knew who I was, and if readers wrote to me I always answered, signing myself 'Dora Saint (Miss Read)'. A few years ago, my publishers felt it might be a good idea to reveal my identity, and I was quite agreeable. I cannot say that the disclosure made banner headlines anywhere, but I think it has made things easier for me, and for my marvellously protective publishers who kept the secret for so long.

I am sometimes asked: 'Is Miss Read really you?' The answer, of course, is 'No'. Obviously, I am not a single woman living in the school-house, and running a village school, although it is true that I am a teacher by profession, and have taught in a number of rural schools.

Although she is my other half now, Miss Read is a far more sterling character than I am. For one thing, she does far more in the community in which she lives. I think, too, that she is made of sterner stuff. I look upon her as the sort of person I admire, and see in her something of the many single women I know, who contribute so much to those who share their lives. She faces life's little ups and downs with courage and humour. As a spinster, she has to make decisions alone. As a public figure, in the small world of Fairacre, she has to stand a little apart, exercising discretion, patience and wisdom, and setting an example to her young charges. My own life is very much less lonely than Miss Read's.

Miss Read's way of living in a somewhat idealised village reminds many readers, I like to think, either of happy days in their own childhood, or of visits to older relatives living in similar rural surroundings. I feel sure that the country settings of both Fairacre and Thrush Green contribute to the fact that all the books are still in print. As Walter de la Mare said: 'Even a Cockney's starven roots may thirst for the soil', and most of us are countrymen at heart.

Miss Read, who started life at around forty years of age, some quarter of a century ago, should now be retired. Joseph Coggs, who was five in *Village School,* should be thirty, with perhaps children of his own at Fairacre School. This is the kind of problem which perplexes a writer of a series of books having the same characters. I remember saying casually to wise Michael Joseph that I thought I might kill off Miss Clare in the next book. His alarm was considerable. 'For pity's sake,' he begged me, 'don't kill off *anyone*! You never know when you may need them.' It was sound advice.

And so, like Mrs Bruin and her pupils of *Rainbow* fame, and Billy Bunter and his Greyfriars friends, Miss Read and her children remain the same over the years, like flies in amber, caught in a small golden world of little change.

TALES FROM A VILLAGE SCHOOL

Harvest Festival

A sheaf of corn sags drunkenly against the needlework cupboard. The children squat on the floor among the straw like so many contented hens. They are busy making small bunches of corn to decorate the pew ends of the church which stands next door, and their eyes are intent on their handiwork. It is peaceful.

Every year, at the vicar's invitation, they spend the Friday afternoon before Harvest Festival Sunday in decking certain parts of the church, and this privilege they guard jealously.

'Shall we take some flowers for the font?' asks Ann, eyeing a fine pot of dahlias on my desk.

This innocent question creates a flurry among the straw. Hubbub breaks out.

'Us never does the font! The ladies always does the font!'

'That's right! Just the pew ends, vicar said.'

'No, he didn't then! The bottom two steps us always does. The ladies does the top two. Why, don't you remember how we done it with apples and marrows last year?'

'Me and Eric done it, Miss. Apple, bunchercorn, marrow; apple, bunchercorn, marrow . . . all round, didn't us?'

The point is settled. Pew ends and the bottom two steps of the font are in our safe-keeping, and peace reigns again.

'Make the bunches roughly the same size,' I suggest. 'Somewhere about thirty stalks, I should think.'

They lower their heads and their lips move as if in prayer.

'Twenny-two, twenny-three, twenny-four . . .' they murmur, brows furrowed. The line of completed bunches on the side bench by the wall grows longer and longer, and I call a halt.

'Sixteen pews on one side and fourteen on the other,' I announce. 'We need two bunches for each pew, so how many bunches shall we want altogether?'

There is a bemused silence. We can hear the vicar's lawn mower in the distance. At last John says he reckons us might need fifty or sixty, maybe. No one else has any other suggestion on this matter, and I put

$$16 + 14 = 30 \text{ pew heads}$$
$$30 \times 2 = 60 \text{ bunches}$$

on the blackboard. The side bench holds more than this number, so we tie up the rest of the sheaf with its hairy binder twine, collect our bottles of milk, and have a short interval for refreshment.

As they suck solemnly, the children swivel their eyes round to the splendour of their achievement . . . sixty-odd bunches of corn, each tied neatly with the yarn that the smaller children use to knit rhomboid dishcloths for their mothers, a wastepaper basket filled with polished apples, and a monster bunch of scrubbed carrots.

When the last milk bottle has clattered into the crate, we go to the school door, bearing our gifts with us, Ann and Jane lead the way at a seemly pace, carrying the wastepaper basket between them. Behind them straggles the rest of the school, wisps of corn drifting from clutching hands to join the yellow elm leaves that flutter on the path between the school and the church.

I struggle along in the rear, trying to find the best way to carry the slippery remains of the sheaf of corn. It pricks cruelly, and I dump it thankfully in the church porch for the other decorators to handle.

The door is heavy and opens with an ecclesiastical creak. The cold church smell, compounded of hymn books, mildew and brass polish, greets us, and the children tiptoe in with a subdued air. Four boys and four girls are dispatched to one end to attend to the font steps. The rest of them wrestle with their bunches of corn and the pew heads, lashing them securely with the lengths of knitting yarn which I snip with the big cutting-out scissors.

Above us, from the wall, look down the marble busts of the long-dead. Chill and aloof they wait, their sightless eyes gazing down at the perspiring children who are so zestfully enlivening their cold temple with the cheerful fruits of the warm earth. At last all is finished, and we go to see the final touches put to the font steps.

John is crouching there with an enormous apple in his cupped hands. He looks up, squirrel-like, as we approach.

'Us've done it, apple, bunchercorn, carrot . . . apple, bunchercorn, carrot, this year,' he says. His voice is lowered to a hoarse whisper, in deference to the dead, but it pulses with a child's excitement.

He puts the last apple in place. We stand back and survey it with our heads on one side. There is no doubt about it. It looks absolutely splendid.

Goldfish and Frog-spawn

In the corner of our schoolroom stands a marmalade-coloured cupboard, curiously grained with scrolls and whorls by some bygone painter's hand. It harbours all the awkward things that have no real home anywhere else. A set of massive wooden geometrical shapes is flung in here, with odd gym shoes, cricket stumps, some Victorian annuals noted for an alarming series called 'Happy Deathbed Scenes', a jostle of maps and modulators, and a distressing wall chart showing the effects of alcohol on the human heart. Every school, that is not hopelessly streamlined and soulless, has just such a cupboard, and it goes without saying that it is this one that important visitors open – and then close hastily, with a nervous laugh.

On top of this useful receptacle stands our fish tank. For over two years six goldfish gleamed and gobbled before the loving gaze of the class, but during the last few weeks their number has dwindled and, one by one, pathetic, limp corpses have had their glinting glory covered by the cold earth in the school garden. Last Monday morning, the sole survivor was found, floating on his side, and there was universal lamentation.

'Poor ol' fish,' said Ernest, compassionately. 'Died of a lonely heart, I shouldn't wonder.' Ernest is sentimental, and a keen reader of the 'Happy Deathbed' series, if given half a chance.

'Stummer-cake, more like,' said Richard, a realist. 'I see a dead fish once . . .'

'Never mind that now,' I said hastily. 'Fred, you'd better bury it at once.'

Fred Mobbs, who had been angling for the body with a wire strainer, carried his dripping burden tenderly away, followed by the sad gaze of the mourners.

During the morning there were many glances at the top of the cupboard, and at intervals there would be a shattering sigh.

'Quiet, ain't it, without the fish?' remarked Richard, who was supposed to be writing a composition.

'Proper awfull!' agreed his neighbour sombrely. Pens faltered to a stop, and somebody in the back row said: 'That tank don't look right, empty like that. Miss, couldn't we have some more fish?'

Twenty pairs of eyes looked hopefully at me. Twenty up-turned faces pleaded. Twenty pens, I noticed, were laid quietly to rest. It was obvious that little work would be done in this aura of gloom unless some ray of hope lightened it.

'Let's have some frog-spawn for a change,' I suggested.

A wave of enthusiasm greeted this remark.

'There's masses up Dunnett's pond. Great, enormous masses . . .'

'More down our way, near the ford!'

'You try and get it, mate! All squishy up over your wellingtons where those ol' bullocks goes and drinks. Up Dunnett's now . . .'

'That ain't frog-spawn, Miss. I see it. It's in long ropes, that is . . . it's toad-spawn, honest! It's poison! My grandma said . . .'

Information, wildly inaccurate, and more allied to witchcraft than natural history, was being bandied about the room.

'Bring some frog-spawn any day this week,' I said finally, 'and the child who works most quietly now can clean out the fish tank.' Peace reigned.

Next morning, Ernest, Fred and Patrick were absent. The hands of the wall clock crept from nine to nine-thirty, and I had quite given them up, when the door burst open, crashing back into the nature table and setting its catkins and coltsfoot aquiver. The three were huddled over a huge saucepan which appeared to be awash with a piece of submerged chain-mail. They dumped their heavy burden on my desk, slopping water in all directions, and stood back, bright-eyed. Their clothes were wet, their boots odorous and slimy, and their hands were an appalling sight.

'We got it for you!' said the first.

'Frog-spawn, Miss!' said the second.

'Wasn't half a job!' said the third. They exchanged proud glances, sniffing happily.

'And could I take the saucepan back now, Miss?' added Patrick.

'Won't it do at dinnertime? You're all very late, you know.'

Patrick twisted his black hands uncomfortably, and Ernest came to his aid.

'Miss, it's Patrick's mum's biggest saucepan, and she'll want it to boil a pig's head in this morning.'

'Good heavens! Does she know you've had it?'

There was a pricking silence. Fred Mobbs shuffled his feet and took up the tale.

'She was up the butcher's getting the pig's head when Patrick went to get something to put our frog-spawn in. We was in the pond, Ern and me, holding the stuff while Patrick run home for something. It's horrible slippery, Miss, and weighs near a ton, and it kep' all on slipping back . . .' He faltered to a stop.

'If you let me take it home now, Miss,' said Patrick beseechingly, 'I'll run all the way, and she won't mind . . . well, not much,' he added, as a sop to common honesty, 'especially if I could take a little note explaining?'

The three bedraggled adventurers looked at me, across their saucepan full of treasure. This, I decided, was no time for petty recriminations. We must all hang together.

'Put some water in the tank,' I directed, 'while I write the note.' Beaming, they departed on their mission, while I sat down to compose a tactful letter of explanation.

The children had stopped work and were watching breathlessly as Ernest, perched on a chair, leant over the fish tank, saucepan poised. With a satisfying splash, the frog-spawn glided in, swirled, sank, and rose again . . . as heartening a promise of spring as the blue and white violets on the window sill. Our cupboard was crowned again.

Lost Property

The procession began during Scripture lesson. The story of Joseph, as colourful and engrossing as ever, was being unwound before my attentive class when the door first opened. In stumped a thick-set infant dangling a navy-blue raincoat belt. Ignoring me, she held it up, snake-like, to the class.

'Anyone lost this off of their raincoat?' she piped in a voice shrill with importance.

' "Off" or "from",' I corrected automatically aloud. ' "His" or "her",' I added silently to myself. I felt unequal to explaining it all to the child, particularly as Joseph was in the midst of recounting his first dream to a decidedly unfavourable audience.

'I said, "Off of"!' protested the child indignantly. I felt even less keen to embark on a grammar lesson on the side, as it were, and anxious to return to Joseph.

My class looked with lack-lustre eyes upon the raincoat belt, but no one spoke.

'Make sure, now!' I rallied them. 'It may be yours!'

'Not mine, Miss.'

'I've got mine all right!'

'Belongs to that new girl, don't it?'

'What new girl? Down our end?'

'No, no! That girl in Miss Whatsername's. You know, with the hair.'

This cryptic exchange had evidently meant more to our visitor than to me for she was already setting off for the door trailing the belt behind her. A few papers fluttered to the floor as the door shut and, after picking them up, we resumed our lesson.

We had just got Joseph comfortably off on his journey to the vale of Hebron when the door opened again. A small child, flaunting a large and distressingly grubby handkerchief like a flag, stood before us.

'Anyone's?' I rapped out, before the child could speak.

'No,' chorused the class. The child retreated before the roar.

'And at last,' I said, 'he came within sight of his brothers.' The class wriggled pleasurably and settled down again. 'But while Joseph was still a long way off, his brothers began to plot against him . . .'

Someone fumbled at our door handle. We ignored the rattling and I pressed on. The rattling became urgent and a faint piping, as of some distant moorhen in distress, was added to the disturbance.

'See who it is,' I said resignedly.

Tutting exasperatedly, the nearest boy flung back the door, almost capsizing a minute creature who was struggling with an outsize pair of wellingtons clutched against his chest.

'These was in our cloakroom,' he gasped fearfully. He advanced uncertainly into the room, tripping over the milk crate as he came. The noise was insupportable.

'For pity's sake,' I roared above the din, 'put those things down and look where you're going!'

The poor child put down the wellingtons obediently and turned to face the amused gaze of his elders.

'Anybody's wellingtons?' I queried with what patience I could muster. 'Look hard, now. And think!'

'No, Miss!' came the chorus again. The wispy child picked up his burden again and staggered out.

'Now, where were we?'

'Joseph's brothers, Miss. Plotting, Miss.'

I took up the oft-snapped thread again. 'They were so wickedly jealous by this time that they planned to kill Joseph. One of them remembered a deep pit near by, and he said . . .'

A hand wavered aloft in the back row.

'You can wait,' I said. 'And he suggested to the others that they should throw Joseph's body into the deep pit, where it would lie hidden.' The children's eyes grew rounder and their gaze more intent.

Still that annoying hand remained aloft. To its silent appeal was added a verbal one. 'Miss, them wellingtons.'

'Well, what about them?'

'They were mine, Miss. I've just thought.'

The class sighed, and turned round to look at the wretched boy with a disgust which equalled my own.

'Go and get them,' I said, dangerously quiet, 'and don't come back until I've finished this story.'

He slunk from the room and I continued doggedly.

'But Reuben, who was much more kind-hearted than his brothers, thought of a better plan. He knew that his old father would be dreadfully sad if anything happened to Joseph . . .'

The door burst open again with an explosive crack. It was not, as I first thought, the luckless owner of the wellingtons returning, thereby adding flagrant disobedience to his other vices, but a beaming boy carrying a brown paper carrier bag with great care. And what might that contain, I mused? A lost train set? Five hundred pieces of jigsaw puzzle? Fourteen gym shoes – all odd?

He stopped beside my desk, still smiling importantly and quite oblivious of the bottled rage that seethed so near him. He held out the carrier bag.

'Would you like to show your class . . .' he said.

I cut him short. 'Anybody own . . .' I began, thrusting my hand into the cavernous depths. I stopped with a yelp. Inside, tightly curled up, was a hedgehog.

Night and Day

'This,' I say, switching on the light, 'is the sun.' The class looks at it with awe.

'And this,' I say, twirling the globe neatly with one finger on Alaska, 'is the earth.'

There is a respectful silence. It is one of those taut moments packed with psychological importance, child wonder and the impact of knowledge.

The spell is broken by Richard, who asks in a fruity Berkshire voice, 'But it don't keep on turning, doos it?'

'Does,' I correct automatically. 'Yes, it does. It never stops. Day and night, week after week.' I tell the children, 'It turns round and round and round and, just here, is Great Britain, where we live.'

The class stands up as one man, and I wave it down again. It is not easy to show the British Isles to a mob of eager children. Apart from its minute nature, this country's peculiar position on the upper slopes of the globe makes it necessary to carry the whole contraption round the class in a pointing position with the brass knob to the front. Fellows of the Royal Geographical Society will have no difficulty in following my meaning.

Half the class say they can't see, while the other half tell the first half to sit down.

I put the globe back on the table and attempt to recapture dawning wonder. I point to the naked light bulb.

'There is the sun shining up in the sky. All the people who live here,' I stroke the class side of the globe seductively, 'are saying "What a lovely day!"'

I drop my voice about an octave.

'But who knows what the people on my side of the globe are saying?'

Silence.

'Well, will they be looking up at the sun?'

Silence becomes unhappy.

'Well, will they? Think! Will they be able to see the sun? John, tell me.'

John, cornered, says he don't know what they says. If they doos say anything, he adds. But, in any case, he don't know.

I start all over again. The sun – heads tip up, the globe – heads tip forward, the seductive stroke – the people *in the sun*!

We are poised again.

'But what about the people on this side of the globe? Can they see the sun?'

Eric don't see why not if they are looking. He is ignored.

Jane says reasonably that all of them as is on her side of the globe is in the sun because the electric is switched on.

I agree. Now we are getting warmer.

'Well, then, if all the people facing the light are in the sun, what are the other people doing?'

Deadlock again.

I begin to go mad. I stick a pin into the steppes of Russia and revolve the globe again with horrible deliberation.

'Here I am,' I say with emphasis, touching the pin, 'and I am just waking up. I can see the sun rising. Now it's the afternoon, now it's the evening. Are you *watching*? It's beginning to get dark. Now it really is dark. Tell me, is it still the daytime?'

'*No!*' A lusty Berkshire roar.

'Where am I now?'

'Round the back!'

Fair enough. Not what the Royal Geographical Society would care to hear, probably, but we progress.

'What am I doing now, then?'

They tell me I be in the dark, I be in bed, it be the night and the day be over.

We smile triumphantly at each other, glowing with effort rewarded and flushed with new knowledge.

I twirl the globe dizzily. The pin flies round and round, and we shout 'DAY – NIGHT' and feel terrific.

'Now,' I tell the class with conviction, 'you really do know what causes the day and night.'

'Yes,' says Jane happily. 'Switching on the electric.'

Larger than Life

It was one of those deceptively bright days of early spring when the sinking sun gilded the sticky buds of the horse chestnut twigs on the window sill and made one believe that it must be warm outside.

The bare elms were etched clearly against a cloudless sky. It was too good to stay indoors among the mingled smells of chalk, empty milk bottles and the hot blacklead from the tortoise stove.

The children stormed into the cloakroom and donned duffle coats and mackintoshes, caps and scarves, and wellingtons or thick country shoes. Within three minutes we were in the lane, kicking up the bright pennies of dead leaves, and gulping down air so cold that it hurt one's lungs. The wind was easterly, and so boisterous that it was like facing the shock of icy water.

We set off downhill, away from the village, and I began to point out all the lovely things that gave winter its particular beauty. With varying degrees of attention, the children duly admired the uncluttered lines of the stark trees, the varnished scarlet of rosehips against the blue sky, and the drops of water that bejewelled a whiskery thistle. The wind excited them and they ran up and down the banks, jumped over imaginary obstacles and collected all manner of treasures as they so cavorted. Their breath billowed before them in silvery clouds as they showed me a pheasant's feather, a red-veined stone and an early violet sheltering below a hedge.

It was Ernest who discovered the bird. Attracted by his cries, the children ran ahead and clustered round him at the side of the road. By the time I arrived, they had taken in all the unsavoury details. It was a rook, and very dead indeed. Suddenly the antiseptic easterly wind seemed very welcome and I moved to get its full benefit.

'Shall we take it back with us?' asked Ernest eagerly, his face alight at the pleasurable idea.

'Certainly not,' I said shortly. 'and I shouldn't touch it either. We can do nothing for the poor thing.'

'I'll sling it up the hedge, shall I?' said Patrick with relish. He bent energetically to pick up the ghastly remains with his bare hands.

I managed to stop him. 'I'm afraid you'll have to leave it, Patrick. We can't lift it without a shovel or something.'

No sooner were the words out of my mouth than Ernest approached with a forked stick. He thrust it expertly under the corpse and carried it to a break in the hedge. The rest of the children watched this manoeuvre intently.

'Come along', I said briskly. 'You will get cold.'

The children left the scene with the greatest reluctance, but gradually recovered their high spirits, and their collections increased rapidly.

That's one thing about country children, I thought philosophically, they don't get upset about such unpleasant encounters with death. After all, what was that dead rook to them? Simply one of the many objects which they had encountered that afternoon, and probably of much less importance to them than the pheasant's feather or the red-veined stone which were giving them so much pleasure.

At last we were back in the schoolroom, bearing forests of twigs and grasses, pockets full of stones and snail shells. The cold wind made one's ears ache, and there was something pleasantly welcoming about the fragrance of hot blacklead.

The rest of the afternoon was spent in arranging the booty. Jars of berries glistened from the window sills. The stones and shells were ranged in neat rows along the nature table. Red and white spotted fungi stood in moss on the side table. The air was suddenly filled with the tang of winter hedgerows as the children wrote up their nature diaries. I walked round the class as they worked, and read their entries.

Ernest's was typical of every one of them. 'Went out for a nature walk. Found a lovely dead rook but Miss would not let us bring it back. It was a butiful bird. We had to leeve it in the hegde.'

Not a word about the dozens of specimens that breathed and bloomed about them in the classroom! Their living beauties remain unsung. The rook, that noisome bundle of feathers lying beneath the darkening hedge, had outshone for them all the bright splendours of the afternoon, and in so doing had gathered to himself a host of belated mourners.

Soft and Hard Boiled

'**W**ell may you weep!' I said severely to the youngest of the three malefactors. She stood about a yard high and felt dismally in her knicker leg for her handkerchief. Tears coursed down her face in fat drops.

Mr Roberts, the farmer, on whose behalf I was doing justice, began to weave unhappily about the schoolroom.

He stands six feet four in his gumboots, played full-back for the county for years, halts mad bulls with one hand and has a heart as soft as a marshmallow. I could see I should have trouble with him if I didn't hurry up the proceedings.

He was gazing miserably at a poster informing him of the processing of cocoa from pod to chocolate bar.

'Look,' he said desperately, approaching my desk, 'let them off this time.'

He spoke in what he thought was a whisper, but half a dozen tracings of South America were blown to the floor. He winced at the sight of the three children standing in front of the assembled school (all twenty-five of them).

The second child, seeing his harrowed face, now began to pipe her eye with some energy.

'Sorry I ever brought it up,' he muttered. 'Poor little things! So small—' His voice broke.

'Nonsense!' I said firmly. 'Not so small that they don't know right from wrong.'

I walked deliberately to the cupboard at the end of the classroom. There was a respectful hush. Tradition had it that there was a cane in that cupboard – never used, but much venerated. This was an Occasion.

I felt among the enormous wooden cones, cubes, hexagons and other massive shapes that these children's grandparents used to use for some mysterious bygone lesson.

Where was that dratted cane, I fumed to myself, with my head among the raffia.

'It's by them maps, Miss,' murmured the head boy, who should go far when he leaves school. He intends, he tells me, to work up the Atomic.

I retrieved the cane from between 'The Holy Land' and 'Muscles of the Human Body'. Mr Roberts was nearly in tears himself when I put it on my desk.

'I shan't use it, silly,' I hissed at him with my back to the class, but I raised it solemnly and pointed it at the biggest sinner. He was of gipsy stock and wore long black corduroy trousers, five jerseys, two waistcoats and a spotted neckerchief. His round black eyes met mine boldly.

'Abraham, you knew it was wrong to take Mr Roberts' eggs?'

'Yes, Miss.'

'And you knew, too, Ann?'

'Yes,' she sniffed remorsefully.

'And Carol?'

The smallest one nodded dumbly. Her knicker leg had failed to yield a handkerchief.

Mr Roberts, I was glad to see, had pulled himself together and managed a creditably reproving shake of the head.

'If this happens again,' I told the children, 'I shall use this cane, not just show it to you.'

The school looked approving. Right's right, after all.

'How many eggs did you take, Carol?'

'One.'

'Then you will have one tap with this cane if you steal again.'

I turned to Ann.

'I took free,' she said.

'Then you know how many taps you would get.'

I could feel the atmosphere relaxing. The end was in sight. Mr Roberts had seen justice done, the cane would return to its dusty habitat and the Occasion was rounding off nicely.

I pointed the cane at Abraham.

'I took a 'ole 'atful,' he said.

Mr Roberts snorted, and began to blow his nose fussily.

'But I never went to the 'en 'ouse, Miss,' pleaded Abraham, a heart-breaking gipsy whine creeping into his voice. 'They was all together, Miss – honest, Miss – atween the 'edge and the tractor shed.'

Mr Roberts wheeled round delightedly. 'Well, what do you make of that?' he exclaimed, rummaging energetically in his breeches pocket. 'That's a real sharp lad! We've been scouring the place for weeks for that pullet's nest!'

Eight-a-Side Cricket

'Us boys is one short, Miss,' says Ernest, 'so we'd better have you, I suppose.'

'That's right,' I agree, ignoring the dying fall of this statement as I rummage for stumps behind a pile of musty wallpaper books at the back of the cupboard.

We have eight girls and seven boys in the class, so that unless one of the girls is conveniently absent on games afternoon, I am invited, in a resigned way, to join the boys. I am one of the opening batsmen, as this not only gets me out of the way quickly, but leaves me free to umpire.

'Lead on, girls, and wait at the church gate.'

We always wait here, so that we can cross the road safely to Mr Roberts' field. The traffic consists, on Tuesdays and Fridays, of the baker's van, which remains stationary outside the farm house for half an hour while Sid Stone, the driver, shares a pot of tea with his sister in the kitchen, an occasional tractor, and four Aylesbury ducks who use the middle of the lane for a dust bath. There is no point, however, in learning kerb drill if we do not put it into practice.

Once inside the field, we get down to business. Kitty, the cart-horse, is driven off the pitch into the outfield, we ram in the stumps, tear off surplus garments – the girls hanging theirs on the hawthorn hedge while the boys have to be restrained from sling-ing theirs down in the muddy patch by the gate – and then we toss.

Ernest wins, and elects that we boys should bat first, so Abraham, a nine-year-old gipsy, and I drag our bats over the bumpy grass and take up our positions.

I catch sight of the layers of clothing still swaddling my part-ner. 'Why don't you take some of those jerseys off?' I shout down the pitch to him.

'Ain't 'ot!' he shouts back.

I give it up, and prepare to face Ann the bowler, who grips the ball in a menacing way as she places her field.

'Come on in,' she commands a shrinking Carol, who is a tender seven-year-old, with no front teeth and weighing about three stone. 'If you're put mid-on, you have to get up close! This ball don't hurt if you catches it right!'

I intervene. 'Put Carol at long-stop and let Jane be mid-on.' It is doubtful if a cricket ball plumb on the thumb would have any galvanic action on the lethargic Jane, and in any case she has reached the ripe old age of ten and has three cricket seasons behind her.

Ann now rushes up to the wicket, a welter of brown arms and pink gingham. The ball hits my bat and rolls a few yards away to a small molehill. As I step out to pat it down, Abraham yells, 'Come on!' as he flashes down towards me. I obey meekly and we run two. Fighting for breath, I face the second ball.

'Don't be afraid to step right out to the ball,' I tell the children, doing so. My off stump lurches sickeningly.

'Treacle, Miss,' calls Ann, meaning I can have another turn.

'Treacle! That's treacle all right! You stay there, Miss,' shout both teams kindly.

I refuse their handsome offer and give my bat to Ernest. He

puts it between his knees, spits on his hands, grips the handle, and swaggers out to the wicket. He looks round at the eight girls with narrowed, supercilious eyes.

'Show off!' shouts Richard from the hedge. 'Thinks hisself a Bedser!'

Ann bowls. Ernest takes a tremendous swipe at it, and falls dramatically flat with his bat outstretched. Kitty, who has been grazing nearer and nearer, now stops midway between the wickets.

'That ol' horse . . .' snaps Ernest irritably, and both teams advance upon Kitty, who gazes at her young friends in a benign way. We are about to put our sixteen shoulders to her flank when Mr Roberts calls from the house and she ambles off.

'I'll bet those cricket chaps up at Lord's and that don't have no ol' horses on the pitch,' grumbles Ernest, picking up his bat.

'They don't even let 'em come on the outfield,' John tells him authoritatively.

Ann bowls again, Ernest skies it towards an ominous black cloud, and everyone shouts at the innocent Carol who, with her back to the game, is waving energetically to someone in the next field.

'Look out! You're supposed to be playing cricket! Wasn't even turned this way!'

'I was only waving to my dad,' protests Carol.

Further recriminations are cut short by a sharp spatter of hail.

'Collect your things quickly,' I call, 'and run in! Mind the road!' I bellow after them, as a gesture to our kerb drill. They straggle off, coats over heads, to escape the pitiless bombardment. Ernest and I wrestle with the stumps, and lumber after them.

With something like smugness in her mild eye, Kitty watches us go. Then she turns back to her own again.

Unstable Element

Ernest had paid a visit to Romney Marsh, and had returned much impressed.

'And all this grass, and little rivers and that . . . they was all under the sea once,' he assured me.

'Grass under the sea!' scoffed John derisively. 'Likely ennit!'

'It's quite true,' I told him, supporting Ernest, whose face was aflame with anger. John subsided.

'And this town Winchelsea,' resumed Ernest, 'it's a shame, really. Used to be right by the seaside, and now it's stuck up there, high and dry.'

' "Below the down, the stranded town. What may betide forlornly waits",' I quoted.

'Eh?' queried Ernest, startled. 'Yes, well . . . there it is, miles away now from the sea. Funny, really, the sea going away like that!'

'It's happening all the time,' I said, 'in a small way. Fetch the map of the British Isles, John, and we'll find Romney Marsh.'

John approached the marmalade-coloured cupboard, whose interior is a hopeless jumble of assorted objects, and, after some rummaging, produced a roll which, when untied, turned out to be 'The Disposition of the Tribes of Israel'. His second attempt brought forth 'Directions for Resuscitating Those Suffering from Electric Shock', noteworthy for the magnificent moustaches of the two chief characters. I found the map myself.

Ernest came out and scrutinised the lower right-hand corner closely. Triumphantly he slapped his ruler across Romney Marsh.

'There 'tis! See the miles of land there is . . . all under the sea once!'

His classmates looked suitably impressed now that this evidence was before them.

'If the sea keeps on going away from the land,' observed Patrick, 'England will get bigger.'

I explained that in some places just the opposite thing happened and, remembering an incident of my own childhood, I gave a spirited account of the gradual encroachment of the sea on the Essex coast, with the dramatic climax of the falling of a cliff.

'And this movement is going on all the time,' I wound up. 'In some places the sea retreats, but in other places the sea is creeping slowly, but surely, inland.'

There was a heavy silence. 'Lor!' breathed Patrick, at length. 'Don't hardly seem safe. I mean, the sea's strong. Could get through anywhere, couldn't it?'

'Remember when we was paddling that time?' said a voice at the back. 'It knocked us clean over.'

'And sort of sucked us under too,' added another. The children surveyed the map with apprehension.

I attempted to allay their fears. 'Of course, it's only a very little every year. Perhaps an inch or so . . .'

'That bit don't look too good!' said Ernest, coming out again, unasked, to put his ruler on the Wash. Fred Mobbs, who had drifted in with the milk crate some minutes before, now dumped it noisily and joined Ernest at the map.

'And just look at the way the sea's busted up here!' he said, indicating the Thames estuary.

'And look,' went on Ernest, with alarm, 'it's only got to eat through Essex, and Hurts, and Bucks, and this 'ere, to be at us!'

'What's more,' said Fred Mobbs slowly, his eyes riveted on the Bristol Channel, 'there's nothing to stop it coming the other side as well!'

I began to wish that I had never embarked on such a difficult subject as coastal erosion or, now that I had been so foolhardy, that I had the support of a Fellow or two of the Royal Geographical Society to help me out of the mess. Time came to my aid. From the church tower floated three silvery quarters.

'I'll explain it all after play,' I said, with more confidence than I felt, and the floorboards shuddered as the children made their way out into the sunshine.

Ten minutes later, I discovered Ernest perched up on the school wall, demolishing an apple with noisy deliberation. His mien was thoughtful but rather more hopeful, and his gaze was fixed upon the comforting bulk of the Berkshire Downs.

'Come to think of it,' he said, pointing towards them with the tattered core, 'it'd take a tidy time to get through that lot, wouldn't it?'

Last Day of Term

The wastepaper basket is pressed down and running over. Two cupboards stand open, displaying neat piles of atlases, nature readers and history text-books, all with determinedly gay colours . . . the sugar coating the pill.

On a lower shelf are ranged most of the children's exercise books, much more shabby and sober than the books above. At the long side desk, two boys have the happy and noisy task of ripping out the few clean sheets left in the almost finished exercise books and making a pile of rough paper ready for next term's tests. The ancient cupboard by the door has been left till last. This is the one that the children call 'the muck cupboard' because the odds and ends are stored here. It is cold and damp. A musty odour creeps forth whenever it is opened, redolent of the tombs which stand close by in the churchyard. Here we keep the clay tin, the chaotic bundle of raffia and the small children's sand trays. We also keep, I suspect, mice; and when I have occasion to visit the cupboard I rattle the knob in a cowardly way so that any bright-eyed creatures within may vanish before I thrust in a trembling hand for the raffia.

The upper shelf has been tidied. Our vases are ranged in size from the gargantuan pink and green 'ark pot' as the children call it, through jam jars covered with stamps, Virol jars and earthenware honey pots down to minute fish paste jars used for wild violets and daisies. Below them two well-patched flannel trouser seats are displayed, as Peter and John tuck wet sacking over the balls of clay. 'Really soaking,' I say. 'It's got to stay moist for about six weeks!' The hubbub is intensified at this joyful thought. Desk lids crash up and down, children trot back and forth to the creaking wastepaper basket and the clatter of paint pots being washed outside in the venerable stone sink adds to the din. I go round the walls, prising out drawing-pins and handing out dusty pictures, painted by the class, to the rightful owners.

Suddenly, there seems nothing more to do. The cupboard doors are shut, the walls are bare and the children settle in their empty desks.

'School starts again,' I tell them, 'on September the seventh. It's a Tuesday.' There are rustles and smiles. September! Think of that . . . months away! No more sitting on a hard wooden bench, clutching a stiff pen and watching the pigeons in the vicarage elms through the school window! But instead freedom! Grass to roll in, flowers to pick and trees to climb . . . six whole weeks in which to tear about in the the sun or loiter in the shade; to help dig potatoes or to steal a warm pod of peas from the row; to shout into the wind or to dream in the sun; to work or to play just as it suits you!

The church clock strikes four. The children stand to sing their grace. Their voices are shrill this afternoon, and in the four short lines of music they rise half a tone sharp with suppressed excitement.

'Good afternoon, children. Have a good holiday, and we'll meet again on September the seventh!'

'Good afternoon, Miss,' they carol. 'Good afternoon, I hope you have a nice holiday. I'll send you a card if I go to the sea. I'll bring you back some rock. Goodbye, Miss, goodbye!' They clatter out; the door crashes behind them; and a rose petal blows across the floor in the breeze.

It is very quiet in the schoolroom. I can hear the pigeons plainly now from the vicarage garden, and there is a stealthy rustling from the cupboard. Can it possibly be a mouse, I wonder for the hundredth time, or simply the raffia stirring in its confining skein? Resolutely, I turn the keys in the locks.

At the door I turn back for a final glance. The calendar, which we have forgotten to put away, stares back at me – 27 July it says. The next time I see it, it will proclaim 7 September, I think, as I unlock my desk and put the calendar on top of the register and hymn book. The elms will have started to drop a yellow leaf or two. There will be dahlia not rose petals on the floor, and the children will bring offerings of mushrooms and blackberries instead of strawberries and raspberries carried carefully in handle-less cups. But all that is weeks away, I tell myself, as I finally lock up. The sun scorches my back as I turn the massive key in the school door.

Swinging it jauntily round my finger, I go, whistling, to hang it up for six glorious weeks in its secret hiding-place at the back of the coalshed.

Bibliography & Acknowledgements

Bibliography

*

Almost all the books were published, in the first instance, in hardback by Michael Joseph Ltd; any variation will be listed. All the books were illustrated by John S. Goodall unless otherwise stated. (The majority of titles were published in the USA by Houghton Mifflin Inc.)

1. *Village School* 1955; Penguin 1960; Orion pbk 2006
2. *Village Diary* 1957; Penguin 1970; Orion pbk 2006
3. *Hobby Horse Cottage* 1958
   Children's book, illustrated by Terence Freeman
4. *Storm in the Village* 1958; Penguin 1973; Orion pbk 2006
5. *Thrush Green* 1959; Penguin 1962; Orion pbk 2007
6. *Fresh from the Country* 1960; Penguin 1962
7. *Winter in Thrush Green* 1961; Penguin 1975; Orion pbk 2007
8. *Miss Clare Remembers* 1962; Penguin 1967
9. *Country Bunch* 1963; Penguin 1988
   Anthology of prose and poetry, illustrated by Andrew Dodds
10. *Over the Gate* 1964; Penguin 1968; Orion pbk 2007
11. *The Little Red Bus* 1964 published by Nelson Books
    Children's book, illustrated by Jennetta Vise
12. *The New Bed* 1964 published by Nelson Books
    Children's book, illustrated by Jennetta Vise
13. *No Hat!* 1964 published by Nelson Books
    Children's book, illustrated by Jennetta Vise

14. *Plum Pie* 1964 published by Nelson Books
    Children's book, illustrated by Jennetta Vise
15. *Cluck, The Little Black Hen* 1965 published by Nelson Books
    Children's book, illustrated by Jennetta Vise
16. *Hob and the Horse-Bat* 1965
    Children's book, illustrated by Terence Freeman
17. *The Little Peg Doll* 1965 published by Nelson Books
    Children's book, illustrated by Jennetta Vise
18. *The Market Square* 1966; Penguin 1969
    Illustrated by Harry Grimley
19. *Village Christmas* 1966; Penguin 1984
20. *The Howards of Caxley* 1967; Penguin 1972
    Illustrated by Harry Grimley. Companion volume to *The Market Square*
21. *The Fairacre Festival* 1968; Penguin 1974; Orion pbk 2007 (with *Over the Gate*)
22. *Miss Read's Country Cooking* 1969; Penguin 1985
    Illustrated by Juliet Renny; Penguin edition illustrated by Sally Seymour
23. *News from Thrush Green* 1970; Penguin 1973; Orion pbk 2007
24. *Emily Davis* 1971; Penguin 1974
    Illustrated by Harry Grimley. Companion volume to *Miss Clare Remembers*
25. *Tiggy* 1971; Penguin 1988; Orion hbk 2007
    Illustrated by Clare Dawson
26. *Tyler's Row* 1972; Penguin 1975; Orion pbk 2007
27. *The Christmas Mouse* 1973; Penguin 1976
28. *Farther Afield* 1974; Penguin 1978; Orion pbk 2007
29. *Animal Boy* 1975
    Children's book published by Pelham Books, an imprint of Michael Joseph Ltd. Illustrated by Gareth Floyd
30. *Battles at Thrush Green* 1975; Penguin 1978; Orion pbk 2008
31. *No Holly for Miss Quinn* 1976; Penguin 1978

Bibliography

32. *Village Affairs* 1977 Penguin 1979; Orion pbk 2008
33. *Return to Thrush Green* 1978; Penguin 1980; Orion pbk 2008
34. *The White Robin* 1979; Penguin 1981
35. *Village Centenary* 1980; Penguin 1982; Orion pbk 2008
36. *Gossip from Thrush Green* 1981; Penguin 1983; Orion pbk 2008
37. *A Fortunate Grandchild* 1982; Penguin 1985
    Illustrated by Derek Crowe
38. *Affairs at Thrush Green* 1983; Penguin 1985; Orion pbk 2009
39. *Summer at Fairacre* 1984; Penguin 1986; Orion pbk 2008
40. *At Home in Thrush Green* 1985; Penguin 1986; Orion pbk 2009
41. *Time Remembered* 1986; Penguin 1987
    Illustrated by Derek Crowe. Companion volume to *A Fortunate Grandchild*
42. *The School at Thrush Green* 1987; Penguin 1988; Orion pbk 2009
43. *The World of Thrush Green* 1988; pbk 1990
44. *Mrs Pringle* 1989; Penguin 1990
45. *Friends at Thrush Green* 1990; Penguin 1991; Orion pbk 2009
46. *Changes at Fairacre* 1991; Penguin 1992; Orion pbk 2010
47. *Celebrations at Thrush Green* 1992; Penguin 1993; Orion pbk 2009
48. *Miss Read's Christmas Book* 1992
    An anthology of prose & poetry with illustrations by Tracey Williamson
49. *Farewell to Fairacre* 1993; Penguin 1994; Orion pbk 2010
50. *Tales from a Village School* 1994; Penguin 1995
    Illustrated by Kate Dicker
51. *The Year at Thrush Green* 1995; Penguin 1996; Orion pbk 2009
52. *A Peaceful Retirement* 1996; Penguin 1997; Orion pbk 2010
    Illustrated by Andrew Dodds

In 2009, *Christmas at Thrush Green* written by Jenny Dereham in collaboration with Miss Read was published in hardback by Orion, with the paperback in 2010.

OMNIBUS EDITIONS

1. *Chronicles of Fairacre* 1964; Penguin 1982; Orion pbk 2005
    comprising *Village School, Village Diary & Storm in the Village*

2. *Life at Thrush Green* 1984 in Penguin; Michael Joseph hbk 1987
    comprising *Thrush Green, Winter in Thrush Green & News from
    Thrush Green*

3. *More Stories from Thrush Green* 1985 in Penguin; Michael Joseph
    hbk 1989 comprising *Battles at Thrush Green, Return to Thrush
    Green & Gossip from Thrush Green*

4. *Further Chronicles of Fairacre* 1985 in Penguin; Michael Joseph hbk
    1990 comprising *Miss Clare Remembers, Over the Gate, The Fairacre
    Festival & Emily Davis*

5. *Fairacre Roundabout* 1990 in Penguin; Michael Joseph hbk 1992
    comprising *Tyler's Row, Farther Afield & Village Affairs*

6. *Christmas at Fairacre* 1991; Penguin 1992
    comprising *Village Christmas, No Holly for Miss Quinn, The
    Christmas Mouse & Other Stories*

7. *The Little Red Bus & Other Rhyming Stories* 1991; Viking Children's
    Books hbk; Young Puffin pbk 1993
    Illustrated by Jonathan Langley

8. *Tales from Thrush Green* 1994; Penguin 1995
    comprising *Affairs at Thrush Green & At Home in Thrush Green*

9. *Early Days* 1995; Penguin 1996; Orion pbk 2007
    comprising *A Fortunate Grandchild & Time Remembered* with a
    new foreword

10. *Fairacre Affairs* 1997; Penguin 1998
    comprising *Village Centenary & Summer at Fairacre*

11. *Encounters at Thrush Green* 1998; Penguin 1999
    comprising *The School at Thrush Green & Friends at Thrush Green*

12. *The Caxley Chronicles* 1999; Penguin 2000
    comprising *The Market Square & The Howards of Caxley*

13. *Farewell, Thrush Green* 2000; Penguin 2001
comprising *Celebrations at Thrush Green* & *The Year at Thrush Green*
14. *The Last Chronicle of Fairacre* 2001; Penguin 2002
comprising *Changes at Fairacre, Farewell to Fairacre* & *A Peaceful Retirement*
15. *Christmas at Fairacre* 2005; Orion pbk 2006 comprising *No Holly for Miss Quinn, The Christmas Mouse* & another story
16. *A Country Christmas* 2006; Orion pbk 2007
comprising *Village Christmas, The White Robin* & other stories including five from *Tales from a Village School*
17. *Christmas with Miss Read* 2011; Orion pbk 2012
comprising nos. 15 and 16 above

Acknowledgements

*

Acknowledgement is gratefully made to the following for permission to include the work of Miss Read listed below which they originally published.

Every effort to clear copyright in all material published in this edition has been made.

BBC: *The Fabulous Coat*
Country Life: *'Embarrassed Reptile'*
Country Living: *My Country Childhood*
The Countryman: *Distant Afternoons*; *The Birth of Miss Read*
Michael Joseph Ltd & *The Author* (journal of the Society of Authors): *At the Sign of the Mermaid*
The Lady: *Georgie Giraffe Comes in Sixth*; *Buying Logs*; *The Peasants' Revolt*; *The Last of Glory*
Observer: *The Lucky Hole*
Sunday Telegraph Magazine: *Return to Arcady*
Times Educational Supplement: *Infants Long Ago*; *Trafalgar Day*; *Restless Young Disciples*; *Scriptural Matters*; *Beyond the Road Sign*; *Feeling Poorly*; *The Lighter Side of Authorship*; *The Author and the Artist*; *Deadly Sins*; *Harvest Festival*; *Goldfish and Frog-spawn*; *Larger than Life*; *Eight-a-Side Cricket*; *Last Day of Term*

The quotations from Evelyn Waugh on pages 139 & 143 are reproduced by kind permission of the Evelyn Waugh Estate and Penguin Books.

The quotation from Harold Nicolson on page 238 is reproduced by kind permission of the Harold Nicolson Estate.

Acknowledgement is also gratefully made to the following artists for permission to reproduce their illustrations which originally appeared in the Miss Read books but not necessarily with the text shown here.

Susan Crowe for the illustrations by Derek Crowe that originally appeared in *A Fortunate Grandchild* and *Time Remembered* on pages: 1, 3, 5, 6, 17, 19, 21, 22, 29, 32, 36, 42, 44 and 47

Kate Dicker for the illustrations that originally appeared in *Tales from a Village School* on pages: 262, 277 281, 290, 299

The Estate of Andrew Dodds for the illustrations that originally appeared in *Country Bunch* and *A Peaceful Retirement* on pages: 93, 111, 129, 130, 160, 162, 179, 185, 189, 227, 259, 307

The Estate of John S. Goodall for the illustrations that originally appeared in the Fairacre and Thrush Green series by Miss Read on pages: iii, 53, 57, 70, 85, 99, 115, 125, 132, 134, 137, 144, 152, 156, 159, 173, 213, 221, 223, 273, 280, 292, 305

Michael Joseph Ltd: page 265

Dora Saint 1913–2012

.